WAR HAMMERS II

THE STORY OF WEST HAM UNITED DURING THE SECOND WORLD WAR

BRIAN BELTON

From a proud grandson
To George Morris
(My maternal grandfather)
Warrior, Firefighter and Socialist

Fire falling from the air,
Bombs blasting everywhere,
So it's to the engines boys to kill the flames,
Only the fire-girls will remember our names,
East London's burning, the docks afire,
Pump the River to douse the pyre,
To save the City so the child may live,
The warrior fireman his life will give.

First published 2015

The History Press
The Mill, Brimscombe Port
Stroud, Gloucestershire, GL5 2QG
www.thehistorypress.co.uk

British Library Cataloguing in Publication Data.
A catalogue record for this book is available from the British Library.

ISBN 978 0 7509 5602 4

Typesetting and origination by The History Press
Printed in Great Britain

CONTENTS

ACKNOWLEDGEMENTS

Roy and Paul Goulden for their time, memories and good humour.

Terry Brown for his kindness and generosity, particularly in passing on the 'Charles Korr tapes' that have proved to be a mine of information not only with regard to this book, but also for the historian/supporter. All images are taken from my own collection. In a few instances the ownership of copyright is unknown. If we have unknowingly used an image without permission then please contact me through the publishers.

FOREWORD

I am delighted to write a foreword to Brian's history of the club during the Second World War. I have to admit to being evacuated to Lanark, in Scotland and later Burnley, so I cannot say I sat the war out in East London, although I do have memories of red skies and tube stations. The latter are interesting because the people of East London marched to The Savoy in the Strand to protest against the failure of the authorities to allow people to take shelter in the underground tube stations during bombing raids (The Savoy had safe underground rooms that were used by many influential people). The stations were opened immediately, which without doubt saved many lives, notwithstanding the awful tragedy at Bethnal Green tube station in 1943 when 113 adults (mainly women) and 60 children were killed when people fell on the stairs leading to the entrance of the station.

Churchill was reported as saying that if the people of East London gave up then the rest of the country would quickly follow. As we all know, they never did, and the club's role in maintaining spirits was recognised at the time and subsequently when we were allowed to repair our bomb-damaged ground and install makeshift floodlights with poles from the London Docks at a time when everyone else was subject to strict rationing.

I like to think that many of the brave soldiers from East London and their families at home, who went through so much lived, long enough to watch a home-grown boy become the best defender in the world and the team bring home the European Cup-Winners' Cup some twenty years later when West Ham United, ironically, beat a team from Munich.

Brian's book is long overdue and I am so pleased to see the club recognised in this way.

Terry Brown
Honorary Life President
West Ham United Football Club

INTRODUCTION

> Then came the war and, with it, the end of my career or so I felt. Surely there couldn't be room for a professional footballer in a world gone crazy? I, of course, being a young, fit man of approaching twenty would go into the services. Meanwhile, in the leisure time I had left I wound up my personal affairs, cursed Hitler and all his rats and occasionally sat down to think of what had been and what might have been.
>
> *Tommy Lawton,* Football is my Business

Writing about West Ham United has become something of a habit, perhaps an obsession, even an addiction, for me over the last (almost) three decades, but to set the club, and its historical footballing context, within the wider environment of the Second World War has been a developing challenge that stretches back to my boyhood days; now close to half a century.

The book that has resulted has been a consistent labour of love, and also the source of frustration and exasperation at times. But for me, as a historian, sociologist and West Ham supporter, the latter have been compensated for by a series of magic moments. These have made up my education in what West Ham United is. My lessons have taken the shape of seminal encounters with club legends and Hammers stalwarts from the wartime era like Ernie Gregory and

Eddie Chapman. My most recent delight and honour has been in contacting Paul and Roy Goulden, the sons of the West Ham player my father most admired, the immortal Len Goulden.

This multi-dimensional learning curve has provided me with a plethora of narrative, a mine of information, but more importantly ongoing understanding and insight that has shaped my personal direction and view of the world. I attained a professional qualification, a Bachelor of Science and then a Master's Degree before achieving my doctorate. Not bad for a bad boy from Plaistow, who left Burke Secondary Modern School as a 16-year-old with a few CSEs (including a grade 2 in 'woodwork' – a qualification, I am proud to say, I have never put to any use whatsoever). However, my consistent and, I think, most profound awareness of the potential for human collaboration and industry has been the result of spending time with the wise, thoughtful, brave, mad, funny, eccentric, depressed, joyful, kind, cranky and generous men who, at one time or another, 'wore the shirt' with the Hammers over their hearts. Many welcomed me into their homes and a few even invited me into their families; all gave me something of their lives. I have worked and associated with so-called educated people, sometimes for many years, and have found most of them incapable of the munificence, simple humanity and social intellect shown to me by these players (there are no 'ex-players' in the lexicon of the Irons), often their wives, children and, once or twice, grandchildren too. I will always be grateful to these people for this.

My privileged journey, with this noble tribe, is reflected in the pages that follow.

PEOPLE

Having published one book about West Ham in war (see Belton 2014), I wanted this offering to be both the same and different. As with the first *War Hammers* (which is concerned with the club during the First World War), I have built the story around games, events and player biographies. My experience of football is that it is, at base, about people; it is something 'made' by managers, players, fans and, to a less palpable extent, directors. This being the case, people, individual players, the men who made the team, constitute a significant part of this story. In this respect I have focused on those players who played as Hammers in the final of the 1940 League War Cup. Several of these men were part of the Hammers team throughout the war and as such they are representative of the bulk of those who played under the banner of crossed hammers in those dark years. I chose to provide as much of their life-stories as was practicable, because they came to West Ham, and the war, with and by way of, the experience of their lives. They contributed the product of those lives to the club, as well as the wider society that struggled through the war years, partly using football to ease that path. I also believe that their lives after West Ham and the war are important. How these men lived and finally died was influenced by both of these aspects of their experience. More importantly, just to cover their time as stoppers or goal scorers is, I think, to dehumanise them. These men were players, but they were also people, and who they were and what became of them is significant, just because of that. However, their former and later lives are also relevant because they, like me, and perhaps you, will always be 'West Ham' – you, me, we, they: that 'is' West Ham and in that we are one.

Around 120 men played first-team football for West Ham during the Second World War. I would have liked to include all of them, but that would have taken about three or four times as many pages as I have eventually filled. Some were at Upton Park before, during and after the war; others were purely 'conflict' players, 'guesting' for the club during the years of hostility. Among them were those who served the club during the war for many dozens – sometimes over a hundred – games; others played just a few times, being football Gypsies for the duration, turning out for several, sometimes many, clubs all over Britain. Such was the nature of the game and the West Ham club during the war. I am sad I have not been able to write about many players who deserve to be included on both personal and sporting merit. These include the likes of Ernie Gregory, Jim Barrett, Jackie Wood and Alf Chalkley. Although I have written about many of these talented players previously, it was hard to exclude them from this book.

I make mention of the wartime international matches that included West Ham players, principally Archie Macaulay and Len Goulden (but also Willie Corbett and Ted Fenton). I considered including the international matches in which the likes of Jock Dodds played (he donned the claret and blue during the 1944/45 season, scoring an impressive 11 goals in 10 games) as well as the many West Ham 'guest' players who represented their countries. However, again, this would have more than doubled this aspect of the book, although Jock was involved in most of the games detailed.

The Charles Korr tapes were a great help in supplying dimension and background to my own primary research. These were kindly passed on to me by Terry Brown. They are recordings of interviews carried out during the first and last in-depth organisational, sociological and historical study of the West Ham club (with total access to organisational records and staff) by Korr, who is now Professor Emeritus at the University of Missouri, St Louis. The tapes were the background for Korr's seminal book *West Ham United* (1986) and include contributions by or about Reg Pratt, Malcolm Allison, Len Cearns, John Lyall, Charlie Paynter and many others.

I also wanted to include something of the wartime supporter experience. The most accessible people were, of course, my family (the support of West Ham goes back many generations in my extended Cockney clan). My closeness to these people I hope provides something of what many of those who identified themselves with the Hammers went through, but also how living with and being part of West Ham helped them through the massive challenges presented by life in war-torn East London.

Overall, I believe this material provides another dimension on football in wartime, demonstrating its relevance and deployment as a psychological and humane resource during a period of worry, fear and tension.

If one writes a book about wartime, one has to include that experience both as background and as foreground. Football could not, between 1939 and 1945, be simply divorced from the historical and social environment, the nature and conduct of hostilities. Given this, I have tried to set the football, the game and its governance, West Ham as a club, its players, management, directors and supporters, in the context of the time. This involves looking at landmark events, but I have also tried to include lesser-known aspects of wartime history, encompassing home defence, in particular around East London, and largely forgotten events, campaigns and characters that I feel deserve attention, if only because of the lack of the same in the past.

WHAT HAPPENED?

While putting together this West Ham United wartime biography, I found that as the story developed it increasingly gave the lie to, or demonstrated the erroneous nature of, an oft-repeated perspective on the Second World War. This interpretation has it that the conflict did little more in terms of the game than end, interrupt or seriously disrupt football careers. While this is certainly true of some, the war also provided a football stage on which many players built and extended their careers. More than a few players would never have got the chance to play for professional teams had the conditions been 'normal'. Many of those who would have got a game or two in peacetime had protracted wartime careers and consequently a playing CV in the post-war football job market. The war also cemented the club's relationship with its supporters; they (we?) went through it together, we got each other through.

At the same time, for the first time, a lot of players were turning out for several clubs, all over the country. They had a unique opportunity to experience different management and organisational conditions; most significantly, this movement created a dialogue between players on a scale never before known. This is not to be underestimated with regard to the organisation of players as a workforce after the war. The latter led to the abolition of the minimum wage and ultimately a complete revision of the way football was organised as an industry. In fact it is probable that the war obliged the boardrooms of professional clubs to move more swiftly towards becoming mature business enterprises, which included industrial relations. This transition was to displace the cultural fiefdoms of local builders, brewers and shopkeepers that many football clubs had been.

CHANGE

There is little point in writing history unless there is an argument about the impact of the past on the present and the future. With this in mind I have provided some analysis of how the war years were to shape the future of West Ham and football overall. Part of this refers to organisational considerations by way of a very general overview. But in places I have personalised other considerations of how the years of conflict moulded the attitudes and motivations of the most perennial aspects of West Ham's human resources. This is mainly focused on the character of support but also the nature of West Ham the board. It includes a reflection on my own experiences as a child who came to the Hammers just a decade after the war, who played on bomb sites, and whose parents, grandparents and teachers were shaped by and in the war. The players who formed my vision of Upton Park and the Hammers, those who played in the first games I was to attend, were products of the post-war organisation of football, itself a creation of the 1939–46 era.

While the First World War played a crucial part in changing West Ham United, altering the class dynamic of the administration of football (following the football class war within the war: see Belton 2014), the Second World War saw the further development of football as a commercial endeavour. The conditions demanded that the final blow be delivered to the practically feudal system, complete with despots and patriarchs, which had dominated the organisation of the game at every level. While there were regional differences in this respect, one only has to compare the position of the managers of the 1940 War Cup Final to intuit this. The war created the room and need to modernise not only the playing of the game (see Belton 2013a, 2013b) but also the running and administration of clubs. As the following pages suggest, at board level, West Ham's Reg Pratt was perhaps the first to see the need for what was ultimately to be a revolution of sorts. To his credit he probably transformed his own approach and attitudes in the first instance; not an easy task for the best of us.

While Len Cearns (the chairman of West Ham for thirty-one years, starting in 1948) also did much to sustain this position, the club remained on something of a plateau, even going into decline, after the 1960s, until the Terry Brown era. For the first time an actual supporter, someone who had stood on the terraces of Upton Park, took a controlling hand in the club, and it was his administration that brought a final end to the dynastic character of the West Ham hierarchy. Terry was wise and loyal enough to value the history of the club (which is something different from tradition or custom), even doing what he could to set up a club museum. But whatever you think of his methods, the overall management of the club under Brown was made fit for twenty-first-century purpose by way of his influence, skill and care. History will remember Terry as a seminal custodian of the club's past and future. A trick of economic history and the failure of international finance during the 'Icelandic period', together with the legacy of Harry Redknapp (see Belton 2007), prevents a secure understanding of events post-Brown at this juncture in time; we still stand too close to that era to make out the wood for the trees.

The current ownership, Davids Gold and Sullivan, continue the interrupted process Brown started, alongside the tremendously hard-working, massively intelligent and dedicated Karen Brady (really the 'First Lady' of the English game). The move to the Olympic Stadium is at the forefront of the ethos they have brought to the club. Again, you or I might not want to 'move' emotionally, I'm not sure the Davids do, but the practical and economic case is clear. Yes, my granddad had fond memories of Bidder Street, Canning Town, with its outside toilet and view of the gasworks, but overall, the three-bedroomed semi in Chigwell is really a better place to bring up your kids. His father was among those who watched Thames Ironworks FC at the Memorial Ground, which was a fantastic sporting edifice in its time (see Belton 2003), but then, as now, economics and finance dictated movement. It must have seemed mad to move from that impressive venue to what there was at Upton Park in the first years of the twentieth century. However, life and history are like that; nothing stays the same – in business, sport and our lives, stasis is usually achieved at the cost of existence.

Once more, Gold and Sullivan are 'fans' and a million miles away from the men who cultivated a sort of 'toffness' as part of an almost *Upstairs, Downstairs* culture that pertained at West Ham before the war. I have met and like Terry Brown, David Gold and David Sullivan; I found them all affable, down-to-earth men, intelligent, interesting, funny and generous. The idea that I might ever have been given the same time, or shown similar kindness by the potentates of the 1940s and those who succeeded them prior to the 1990s is beyond contemplation. I say that from personal experience. One would have more chance of an audience with the Pope or a pint at the Boleyn with Xi Jinping (both Hammers supporters, of course) than a meet with one of the Cearns family round at their drum.

LIGHT

Where we are today started with the coming of war. In those bleak and fearful times, football brought moments of illumination and much-needed distraction. I think of myself as a sort of rogue Protestant; I have always been something of a 'spiritual slapper'. When I have felt the need or the curiosity, I have visited temples, mosques or churches of various denominations, usually on recommendation or pulled by repute; to listen to what the priest, vicar or imam has to say about the world. It was in the 1990s that I took myself over to the West London synagogue to take in the wisdom of Rabbi Hugo Grinn. His connection with the Second World War was as a 9-year-old prisoner in a concentration camp with the rest of his family. In one of his sermons I heard him tell the congregation about one experience he had during this time.

Hugo's father was also a rabbi, and with Hanukkah coming up, he and others thought about the menorah and the concomitant need for candles. But candles, like most other things, were not made available to prisoners, so plans were laid to make them. Each family gave a tiny amount of butter from their meagre rations over a number of weeks for this purpose. The very young children, like Hugo, were given the job of finding material for the wicks. They found that tiny strands of material pulled from the uniforms of the camp guards could be threaded together for this purpose. The quality and strength of the cloth was much more suitable than the rags the inmates had to wear. Each time a child surreptitiously pulled one of these strands from their captors, they took their lives in their hands.

So it was Hanukkah came, and in the cold darkness of one of the camp sheds, the congregation came together to light the candles. But no one knew that butter didn't burn like wax. As soon as each candle was lit, in a split second it was gone in a small flash of flame. Hugo told how he cried bitterly. However, his father held his shoulders, looked into his glassy, tearful eyes and told him, 'There was light. That's all that matters. That there was, even for just a second, light here.'

In total darkness even a glimpse of light signals hope. There is an old Gypsy saying: 'Hope is the last thing to die.' In the Second World War, as the Nazis were raining down fire and destruction on the place I still regard as 'home', West Ham brought hope; they brought light.

My dad and a couple of mates were at a game at Upton Park when the air-raid siren sounded. Two old blokes told the kids to follow them and they ran to a shelter at the back of a house not too far from the Boleyn Ground. The cramped, dark space, lit by a single candle, was packed with frightened people when the explosions started. A young woman, who was holding a baby close to her body, started to sing:

Thou, Whose Almighty word
Chaos and darkness heard,
And took their flight;
Hear us, we humbly pray;
And, where the gospel's day
Sheds not its glorious ray,
Let there be light!

The people in the shelter, including my dad and his pals, who remembered the hymn from school, started to join in. Between the explosions he could hear other people giving their voice too, from shelters along the row of back yards of the little terraced houses that nestled round the home of the Hammers:

Spirit of truth, and love,
Life-giving, holy Dove,
Speed forth Thy flight!
Move on the waters' face
Bearing the lamp of grace,
And in earth's darkest place
Let there be light!

What follows is a story of that hope; it is a tale of light. A time when the Irons of East London went to war and football protected us with its own promise of the next goal, the next game, next week, when Saturday comes; depicting a future that offered an escape from the now. Escape is different from escapism (which is perhaps what football is today). We need to face or escape danger; perhaps facing it and escaping it come to much the same thing, but football and West Ham helped with that. For kids like my dad, amidst the destruction of his dockland home, war workers on shifts or service people, on roaring, freezing seas or fighting in blistering deserts, the game, the 'results', mattered! Hope happened by way of the match still being or to be played – for a moment they were home, for a precious, illuminated second the war was forgotten – 'There was light.' That's all that mattered.

Boundless as ocean's tide
Rolling in fullest pride,
Through the earth, far and wide,
LET THERE BE LIGHT!

From the hymn 'God, Whose Almighty Word'
by John Marriott (1825)

ONE

THE LAST PEACETIME SEASON

> Called up to the Army as Trooper T. Finney 7958274 of the Royal Armoured Corps. I had given up hope of any action in the football sense ... But I was wrong. Football was important.
>
> *Tom Finney,* My Autobiography

The coming of war was something many had hoped might be avoided, but no one was surprised at; the omens had not been good from the mid-1930s with the rise of fascism in Europe. Although on 24 March 1939 Britain had declared that she would oppose any German aggression against Belgium, Holland or Switzerland, and a week later it was determined that the government would stand by France in supporting Poland, the appeasement of German expansionism had become the way of things. This was graphically symbolised by the Nazi salute that the English football team were obliged to provide before their encounter with Germany during May 1938 in the Berliner Olympiastadion.

There was some disturbance in the England camp with regard to the team being expected to give the *Hitlergruß* ('Hitler Greeting'), but the pro-appeasement British ambassador to Berlin,

Sir Neville Henderson, convinced Stanley Rous, the FA secretary at the time, and the Oxford University representative on the FA Council, Charles Wreford Brown, that should the salute not be given by the England team, it would result in an international incident. Henderson also argued that giving the salute would 'get the crowd in a good mood' and that it was the polite thing to do. In retrospect the visitors' 6–3 victory was hardly a redeeming factor. The players, England's Lions, had been clearly led by donkeys – nothing new there in terms of British/German relations. (The final England goal, a crashing 30yd drive, which had torn the German net, came from the boot of West Ham's Len Goulden – Stanley Matthews was to declare that he had never seen a more powerful shot.)

THE IRON '30s

As the opening games of the 1938/39 season were being played out on 27 August 1938, when despite two strikes from Archie Macaulay, West Ham lost by the odd goal of 5 at Craven Cottage, people were wondering if war might sooner rather than later override such considerations.

A few weeks later, on 17 September, Macaulay repeated his performance against Fulham at Upton Park as, with a 2-goal contribution from Ben Fenton, the Hammers achieved a 4–1 trouncing of Coventry City (Lol Coen got the only Sky Blues goal). West Ham appeared to be making something of a comeback from a disastrous opening to the season; three consecutive defeats were followed by a run wherein the Irons lost just 1 match. The 16-goal, 5-match sequence culminated in the 6–1 East London defeat of Tranmere Rovers (Macaulay hit a hat-trick, which was equalled by the combined efforts of Joe Cockroft, Norman Corbett and Stan Foxall).

At the same time, things were beginning to look a bit more hopeful on the international front too as the British

Prime Minister, Arthur Neville Chamberlain, was working hard to placate Hitler in Berchtesgaden and Bad Godesberg. More than a few saw this frantic diplomacy as only delaying the inevitable, and perhaps it was something of a desperate tactic to give Britain some time to prepare for war. The latter was to some extent confirmed when the Royal Navy was mobilised on 27 September. The Football League gave notice that the weekend's fixtures would be completed if war did not break out before the start of October.

The notorious 'peace in our time' message brought back from Germany allowed football and Britain some respite, although the commotion and general mood of pessimism made it hard for people not to be conscious that the world was on the brink. The statement looked more than hollow when Hitler's forces invaded the Czechoslovak Sudetenland on 1 October 1938. In Britain this was the prelude for the ominous distribution of gas masks, the hurried digging of air-raid shelters in public parks, and the erection of anti-aircraft batteries around London.

Before the kick-off of West Ham's game at the Saltergate Recreation ground and every Football League match on 1 October 1938, there was a service of thanksgiving 'to express thankfulness for the preservation of peace'. Chesterfield ended the Hammers' short-lived purple patch with a single-goal win. The Irons managed just nine more League wins until a 6–2 away win over Norwich on 11 March 1939 (Sam Small's hat-trick was the foundation of the Carrow Road victory).

By Easter 1939 Germany had occupied all of Czechoslovakia. The government announced the introduction of compulsory military service for men aged 20 to 21, limited to a period of six months' training, although the call-up would eventually take in all fit males between the ages of 18 and 41. This potentially would have a huge, and at that point seemingly disastrous, impact on professional football.

West Ham finished eleventh in the old Second Division, 11 points adrift of Champions Blackburn. Spurs had done the double over the East Londoners but the Hammers, after 3 games, had put Peter McWilliam's boys out of the Cup (Stan Foxall claiming 4 of the 6 goals put past the Tottenham defence over what was a truculent triptych of tussles). It was a pity Portsmouth killed off any further advance by the Irons. It was the sixth time since 1928 that the Hammers had been eliminated by a club that would make the Wembley final.

The Boleyn Boys had by that time played their seventh successive season in the second tier of English football. There were few high-points during that period; perhaps the semi-final stage of the FA Cup in 1933 (a defeat by Everton) was the apex of footballing prowess during what, in retrospect, looks like a relatively grey era in the history of the Hammers. In that same 1932/33 season the Irons avoided the drop to the Third Division South with a 1-point advantage over Chesterfield. Subsequently, the Irons got to third and fourth spots in 1935 and 1936 respectively. In 1935 a single point would have meant the East Enders leapfrogging Bolton (the Trotters had a better goal average) and taken them up to the top flight with Brentford. A season on, 4 more points would have seen the Cockney club taking Charlton's place and going up with Manchester United. So, with a less pessimistic second look, the 1930s did have a fair share of drama and interest for those who followed the fortunes of the Upton Park cadre.

But at the dawn of 1939, West Ham were beginning to look like something better than what had gone before. As the side's young goalkeeper at the time, Ernie Gregory, recalled: 'We began to feel like a side that could be promoted.' Ted Fenton (in his book *At Home With The Hammers*) agreed: 'In 1939, we really and sincerely thought we were going to do it. We had the balance, the power and the experience necessary. We saw it as our season of fulfilment.' There had indeed been, for some time, a show of will to succeed at Upton Park. When Everton officials approached the Hammers directors in the late 1930s, asking if the club would be prepared to sell Goulden and Jackie Morton, the board gave a definite refusal. Around the same time, West Ham made the bold and successful bid that brought Archie Macaulay to the Boleyn Ground from Rangers.

UMBERTO THE MAGNANIMOUS

As spring turned to summer in 1939, the FA decided to call a joint meeting with the Football League the moment that war was declared to make plans for the game during hostilities. This was indicative of the prevailing gloomy ethos that had shrouded the last peacetime season. The campaign had been played out in a mood of near-excruciating tension as politicians and diplomats continued their apparently unending dance of negotiation and scheming. But for years one international crisis had followed another as football, along with the rest of British society, endeavoured to establish some sense of stasis and predictability.

Following the penultimate season of the 1930s, one of the great heroes of that Hammers side, Len Goulden, was with the England team for a 3-match tour of Italy, Yugoslavia and Romania. He had staked his claim in the 3–0 victory over the Rest of Europe at Wembley in October 1938, again with the final goal of the game.

Before and during the initial match of the tour, the San Siro Stadium in Milan was drenched in torrential rain. In the soaking conditions the German referee (Dr Bauwens) gave an Italian goal, which had clearly been hit home by a fist of one of the home players. This was so blatant that Italian Crown Prince Umberto offered to ask the officiating Deutsche to review this decision, but the offer was diplomatically refused by the FA. The match concluded in a 2–2 result following a late England goal.

A few months earlier, in April, Umberto, returning with troops from action in the Spanish Civil War, had flouted Italy's newly formed racial legislation. Reviewing the Italian wounded as they were disembarking at the docks in Naples, the crown prince extended a special greeting to the 27-year-old Lieutenant Bruno Fernari, a Jew. Umberto posed with the young man for a picture. Bruno had given up an engineering career four years previously to join the Italian Army. He had suffered a leg wound during the Christmas fighting in Spain and was twice decorated for his bravery. He also received a gold medal for horsemanship.

A few Jewish volunteers remained with the Italian forces in Spain. Most of those who returned were to find that they were no longer considered Italians, so were not able to take up the jobs and trades they had left to serve their country. A disproportionately high percentage of Jewish volunteers were decorated; many were wounded in the last three months of the Spanish Civil War.

Following a long train journey, England were beaten 2–1 by Yugoslavia in Belgrade, but subsequently the tourists claimed a 2–0 victory over Rumania in Bucharest (Len Goulden scored England's second). This was the last peacetime international for England. Over the following seven years, players would receive unofficial recognition only, which of course translated into no recognition at all.

THE END OF THE START

Soon after Len's and England's twenty-four-hour trip back to London, the Air Raid Precautions (ARP) Department of the Home Office laid plans for closing all forms of entertainment on the outbreak of war. The arrangements allowed for the possible reopening of such facilities after a week, depending on the intensity of what was thought to be the practical inevitability of aerial bombing and related decisions to be made by the police.

In the summer of 1939, when the West Ham players reported for pre-season training, talk of war was rife. Sir Edward Grey's words of 1914, 'The lamps are going out all over Europe', seemed as relevant at that time as they had been on the eve of the Great War. A type of fearsome gloom, tinged with uncertainty, was pervasive, but there was also a feeling that the normality of life, of which the ticks and tocks of football were a part, with its regularities, every Saturday, kick-off at 3 o'clock, the results, scores, scorers, leagues and reports, was about to be suspended. The ominous, omnipresent insecurity was fuelled by the newspapers, which seemed to speculate endlessly about the game being stopped, or in some unspecified way curtailed, if and when war broke out.

As early as September 1938 the Hammers chairman had pre-empted a Football Association circular of April 1939, which expressed the hope that the game might be an example of patriotism to British youth by professional players signing up for the Territorial Army (known affectionately as 'The Terries') or other national service organisations. West Ham's chairman, Will J. Cearns, in the face of the threat of the club's players and other staff being called to defend the far reaches of the Empire, counselled that 'the first-team join the Reserve Police and the second team get into the Territorials'. This gave these employees a fair chance of not being called to service too far from Upton Park, at least over the immediate period, and provided some hope that the Irons could field a decent side in time of war. Leonard 'Len' Crittenden Cearns, the 24-year-old son of W.J., also enlisted in the 'Terriers'. The 'Crittenden' aspect of Lenny's moniker resonated John J. Crittenden, US attorney general, a slavery compromiser and member of the 'Know Nothing' Party.

The 'local service' tactic had become something of a trend in football for most of the 1938/39 season. Liverpool staff and players had enlisted with the Terries as a club. This included their manager and former Hammers 1923 FA Cup Final skipper, George Kay. Like West Ham, their combatants from that final, Bolton Wanderers, also joined almost as a unit. However, the Manchester United board completely rejected the idea, seeing it as 'a matter for the individual to decide'.

When war did finally break out, many of the West Ham playing staff joined the forces and not a few served together in a searchlight unit of the Essex Regiment in East Anglia. So for a good part of the war years, that part of the world was defended against the airborne foe and invasion by men who were more at home with a ball than a gun. Typical of the man, Dick Walker left the police after three months, volunteering to have a more direct impact on the enemy. But less than a week before war broke out, Charlie Paynter got Archie Macaulay a job as a toolmaker in essential war work.

The summer brought a call-up of more reservists, and in July the Football League Management Committee decided that there should be no obligation on clubs to pay players while they were training with the armed forces, but given that an arrangement with the military authorities might be made to make players available, they could be paid for the time they were available for playing football. Perhaps inevitably, the game, as a business, was aware that paying players who were not available for selection made no financial sense. Thus they sought to gain latitude on the six-month conscription period, looking to get it shortened to four months during the summer for footballers.

Around the same time the Army Cup rules were amended to allow soldiers to play for professional clubs as long as consent was obtained from commanding officers. However, with the future uncertain, any arrangements were inevitably provisional. This was illustrated at the Boleyn Ground during August 1939; no new players were recruited as the cost was likely to represent money down the drain should they be called to serve King and Country.

Predictably perhaps, Charlie Paynter found that fourteen players were absent for the opening session of pre-season training, many of whom had been ordered to report to Huntingdon to undergo training with the 64th Searchlight Regiment. However, they returned to make the public trials that traditionally heralded the start to the season in support of the Football League's Jubilee Benevolent Fund. Clubs all over England took part in this project, using it to provide try-outs for potential players (playing alongside established professionals). West Ham and Fulham contested this season's curtain-raiser, home and away on the same day with both the first team and reserves. The West Ham sides lined up thus on 19 August 1939:

Reserves (at Craven Cottage):

Ernie Gregory
Steve Forde
Arthur Banner
Norman Corbett
Jim Barrett
Jim Harris
Terry Woodgate
Dick Dunn
George Foreman
George Proudlock
Dick Bell

The West Ham second team won 4–2 at the Cottage.

At Upton Park, West Ham faced the Cottagers on what was to be the hottest day of the year.

First team (at Upton Park):

Harry Medhurst
Charlie Bicknell
Charlie Walker
Norman Corbett
Dick Walker
Joe Cockroft
Stan Burton
Archie Macaulay
Cliff Hubbard
Len Goulden
Jackie Wood

The Hammers had met the West Londoners in the same Jubilee encounter of the previous year, wining 4–2 at the Boleyn Ground. More than 10,000 supporters meant a £521 donation would be made to the Football League's fund. In the roasting temperatures, players and officials slogged through to produce an exciting game, the sides sharing 6 goals (Jackie Wood and Archie Macaulay were on target for the Hammers, who were assisted by an own goal).

On Monday, 21 August the FA waived Rule 33 which stated that 'no player serving in His Majesty's Forces could be registered as a professional footballer'. The following Saturday, West Ham opened the 1939/40 season at Home Park – a venue that would be destroyed in the bombing to come. Plymouth Argyle were beaten 3–1. Cliff Hubbard (2) and Jackie Wood were the Hammers' scorers in front of 18,000 of the Pilgrim persuasion.

The Irons' Second Division schedule continued a couple of days later with Fulham returning to the Boleyn Ground. Jackie Wood was on the mark again, and with a goal from Ted Fenton, Upton Park saw what was to be the first and last home Football League Second Division victory for the Irons that season, seeing their visitors off 2–1.

EVACUATION AND TALES OF WAR

The blow of the East End having to say goodbye to its children as evacuation kicked in (the process officially started on Friday, 1 September) was unsurprisingly not softened by the Hammers' result against Fulham.

This was perhaps the final recognition that war was stalking London. West Ham's children brought home notes from their school giving details of the plans for their evacuation. Parents read the list of the things their kids would need or be allowed to take with them, which included a change of underwear, stout shoes, spare socks and a raincoat. Everything was to be packed in a small case.

As the crocodiles of schoolchildren converged on Barking railway station, a sea of tears was shed. Each child had a cardboard label tied to them by a piece of string, detailing name, address and school. A particular fear at this time was the potential use of gas, and many parents knew about the activities of the Luftwaffe against civilians in the Spanish Civil War, so every child had a box respirator slung across their shoulders. Many of the younger ones, with this and their 'small case', sometimes a brown paper bag, or a sad little bundle containing their bits and pieces, looked like tiny Sherpas.

My 5-year-old mother was one of those children. The second youngest of thirteen, she left dockside Poplar not to return for more than five years. She came back, having been billeted in Wales, speaking fluent Welsh. The entire time she was away is a blank to her, apart from a visit from her dad. He brought a children's china tea-set from her older sister. When she opened it after he left, she found it had been smashed to pieces. Almost half a decade of the most precious years of her childhood life was blotted out. God knows the fear, anxiety and horrors she experienced that caused this to happen. Many children, remote from love and protection, were used as nothing better than mini-slaves, and although there are numerous stories of the kindness of strangers, we will probably never know the level of abuse that many of these isolated children suffered. This is one of the several hidden casualty lists of the Second World War. My mum at 80, like many who had similar experiences, had coped well with the consequences, although who would want their child to have this exile as a seminal part of childhood?

Her father, George Morris, a veteran of the trenches, one of the Middlesex Regiment who played football with the Germans on Christmas Day 1914, joined the Auxiliary Fire Service. Sorrowfully ironic in his case, schools left empty by the evacuation of pupils were allocated to the Auxiliary Fire Service as surrogate stations.

Sheds and warehouses had been made available for firefighters in the docks by the Port of London Authority. The majority of the outer London brigades numbered their auxiliary fire stations consecutively after their regular stations. West Ham, for example, having three regular fire stations, commissioned twenty auxiliary stations and numbered them 4 to 23.

George was a pioneer of the 'Poplarism' revolt of the early inter-war years; a socialist, he educated himself in conjunction with the Workers' Educational Association. George had, of course, seen terrors in the Great War, but the dreadfulness he would witness in his own manor over the duration of the London bombing was to stay with him to the grave. He rose to officer level and was decorated for his bravery in the face of the wildly blazing East End that spat rivers of molten fury and created chasms of fire, like a massively expansive dragon. For me he was a tiny St George who, alongside his small regiment of fellow volunteers, pumped the Thames in the defence of their home. The old river, by which so many had made their living, once more became the water of life, deployed to drive the volcanic monster down. When you next look at our river, maybe for a moment give a thought to how it saved London and defied and denied fascism.

George related nothing of his experiences as a firefighter; his time as a literal fighter-of-fire; but each time it was mentioned, the history of carnage, the flames, could be seen in his eyes as they stared into the scorching past. The courage and tenacity of home front, Blitz-time heroes like him has too easily come close to being forgotten.

COMMITMENT TO SUPPORT

As a boy, when lonely or afraid, the warp and weft of football was a recourse and resource for me. In a police cell, or waiting outside the headmaster's room, in a tent alone in Tassili n'Ajjer, I have loudly, under my breath or in my head, sung 'Bubbles' or recited to myself the 1923 cup final team, the 1958 promotion side, the FA Cup winners of 1964; distraction yes, but also making myself part of something stronger, bigger than just me.

Not a few of those kids, those evacuated, disoriented little East Enders, dispersed all over Britain, would have carried out much the same rituals as I have, and felt something similar in their times of foreboding. Having, in their heads, hearts and spirits, something of home in West Ham United would have united them with the feel and memory of family and the place where they had first seen the light of day; when they listened to or read the football results or kicked a ball. Perhaps more than a few spent part of their journey to what must have seemed like the ends of the earth, finding distraction, comfort and maybe a little sense of courage, recalling or talking about the team, the result and, most importantly, tomorrow.

THE COMING STORM

With two wins from two games, most Hammers supporters looked towards the weekend and the Boleyn Ground game against Leicester City with some hopes of the development of a winning streak. However, after the final day of August, at 4.45 a.m. on 1 September 1939, Hitler ordered the German invasion of Poland. On that Friday the Luftwaffe bombed Warsaw, while Nazi tanks breached the Polish border.

Although London was under the threat of potential aerial attack from Nazi bombing, a communiqué from the Home Office declared that circumstances did not merit the cancellation of matches, although throughout the country theatres were darkened, cricket matches were cancelled and at West Ham Stadium in Custom House greyhound racing was abandoned, as it was at tracks all over Britain.

Saturday, 2 September saw West Ham taste defeat (2–0) in East London. The travelling Foxes got home to find Leicester, late on

Saturday evening, with the blackout already in force. But despite the obvious difficulties this presented, many people were out in the streets; seemingly folk didn't want to go home, even in the face of a ferocious thunderstorm. There was a clear sense that something was about to happen.

The next day, 3 September, at 11.15 a.m. the Prime Minister, Neville Chamberlain, announced that the British deadline for the withdrawal of German troops from Poland had expired. At a point when the BBC became restricted to two wavelengths, the world heard him over the 'wireless' tell how the British ambassador to Berlin, Sir Nevile Meyrick Henderson, had handed a final note to the German government that morning stating that, unless it announced plans to withdraw from Poland by 11 a.m., a state of war would exist between the two countries. The British Prime Minister continued: 'I have to tell you now that no such undertaking has been received and consequently this country is at war with Germany.' As he uttered that last word, the air-raid sirens sounded all over the country. Many took this to be the first air raid, but no bombs fell before the sirens sounded the all clear. For some time it was thought that what had happened was a sort of heralding of war, but in fact it had been a false alarm, caused by a French light aircraft entering British airspace unannounced. Nevertheless, it was a poignant moment.

All League football was suspended and for a short period no football was played in Britain, apart from the Services, as players were called-up for ARP or other wartime duties.

The new season was over by its second Saturday, hostilities sending the national game into what was to be a partial hibernation, but West Ham 'finished' in a respectable position – notionally their best since 1936, albeit that none of what they had done, or what anyone else had done, counted at all.

Football League Division Two, 1939/40							
	Played	Won	Drawn	Lost	For	Against	Points
Luton Town	3	2	1	0	7	1	5
Birmingham	3	2	1	0	5	1	5
Coventry City	3	1	2	0	8	6	4
Plymouth Argyle	3	2	0	1	4	3	4
West Ham United	3	2	0	1	5	4	4
Tottenham Hotspur	3	1	2	0	6	5	4
Leicester City	3	2	0	1	6	5	4
Nottingham Forest	3	2	0	1	5	5	4
Newport County	3	1	1	1	5	4	3
Millwall	3	1	1	1	5	4	3
Manchester City	3	1	1	1	6	5	3
West Bromwich Albion	3	1	1	1	8	8	3
Bury	3	1	1	1	4	5	3
Newcastle United	3	1	0	2	8	6	2
Chesterfield	2	1	0	1	2	2	2
Barnsley	3	1	0	2	7	8	2
Southampton	3	1	0	2	5	6	2
Sheffield Wednesday	3	1	0	2	3	5	2
Swansea Town	3	1	0	2	5	11	2
Fulham	3	0	1	2	3	6	1
Burnley	2	0	1	1	1	3	1
Bradford Park Avenue	3	0	1	2	2	7	1

The Consultative Committee of the Football Association, which had met in September the previous year, had agreed to have a meeting (as committees so often do): 'In the event of war a meeting [will] be convened comprising the officials of the FA and the Management Committee of the Football League for the purpose of deciding the course of action to be taken with regard to the game.' This had effectively been an expression of resignation to the predictable, even though that same month Chamberlain had flown back from Munich apparently having appeased Adolf Hitler. There were cheers as he held up the piece of paper that he took to assure 'peace in our time'.

Most of the British population had hoped their Prime Minister's message would prove to be true, even though preparations for war had been going on for years. For instance, the stipulations of the Air Raids Precautions Act of 1937 had been kicking in for some time. This required local authorities to draw up emergency fire schemes for their area and submit them to the secretary of state. The County Borough of West Ham was an area of 7.5 square miles, but considering the dockside importance of the district, the crowded little borough was a prime target for the worst ravages the Luftwaffe might unleash.

Initially, West Ham Council had refused to carry out its obligations under the Act, until more financial help for the protection of relatively poor districts like West Ham was made available. However, plans were eventually laid for the recruitment of an Auxiliary Fire Service, even though the local authority continued to argue with the government about the level of direct funding for the new service.

The Home Office was not too concerned about sport, so what restrictions were to be put in place in the circumstances was subject mostly to guesswork. After a short period the ban on sports activities outside the evacuation areas was lifted and the FA was advised that friendlies could be played, but only in areas that did not come under evacuation orders (big towns and cities, and centres of military importance).

On 5 September 1939, William Charles 'Everton Charlie' Cuff, the Football League president, in the light of the government's closure of places of entertainment, announced that clubs needed to maintain player contracts. The following day an emergency meeting of the League Management Committee took place at Crewe, which effectively ended League competition. The main means of shaping and restricting football at least for an interim period included the following:

- The formal advice that clubs should keep players standing by was rescinded – clubs had to pay players up to 6 September.
- Signing-on bonuses and removal expenses were to be immediately paid up.
- Refunds for season tickets had to be held up, but had to be consistent.
- Matches already played in the League would stand as cup-ties – if the regular schedule resumed, the return matches would be played on a like basis.
- Injured players were to stick by end-of-season procedures when making claims.
- Proposed inter-league matches against Scotland and Ireland were cancelled.
- Any different format for competition when soccer resumed was postponed.

QPR played the first official wartime friendly on 9 September *v.* the Army. The Hoops won 10–2. The Army team was never named and the game was played behind closed doors. Posters were put in place at all games, telling supporters what to do if an air raid took place (the same instructions were included in programmes).

On 11 September the Players' Union suggested that the FA might introduce regionalised competition, allowing clubs to charge for admission to matches. The Union was prepared for its members to play for nothing on condition that clubs donated any income from gates to charity. The Football League Management Committee pronounced that players would, initially at least, turn out for free (as the FA had annulled player contracts). Players could claim valid expenses, but they were covered for accidents by insurance through the Workmen's Compensation Act.

On 14 September it was announced that it would be possible to organise friendly games in areas barred by the Home Office under the Defence Regulations, on condition that the local police gave the go-ahead. The first series of friendly games took place on 16 September and were said to be chiefly for 'recreational entertainment for the young people'. More than 30 friendlies were played. These were first-class games, and although they were organised along amateur lines, they pulled in more than 120,000 people, so demonstrating the demand for quality football even in (perhaps partly because of) the worrying times.

The London Combination, which had scheduled first-team competitions during the First World War, had laid plans to organise games on much the same model. After discussions with the Home Office, the FA, on 21 September, declared its support for friendlies being organised and competitive matches in local and district groups on Saturdays and public holidays, on condition that there would be no detrimental effects for the war effort, which, of course, included National Service.

SAFETY FIRST(?)

However, public safety needed to be considered and a restriction was put in place on the numbers of people allowed to attend matches in evacuation areas. This was set at half the capacity of grounds or 8,000, whichever was the fewer, or as sanctioned by the local police. It was felt that there was a need to avoid the possibility of large crowds moving to or from football grounds.

The government evacuation scheme had been put together over the summer of 1938 by the Anderson Committee. The Ministry of Health implemented the scheme with the country being divided into zones, designated as 'evacuation', 'neutral' or 'reception'. Priority evacuees were moved from the big urban centres and billeted on the available private housing in more rural districts. Each area covered approximately 30 per cent of the population. However, a number of urban areas that were bombed during the war had not been classified for evacuation. In early 1939, the reception areas generated lists of available housing. Room for a couple of thousand people was found. The state also built camps which provided a few thousand spaces.

In non-evacuation areas, for football grounds with a capacity of 60,000, the chief constable was given the discretion to allow up to 15,000 spectators to enter all-ticket games (the tickets would need to be purchased in advance). The latter regulation quickly proved to be unfeasible. Ultimately, London clubs were allowed crowds of up to 15,000, using tickets bought on match days via the turnstiles.

The secretary of the Pools Promoters' Association, E. Holland Hughes, declared on 20 September that public demand, alongside the desire of members to provide employment, had led the association to agree to the reintroduction of football pools. Irish League matches and what English and Scottish games might be scheduled would form the basis of, for all the seemingly philanthropic language used by Holland Hughes, this nice wartime earner for the promoters.

It was decided, on 22 September, that English professional players would receive up to £2 for each game played. This was subsequently 'reviewed' and cut to 30*s* (£1.50). For any given match, eleven players and one reserve would be eligible for remuneration (this would later be raised to fourteen players). There would be no championships or trophies and players would not receive bonuses. The League contacted clubs, letting them know that their joint response would decide how games would be organised on a regional basis. It was announced that registered players would be allowed to assist clubs (that they were not registered with) within a reasonable distance of where they lived or worked, on the understanding that the clubs they were registered with approved. A set minimum admission price to matches of 1*s* (5p) was put in place, although clubs were free to allow entry to those in the Services, women and boys at a lower cost. Partly as a consequence of insurance considerations, 2 per cent of net receipts would be taken by the League.

Another batch of friendlies was organised for 23 September. A couple of days later, the earlier stipulation that games could only be played between clubs no more than 50 miles from each other was rescinded. The only limitation on travel was that away sides needed to complete round trips in a day. The majority of boards believed (or might have said they believed) that most clubs could get to any other club in a day. The limiting factors at club level were firstly the cost of getting to a venue and secondly if the crowd at the end of the journey warranted the outlay for getting there. Everything else was noise in the machine.

Not long into the war, the authorities disallowed anyone below the age of 23 from being eligible for the police because of the demands of the Armed Forces. So all plans for maintaining team continuity at Upton Park were at least partially scuppered and life would only get harder for West Ham and other professional clubs. But the game did what it could to continue. On 23 September, West Ham, in compliance with restrictions, played their first friendly of the new season in the 'safe' area of Bournemouth (which contradictorily during the war seemed to get more than its fair share of bombing). At Dean Court, Stan Foxall and Sam Small saw to it that the Irons claimed a 2–1 victory. The Hammers lined up as follows:

Ernie Gregory
Charlie Bicknell
Steve Forde
Ted Fenton
Dick Walker
Jim Barrett
Stan Foxall
Sam Small
George Foreman
Len Goulden
Jackie Morton

SO WHAT NOW?

On the last day of September, two grounds hit the 8,000 crowd limit. At Elm Park, Arsenal met Reading (the North Londoners won 3–1), and at Upton Park, West Ham beat Millwall 2–1 (George Foreman got both goals for the Hammers). The team:

Ernie Gregory	Stan Foxall
Charlie Bicknell	Sam Small
Steve Forde	George Foreman
Ted Fenton	Len Goulden
Dick Walker	Jackie Morton
Jim Barrett	

For the initial friendly matches, West Ham drew on players from both teams that had faced Fulham back in August (even that seemed a world away), plus John ('Jackie') Morton.

WARTIME FOOTBALL

At the end of September, the joint FA/League War Emergency Committee announced its plans for wartime football. There were to be eight regional competitions. Two would be designated 'South', with divisions 'A' and 'B'. These competitions would include clubs from London and the south of England. Other sections would be East Midlands, Midlands, North-West, North-East, Western and South-Western. Players would be paid 30*s* (£1.50) a match (the maximum pre-war weekly wage had been £8) and guest players would be allowed, with the proviso that the club they were registered with gave permission.

Just half-a-dozen of the eighty-eight League clubs rejected the chance to take part: Sunderland, Aston Villa, Ipswich Town, Derby County, Gateshead and Exeter City. Because of wartime exigencies, Birmingham and Arsenal would not be able to play on their own grounds (the Gunners had made arrangements to share White Hart Lane with Spurs).

All the regional leagues would, as was usual in the British game, award 2 points for a victory, 1 for a draw. However, twenty-one clubs had indicated that they wanted to be part of a London area competition. Luton Town was ultimately placed in the Midlands section, but this didn't resolve much as the capital's eleven clubs were loath to be split up by the regionalisation. Every team wanted to play Arsenal as matches *v.* the Gunners promised better pay days on the gate. London clubs were also less than happy about the prospect of travelling to the south coast for games (Southampton, Portsmouth and Bournemouth had been slotted into the South 'B' Division) when a completely feasible competition could have been created by the capital's clubs alone.

For the London clubs there was no good reason why the Football League had to be involved. They believed that the London Combination, under the governance of the London Football Association, could run a perfectly good competition. For a while it looked like the Cockney clubs might break away, although this possibility was always denied by the League.

Fred Howarth, the League secretary, had envisaged up to eighteen clubs competing in each league. This number was in part dictated by the fact that there were at best thirty-four playing days left in the season by the earliest start date. Eventually the eleven London clubs agreed to groupings that provided two divisions and eighteen games for each club, as long as they were able to stage matches on successive playing days. This was something of a compromise but it allowed them to organise a competition for the second half of the season, under the auspices of the London Combination, with the clubs shuffling around – for West Ham this was the 'C' Division. The new season would kick off on 21 October. In the meantime, friendly matches continued, although interest was minimal; in fact the drawing power of these fixtures was relatively pitiful. James Fay, the secretary of the Players' Union, was predictably discontent with regard to player payment, grumbling that it was 'not adequate'.

On 7 October the Hammers faced Spurs in a friendly encounter at White Hart Lane. George Foreman and Jim Barrett gave the visitors a 2–0 win. A week later Charlton were walloped at Upton Park 9–2 (Sam Small 3, George Foreman 3, singles came from Almeric Hall, Len Goulden and Stan Foxall). Most of the West Ham XI that day would serve the club during the difficult years of war. The Hammers side was:

Harry Reed Hooper
Charlie Bicknell
Steve Forde
Ted Fenton
Dick Walker
Joe Cockroft
Sam Small
Almeric Hall
George Foreman
Len Goulden
Stan Foxall

Four days later, what was to become a wartime tradition of representative friendlies was inaugurated at Aldershot. An FA XI, which included eight internationals, met a combined side known locally as 'Camp and Town' in aid of the Red Cross and St John Ambulance. This team included five players registered with Aldershot FC alongside half-a-dozen capped professional players who had joined the army. Hammer Len Goulden was a late replacement for the unfit Everton and England man Cliff Britton. This match revealed much about the character of football in the Second World War. The gate of close to 10,000 raised over £350 (so much for the 8,000 crowd restriction).

The FA's Lester Finch, who had played for Great Britain in the 1936 Berlin Olympics, scored the only goal of the game. He was one of two amateurs in their side. He had scored a goal in the first round at 'Hitler's Games' in Britain's 2–0 victory over China. Sadly, 2 goals from Arsenal's Bernard Joy were not enough to beat eventual bronze medallists Poland in the quarter-finals, but team GB went out fighting in a 5–4 defeat.

FIGHTING FOR ARRIVAL …

So the chilly winds of wartime football began to blow as winter approached the Docklands of East London. Soon Britannia and her Empire would be standing alone against the grim evil that was engulfing Europe and casting shadows over the rest of world. Soon the death camps would be established, just a day or so away by ferry and train, no one knew what to expect, apart from the worst.

My father was a 9-year-old living in Custom House, the bull's-eye for the Nazi bombers as part of the dock-side storehouse of the country. He looked into the coming night, with my grandfather making his way to face the nightmare in northern Europe and my grandmother (Eleanor, known universally as 'Nell') refusing to allow him to be evacuated, believing her – their – London was where they belonged, where their support mechanisms were and so the best and safest place for her and her only child.

My grandfather, Jim Belton, was a stoker, son of a stoker and a Gypsy mother, in Beckton Gasworks. These men toiled in the bowels of the earth, feeding the hell-like furnaces, practically naked in the atrocious heat, except for the iron boots that protected their feet from the burning embers that fell to the ground. Drinking salty milk to sustain themselves, they were a massively muscled, industrial barbarian breed. With the coming of war, although they were in a reserved occupation, many like my grandfather rose from the grim engine rooms of the most awesomely gigantic city on earth, with all the pent-up odium of generations of excruciatingly exhausting shift exploitation. These rolling twelve-hour tortures excoriated the body and distorted the mind; the havoc that Jim and his kind were to wreak among the Nazis is a chilling tale. Such confessions (for that is what they were) were told only on remote, cold, dark nights, round an open-air fire, to an audience of a single wide-eyed grandson. His enemy would have seen nothing like him – many would not live to relate the experience. Once he told me how he tore three of the foe apart with his bare hands … and teeth. In the telling of such tales was the only time I would see the few tears he had.

FIGHTING FOR SURVIVAL

The whole of my grandfather's life before and after the war was a series of battles; the last was the one he lost, writhing against pain, on a grim iron bed, set in a dingy, fifty-bed cancer ward in Stratford, a far cry from 'Olympic City', forty-odd years on. Nell told me about the time when they were homeless in the late 1930s, when my dad was a baby. There was a one-room flat available in Poplar, in a dark tenement, long since and rightly demolished. The landlord took pity on the little family, although he had promised the flat to an Irish family. So for sport, he proposed the right to lodge in his slum would be settled by a bare-knuckle fist-fight, to be held in the gloomy yard encompassed by this black building. Jim's Irish opponent was a giant of a labouring man, towering over the man from Canning Town and perhaps twice as wide. Bare-chested, the pugilists met one another in front of a huge crowd that had gathered in the yard; women and children hung out of the tenement windows for a grandstand view of the event; it was a gladiatorial atmosphere. The Irishman was powerful and brave, but the spite and venom from the stoker, protecting and fighting for his family, came by way of some primal place. Swinging and battering, a blind and mad fury from Jim engulfed the opponent, as blood flowed, sputum splashed and bone shattered. The end came on the low crunching tone of a head-butt, shockingly delivered from the thighs, via a heavily sinewed neck. The landing caused even the most hard-eyed spectator to divert their gaze.

That night Nell and little Jim had a roof over their heads as my grandfather left for the night-shift. Such is the cost of the lack of social housing; in the last analysis, we are dehumanised by trying to stay human. The post-war Labour government, understanding this, built over a million homes; some semblance of a will to fulfil the largely reneged-upon promise of 'homes for heroes' after the Great War. Yet we have since drunk sour milk from the Thatcherite teat, at a high price that we are perhaps yet fully to pay.

Nell came from a Gypsy site in Barking. Her brother (another Jim) would play a role in liberating the concentration camps; he drove one of the bulldozers that were used to clear the bodies of murdered Jews, Catholics, communists and ... Gypsies. The two Jims, volunteers for the fight, were great friends after the war. They were often silent in their brotherhood; not hard to understand why.

Football's survival, and West Ham's continued existence, would be part of the nation's resources, although in 1939 few had anything but doubts that Britain had the ability to endure what was to come. However, football is a game, a cultural asset, founded on human hope, and as Sir Geoff Hurst was to say, 'football is a game of tomorrows'; at the start of the war years, there was hope for tomorrow (certainly according to Walter Kent and Nat Burton by way of East Ham's Vera Lynn) 'when the world is free' ... Up the 'Ammers!

TWO

THE HAMMERS GO TO WAR

> ... the general opinion was that war would not come. But it did. On Sunday morning we all reported to White Hart Lane, for we were due to play Southampton on Monday, but no preparation was necessary. War had been declared.
>
> *Ronnie Burgess, Spurs*

Even in the first few weeks of the war, Mass Observation, an organisation established in 1937 to record public opinion and reactions, found that the abolition of competitive professional sport, making another change in the routine of everyday life, risked having 'deep repercussions' across British society. It was 1940 when Mass Observation argued:

> Sports like football have an absolute effect on the morale of the people and one Saturday afternoon of league matches could probably do more to affect people's spirits than the recent £50,000 Government poster campaign urging cheerfulness.

In short, football might not have had the means to win the war, but it would help to prevent Britain from losing it. Mass Observation was unable to identify a single pre-war football fan who believed that the sport needed to be stopped for the duration of hostilities. Indeed, the organisation found that just 2 per cent of people uninterested in the game in peacetime were in favour of football's suspension in wartime. However, just after the start of conflict Mass Observation found that only 65 per cent of supporters who turned up for games before the war could do so after war was declared – travel restrictions, Saturday shift-work in factories and obligations to family prevented them from attending matches.

ESTABLISHING A WAY FORWARD

War brought an end to transfers in football and a couple of days after the Scottish FA suspended contracts between clubs and players, effectively convening the initial meeting of the War Emergency Committee, fifteen representatives from the Football League and the Football Association got together to replicate the Scottish decision, but in actuality they were merely actioning a resolution made a year previously.

The First World War had, up to 1916, been totally fought by volunteer servicemen. During 1939 conscription was introduced almost immediately, creating quite different conditions. Added to this the threat of aerial bombardment was more of a certainty than was the case in the Great War (although Germany carried out air raids and naval bombardments on Britain from Folkestone to Hartlepool in the First World War). There was hardly a British community or family unaffected by the slaughter of 1914–18, but in the main men were transported to the relatively remote front line. In 1939, the prospect of air raids, something that had been a constant worry for the several years over which war had been seen as a distinct possibility, was understandably the source of huge public trepidation. The world had seen what this type of warfare could do in the Spanish context; how much worse would it be, given that British cities were so much more densely populated than their counterparts in Spain? So when the war started, it was not unexpected when the government banned the assembly of crowds, which translated into the immediate suspension of public entertainment, including sport. What was surprising is that, with regard to football, this decision was so swiftly binned.

None the less, football, for a time, had been in a sort of no-man's-land of its own, which placed the players in an invidious situation. The retain-and-transfer system that pertained in 1939 – and which was to do so until the 1960s – tied professionals to their clubs. As war loomed large, so the players were discarded by their clubs, just like any other unnecessary expense, which in practice they were. This left many with little alternative than to sign up for service.

However, the clubs retained the registration of players, so maintaining their control over them in footballing terms. From a contemporary perspective it is hard to see why the players seem merely to have accepted this situation, but this was how the game had been run since the beginning of professionalism and they were dependent on the structure. If the players had become free agents, there would have been no foundation on which to restructure football in order to acclimatise to the wartime circumstances. If clubs had been forced to close down completely for the duration of hostilities, there would have been little if any financial basis on which to continue a professional structure when peace came. Added to this, plant (meaning equipment, facilities and, most importantly, the maintenance of grounds) and a rising generation of players (and skills development) would also have been sacrificed. For the game to survive the war in any recognisable form, the clubs' determination, alongside the ambition and desire of the players, was required.

Ultimately the Players' Union accepted whatever minimum payment the Football League agreed to for an experimental period, understanding that regional competition could benefit football much more than the relatively meaningless friendlies that were proving less and less of an attraction. They also wanted to look at the potential for pooling the gate money, any surplus being passed on to the players as a bonus, together with the interest from the Jubilee Fund. With numerous players going through straitened times financially, the Union made many grants to its members.

The Management Committee of the League resolved that:

> Permission is granted to any club to implement any promise made to players on joining HM Forces up to and including 8 September when all players' service agreements were suspended.

In effect this meant the maximum payment of 30*s* a week; there would be no extra money for playing. However, West Ham came to the decision to pay all their players 30*s* a week regardless of whether they played or not (probably looking to inspire a sense of loyalty). Around two dozen Hammers were by this time serving in the army and the board agreed that these men should not be at a financial disadvantage because of their patriotism.

REGIONAL LEAGUE SOUTH 'A' DIVISION

Crystal Palace came to Upton Park for the opening game of South 'A' Division. Despite 2 goals from Stan Foxall, West Ham lost that first match (Palace hit half-a-dozen). But while the result wasn't unimportant, more importantly, just forty-eight days from war being declared, football had overcome almost every obstacle placed in its way and had laid the ground to maintain the competitive game, as well as something of its professional ethos. This might be thought of as a small but significant victory of faith and determination over adversity.

However, while disruption in London and elsewhere in Britain was not as bad as might have been expected, considerations such as transport alone would have been enough to scupper the countrywide excursions demanded of 'normal' football. This said, there was a clear will to keep football alive and working at a level that would capture the passion of the people and provide a significant means of deflecting attention and improving morale.

For all this, initially there was no mad rush to attend games in the regional competitions. The visit of Palace to Upton Park pulled in a crowd of 6,700, and by the time the 'expenses' had been settled (according to one player I spoke to some years ago, this was a somewhat 'creative' exercise on the part of the Upton Park administration), Palace hardly covered their travel costs.

In the main, attendances were not much improved compared to friendlies, and while the expenses that clubs had were not as great as in the peacetime game, income was way too close to running costs. Five per cent of net gate receipts went straight to the League; what was left was shared between the two clubs involved in any particular game. Four weeks went by before the first five-figure crowd (12,000) watched Norwich entertain Arsenal (the match ended 1–1, with Cliff Bastin on target for the Gunners). West Ham's first four matches, comprising the 6–2 beating by the (then) Glaziers, a 5–3 defeat at Carrow Road, a 2–1 Boleyn Ground win over Spurs and a 2–2 draw at the Den (Archie Macaulay and Dick Dunn had put the Hammers 2–0 up at half-time but Tom Brolly and Jimmy Jinks hit back for the Lions), were watched by an aggregate 24,500. However, the forty-one regional wartime games played up to the week before the latter match (4 November) produced a combined turnout of just 101,000; a year earlier, forty-four Football League matches had been attended by 685,000 people. Nonetheless, West Ham was doing a lot better than average.

THE GAME TAKES SHAPE

Despite an apparent reticence to go to matches, the public continued to bet on football (the great perennial of the professional game). During that November of 1939, the new 'Unity Pools' was put together, uniting the giants of the pursuit: Littlewoods, Vernons, Copes, Shermans, Socapools, Bonds', Jervis and Screens. The combined coupon conserved paper, minimised handling and so maximised profits. In January, a Hull woman won a record Unity Pools payout; for her 1*s* and 6*d* (7½p) she attracted a dividend of £8,059 (odds of over 107,000 to 1!).

On 11 November at Ninian Park, Cardiff, a crowd of 28,000 watched Wales draw 1–1 with England with proceeds going to the Red Cross. This reiterated the public thirst for the game, particularly representative encounters. The home side led by an Ernest Glover goal at half-time, but one of two West Ham players on international duty that day, Len Goulden (the other was Ted Fenton), equalised for the visitors.

Retrospectively the 'war game' can be seen emerging; a type of football was evolving to the conditions, finding the means first to adapt, in order to survive, with the ambition to thrive. To provide more income, many clubs continued to arrange friendlies, but in November 1939 the relatively stroppy London clubs organised fixtures to take them from the end of February to the start of June. 'South C' League was made up of pre-war First and Second Division clubs, while peacetime Division Three clubs formed a 'South D' League. The clubs involved were unable to complete their South A and South B schedule before the start of these competitions, but with just one omission all outstanding games were completed, generally as midweek matches.

Early December saw winter hit Britain with full force. With newspapers and radio prohibited from forecasting the weather (as a result of anxiety about aiding the enemy), a level of mayhem became unavoidable; supporters could not be forewarned of cancellations. Two days before Christmas, football postponements became endemic due to fog, but this didn't stop West Ham beating Norwich (4–1), and the day after (Boxing Day) Tottenham were put to the proverbial sword (the only goal of the game came from George Foreman). Early in January rationing started, initially restricting the availability of butter, bacon and sugar. On the 27th of that month a mere 7 out of 59 matches were played in the lowest temperatures recorded since 1894; hundreds of people died as a result of the conditions.

Indeed, the first three football seasons of the Second World War were notable for their harsh weather conditions. In 1939/40, however, not only was snow a significant problem, the winter also contained the longest-lasting ice storm Britain had known (27 January to 3 February 1940) and gale-force winds in south-east England created drifts well over 15ft (nearly 4.6m). The game was, of course, hard hit, but there was a feeling that 'if we can survive this, we can deal with anything'.

If the 1939/40 season had not been a wartime contest, the Irons might have been well pleased with the outcome – lots of goals, with decisive results over long-established adversaries like Spurs, who were defeated in all of their 4 games against West Ham (11–3 on aggregate). Chelsea were equally embarrassed, losing by a combined score of 14–5 in their two encounters with the rampant Hammers. The rampaging East Enders were involved in just one goalless match in all their games following the abandonment of the Football League programme; the side failed to score in just a couple of the others. Finishing runners-up to the mighty Arsenal, together with their performance in the Football League War Cup, constituted a great season for West Ham.

South 'A', 1939/40							
	Played	Won	Drawn	Lost	For	Against	Points
Arsenal	18	13	4	1	62	22	30
West Ham United	18	12	1	5	57	33	25
Millwall	18	8	5	5	46	38	21
Watford	18	9	3	6	44	38	21
Norwich City	18	7	6	5	41	36	20
Charlton Athletic	18	8	1	9	61	58	17
Crystal Palace	18	5	3	10	39	56	13
Clapton Orient	18	5	3	10	28	60	13
Tottenham Hotspur	18	5	2	11	37	43	12
Southend United	18	4	0	14	30	61	8

Football's initial response to war was a resolve not to make the same errors as those made in 1914, when the Football League and the FA Cup had continued as normal for a complete season. This had resulted in something of a class war within the general hostilities (see Belton 2014). Everyone associated with the game was at some point condemned as lacking in patriotism and/or being unproductive in terms of the war effort; in short, traitors.

However, society had learnt lessons from the Great War with regard to football. Between 1939 and 1945 the game would be part of the country's defensive strategy, a means of diversion via entertainment (for the most part) and solace, but also part of the means to hold firm to a British way of life; a semblance of normality. As such, the game played a role in establishing a firm foundation on which to strike back at the evils of international fascism. Football would, in this conflict, be a vibrant and meaningful force for good!

With West Ham playing their Division 'C' football well into the late spring, supporters were coming to games at a time of almost inconceivable international tension. On 9 April 1940, Germany invaded Norway and Denmark, so starting the war in the west.

By the beginning of March, the clubs were asking for an extension to the season, not least so that a knockout competition, which they viewed as a potential money-spinner, could be fitted in. It was agreed that the season could run until 8 June and the preliminary rounds of the War Cup would begin on 13 April.

On 4 March it was decided that players could be paid a bonus of £1 for a win and 10*s* (50p) for a draw in War Cup ties.

The 'C' Division was really a great success. Winding up on 5 June, it attracted the best part of 130,000 over West Ham's 18-game schedule. The most amazing game was the 10–3 pummelling of Chelsea on their own Stamford Bridge turf; a Ted Fenton hat-trick was added to by 4 from Sam Small, 2 from Foreman and a single from Foxall – a day for the 'Fs' – while Chelsea's reply was a Joe Payne hat-trick. As in the South 'A' Division, George Foreman was top scorer with 19 goals (he hit 17 in the early season schedule).

'C' Division, 1939/40							
	Played	Won	Drawn	Lost	For	Against	Points
Tottenham Hotspur	18	11	4	3	43	30	26
West Ham United	18	10	4	4	53	28	24
Arsenal	18	9	5	4	41	26	23
Brentford	18	8	4	6	42	34	20
Millwall	18	7	5	6	36	30	19
Charlton Athletic	18	7	4	7	39	56	18
Fulham	18	8	1	9	38	42	17
Southampton	18	5	3	10	28	55	13
Chelsea	18	4	3	11	33	53	11
Portsmouth	18	3	3	12	26	45	9

Charlie Bicknell had appeared more times than any other West Ham player with 41 League and War Cup outings.

'There'll Always Be An England' had been written and distributed in the summer of 1939. The song had become massively popular after war had been declared. It was composed and written by Manchurian Ross Parker (born Albert Rostron Parker in 1914) and Hugh Charles (born Charles Hugh Owen Ferry in Stockport, 1907).

The song was first heard in Carroll Levis's film *Discoveries* (1939), sung by Glyn Davies, a boy soprano. On 1 September, the song, sung by Vera Lynn, became a huge hit and by November 200,000 copies of the sheet music had been sold.

Parker died in 1974. Ferry composed many other songs, including another big Vera Lynn hit, 'We'll Meet Again'. He was the manager of the famous and popular Jack Hylton band during the war. He left his wife and family to live with Jack Hylton's sister, Alice. He died in 1995.

Apart from un/official internationals, other representative games were prolific in number during the 1939/40 season. On 18 October 1939, Stan Foxall played for an FA XI *v.* an Aldershot and Army side (the FA won 1–0), and on 25 November, Hammer Joe Musgrave was part of an Army XI defeated 4–1 by an FA XI. Len Goulden ran out for an England XI that turned over the Army 4–3 on 20 January 1940, and he was in action again for the London Pros *v.* London Amateurs in the Pros' 4–2 victory.

THREE

THE WAR CUP

(1940)

In a life and death struggle,
we cannot afford to leave our destinies
in the hands of failures.

Clement Atlee, Labour Party leader,
on the British management of the war in Norway

The Football League War Cup tournament of 1940 was hurriedly organised and took place over nine weeks. This was during what came to be known as the Phoney War, a strange period of uncertainty when few people knew if the war was a flash in the pan or Armageddon. It was a massively popular competition; more than 260,000 people watched the 32 first-leg ties.

On 13 April 1940 the preliminary stage of the tournament involved thirty-eight peacetime Third Division teams, brought together on a regional basis. They played one-off matches. For the first round proper, restrictions on attendance were relaxed, allowing crowds of up to 50 per cent of ground capacity, reliant on the permission of the local chief constable. Any replays were sorted out by way of mid-week games.

On the same day, at Wembley Stadium, a crowd of 40,000 watched Wales defeat a fine England team that included Hammer Len Goulden. Arsenal's Bryn Jones (who served in the

Royal Artillery during wartime) scored the only goal. Although George 'Willie' Hall missed a penalty for England, the Welsh fighting spirit won the day.

The Football League War Cup rules stipulated that guest players could not be used except in emergencies; that the whole of football was a bit of an emergency procedure seemed to have been forgotten by officials, and retrospectively this idea can be seen as a pretty thoughtless effort to enforce a sort of peacetime ambiance. An appreciable number of players flatly refused to go back to the clubs they were registered with to play ties, given where they were stationed in the Services or employed in war work. As a result, the 'no-guest' tenet soon proved to be an unreasonable and impractical rule to implement consistently.

The preliminary ties were followed by the first round; this was decided over two legs with the pre-1939/40 First and Second Division clubs entering the fray. The draw at this stage was regionalised, the ties taking place on Saturday, 20 April with the return games scheduled a week later.

NAMSOS

At this time the Allies were doing what they could to counter the German invasion of Norway that had started on 9 April. On the day of the first leg of the Football League War Cup, the small town of Namsos, a base for Anglo-French forces in central Norway, was bombed. The buildings in the town were for the most part made of wood and therefore the destruction was complete and, as reported at the time, 'without consideration of the civil population'.

The Namsos campaign involved heavy fighting between Anglo-French and Norwegian naval and military forces against the German Army, naval and air forces, which continued up to early May 1940. It was one of the first significant occasions during the Second World War when British and French land forces fought the German Army together. It was a desperate attempt to deny Nazi access to the iron-ore resources of northern Norway. But the Germans' superior equipment ultimately led to the evacuation and defeat of the Allies.

BATTLING BLUES

West Ham's debut in the War Cup was a tie against Chelsea at the Boleyn Ground and 15,200 home supporters turned up for this inaugural confrontation. Fresh from their league domination of the West Londoners, the confidence in the West Ham dressing room had to be high. But Chelsea might have seen the tie as a chance to redress the balance and get some dignity back. Billy Birrell was the wartime manager at Stamford Bridge; he was the man who would bring Ron Greenwood, West Ham and England manager-to-be, into the Chelsea side from their youth set-up in 1940. As a player, Birrell had turned out for Raith Rovers and Middlesbrough, winning the Second Division title with the latter in 1927, before moving into management. He returned to Raith to become manager before going to Bournemouth in 1930 and then in 1935 joining Queens Park Rangers. After guiding Rangers to third place in Division Three South in 1938, he was appointed manager of First Division Chelsea shortly before the outbreak of the Second World War.

During Birrell's time at Stamford Bridge, the Blues consistently finished in mid-table, but narrowly avoided relegation to the Second Division in 1951 on goal average. However, Bill guided Chelsea to two FA Cup semi-finals, in 1950 and 1952, on both occasions losing out to Arsenal in replays. So this man was a fighter in knockout football.

Birrell retired following the final defeat at the hands of the Gunners in the Cup, to be replaced by Ted Drake. Billy played a significant part in the development of Chelsea's youth system, which was to pay dividends for future managers.

HERMAN (NOT A GERMAN)

For most of April, Charlie Paynter had turned to the man who had kept goal for the Irons for much of the last part of the final season of peacetime football, Herman Conway.

Born in Gainsborough, Lincolnshire (11 October 1908), Conway was to make 37 appearances for the wartime Hammers in the 1939/40 and 1940/41 seasons, taking a bit of stick given that he shared a first name with the commander-in-chief of the Luftwaffe.

A strapping 6ft-tall, reliable keeper, Conway had moved to Upton Park from Turf Moor in 1934. He had broken into the Burnley side in February 1930. Prior to signing for the Clarets he gained a reputation with Gainsborough Trinity, playing from March 1929 in the Midland League.

As a boy, Conway had been inspired by the Aston Villa, Liverpool and England goalie Sam Hardy, but went to Burnley on the recommendation of another former England custodian, Jerry Dawson, a twenty-one-year (and more than 500-game) servant of the Lancashire club.

At Upton Park, providing defenders with assurance by way of his secure handling, Conway turned out 41 times in the League during 1934/35 term, a campaign wherein Bolton Wanderers gained promotion to Division One by a nose, bettering West Ham on goal average only.

In December 1938, with more than 100 senior outings under his belt, Conway's reign between the posts at the Boleyn Ground was ended by Harry Medhurst. During the first half of the 1939/40 season he played for Tunbridge Wells Rangers before taking up duties in defence of King and Country. Rising through the ranks, Conway was to become commandant of a supply camp in Accrington, fulfilling the role of adjutant-quartermaster.

During the war years, Conway's military commitments allowed him to turn out for Blackburn Rovers (ironically the team he effectively locked out of the 1940 Wembley War Cup Final).

After the conflict he was offered a place at Ewood Park, but he chose to return south to carry on his interests in the construction industry.

In August 1945 Harry Warren, the immediate post-war manager of Southend United, brought Conway to Southend Stadium (Grainger Road) to play in the transitional, regionalised Third Division; he lived in Chadwell Heath at this point (not too far from the current West Ham training ground). He packed up playing in May 1946.

Conway and his wife were regulars at Upton Park up to his death in April 1983. He played more than 200 Football League games for Burnley and West Ham United; he made 122 League (and 5 FA Cup) appearances for the Hammers (1934 to 1938) and between 1930 and 1934 he had protected the Burnley nets on 81 occasions in the Football League.

The East End's local press recorded the Hammers' first hurdle of the War Cup.

Hammers Just Home – Late Winner at Boleyn

West Ham 3, Chelsea 2

West Ham yesterday won this match representing the first half of the first round of the Football League Cup at Upton Park because apart from the balance of play, they showed more determination in front of goal. Their more forceful tactics brought them a greater number of scoring chances than came the way of the Chelsea forwards, and that they did not win by a larger margin was due to the fact that on occasions the ball did not run kindly for them and that Jackson, the Chelsea goalkeeper, brought off one brilliant save from Fenton. Whether the goal advantage will prove enough for West Ham to enter the next round remains to be seen. The teams meet again to decide the aggregate of goals on Saturday at Stamford Bridge.

The Hammers had to struggle hard to secure their narrow advantage for they were twice pegged back from a goal lead, but in the end obtained the winning goal a quarter of an hour before the finish. Their first point soon after the start was a fortunate one. O'Hare turning a centre from Fenton into his own goal, and after half an hour Kiernan netted a clever equaliser for Chelsea. Three minutes later Fenton scored with a grand first-time drive to give West Ham the lead again, and they maintained the advantage until fifteen minutes before the interval, when Hanson scored (apparently an accomplished baseball player) the best goal of the match, after neat play with Payne. The winning goal came from Macaulay, who headed through from a corner kick by Foxall.

The team:
Herman Conway, Charlie Bicknell, Charlie Walker, Joe Cockroft, Dick Walker, W. Masson, Sam Small, Ted Fenton, George Foreman, Archie Macaulay, Stan Foxall.

Chelsea fielded a decent side that included Tommy Kiernan (who would also turn out for Spurs during the war years). After hostilities Kiernan would return to Scotland and play 24 League and Cup games for Celtic, scoring 15 goals. He would be selected for the Scottish League before moving to Stoke in 1947.

The Chelsea side: John Jackson, John O'Hare, George Barber, David Alexander, Bob Griffiths, Sam Weaver, Dick Spence, Tom Kiernan, Joe Payne, Sid Foss, Alf Hanson.

West Ham's first sortie into the Football League War Cup had been an exciting game, played just a week after the Hammers' hard-fought 1–1 Upton Park draw with Brentford in Division 'C'. The fact that the Cup combatants were only separated by John O'Hare's own goal set up an intriguing second leg. But the Hammers were taking a very slender lead to Stamford Bridge.

TREPIDATIOUS SKIES

On the day of West Ham's first Football League War Cup tie, all over London there were signs of preparation against air attack, but over 8 million Londoners, living in the biggest bombing target in Europe, were still waiting for the attrition to start. It was a city of sandbags, piled high round the windows and doorways of public buildings, shop fronts and underground shelters. The bags, however, were beginning to turn green as they weathered and began to leak at the corners.

Estate agents' boards blossomed in Belgravia and Mayfair, as the rich and titled escaped to safer venues in the shires. In Eaton Square only six houses out of 120 were occupied. There were no takers.

But in the City, which had been so quiet six months previously, when 3,500 firms had fled to the provinces, daily life had returned to near-normal. At least 700 companies had returned, and thousands of office workers poured along almost traffic-free streets. Hardly one carried a gas mask.

There were no paintings on view at the National Gallery – they had been stored in a slate quarry in Wales – but the gallery was filled every day with music lovers who attended Londoner Myra Hess's lunchtime piano concerts; during the war years, with public concerts darkened, she organised around 1,700 afternoon bashes, knocking out around 150 Joanna performances herself.

The middle of Hyde Park was wired off as a military area; indeed sandbagged shelters disfigured all the parks. But the barrage balloons, shining in the evening sun, looked almost romantic – like pearls strung from clouds.

On 20 April, Hitler celebrated his 51st birthday. He is known to have eaten copious amounts of cake, so one can surmise this was on the menu. He was particularly partial to 'Führer Cake' – an apple cake laden with nuts and raisins, which had to be baked each day and left out every night. This, along with his vegetarian diet, might explain his medical records (commissioned by the US military). The latter evidences that he took around thirty different drugs in the hope of moderating his farting. In the process he imbibed strychnine, a poison, which probably explained his constant stomach pains. Propaganda minister Joseph Goebbels, with a characteristically forced joviality, declared in a radio broadcast that 'The German people have found in the Führer the incarnation of their strength and the most brilliant exponent of their national aims.' He made no mention of his prestigious trumping. American journalist William L. Shirer quoted this passage in his *Berlin Diary* (1934–1941), noting that the birthday celebrations were poorly attended that year. The fighting in Norway continued and German casualties were mounting. However, to celebrate his birthday, Hitler ordered a new SS regiment to be set up, made up of Norwegians and Danes as well as Germans.

Norway was never the prize that Hitler had hoped it would be. Yes, it acted as a base from which Germany could attack the Allied Arctic convoys to the USSR, but the defence and holding of Norway took more Nazi resources than the country's strategic usefulness warranted.

While the Namsos campaign was still going on, it was understood to have gone so badly for Britain that a vote of no confidence in Parliament saw the government suffer a reduced majority, causing Prime Minister Neville Chamberlain to resign.

Winston Churchill, as the First Lord of the Admiralty, was the man with responsibility for the Norwegian campaign. He had made many of the tactical decisions involved that turned out to be huge mistakes. Of course, in political and historical terms he came out on top and led Britain throughout the rest of the war years. History is indeed paradoxical.

THE LITTLE SHIPS

Despite the frenetic preparation for war, London was hardly touched physically between September 1939 and April 1940, the period that would come to be known as the 'Phoney War'. However, a month after West Ham's games with Chelsea in April 1940, Hitler's forces overran France, trapping largely British forces at Dunkirk, on the French north coast.

Evacuation started on 26 May, but heavy German bombing had destroyed Dunkirk's harbour, stranding hundreds of thousands of Allied troops on the beach, with little option but to hope for rescue. Whenever the weather allowed, the Luftwaffe attacked until Dunkirk was not much more than rubble.

On 29 May, the British public were told of the evacuation, and responding to pleas from the government, a flotilla of privately owned boats made for Dunkirk, looking to bring the beleaguered troops back to England. This brave, humane armada was forever to be known as the 'Little Ships'. Many of these vessels came out of London's docklands, estuary towns and villages to the east and west; among them were hard-working cockle boats from Southend and Leigh, posh river cruisers that had never tasted sea water, and sixteen Thames sailing barges, their shallow draft allowing them to get close to the Dunkirk beaches. Eight of them ran aground and had to be abandoned. Several Thames paddle steamers, which had been used before the war for pleasure trips, also made the trip. One such was the famous *Crested Eagle*, which was bombed and sunk, but the *Royal Daffodil* got back to London after rescuing 9,000 troops, even though she had been machine gunned, bombed and torpedoed. Some of the craft were made by Thames Ironworks, the company out of which West Ham United evolved, including the *Jane Hannah MacDonald* lifeboat.

There was a fervent welcome home for the London fireboat *Massey Shaw* on her return from Dunkirk. Her heroic passage started at Ramsgate. Placed under the command of an officer of the Royal Navy, the White Ensign was hoisted over her decks.

Massey Shaw's shallow draught meant she was able to run close in to the beaches and ferry around 500 servicemen to bigger craft lying further off shore. She was the final 'little ship' to disembark and on her last crossing rescued ninety-six men, bringing them back to Ramsgate.

In the *London Gazette*, Rear Admiral Sir Bertram Ramsey, KCB, Flag Officer Commanding, Dover, wrote:

> Of the civilian manned craft, one of the best performances was that of the London Fire Brigade boat *Massey Shaw*. All the volunteer crew were members of the London Fire Brigade or AFS, and they succeeded in making three round trips to the beaches in their well-found craft.

After 'Operation Dynamo' (the name given to the evacuation of Dunkirk) ended on 4 June, 198,000 British and 140,000 French and Belgian servicemen had been rescued, but most of their heavy equipment had been discarded in northern France. Six destroyers were lost as were eight personnel ships and some 200 small craft, from a total of approximately 860 craft of all sizes.

Another 220,000 Allied troops were brought back to England by British ships from other ports in France (Brest, Cherbourg, Saint-Malo and Saint-Nazaire). So in all 558,000 Allied personnel were evacuated.

While more than a million men were taken prisoner by the Nazis over three weeks, at a cost of 60,000 casualties, the evacuation was a major boost to British morale and enabled the Allies to fight another day – even if that fight was to be on home turf, resisting the expected German invasion of Britain.

On 7 May 1940 questions were asked in Parliament about the ease with which professional players on army service had been released to play for their former clubs in the previous Saturday's War Cup competition. The secretary of state, Oliver Stanley, asked what authority was necessary for special leave. At the end of the month it was reported that Chelmsford were paying former league players £4 a game.

But it seemed football would not be cowed; the 16 second-round War Cup ties had attracted 150,000 supporters.

FOUR

PAYNTER

> Football is not really about winning, or goals, or saves, or supporters – it's about glory. It's about doing things in style, doing them with a flourish; it's about going out to beat the other lot, not waiting for them to die of boredom; it's about dreaming of the glory …
>
> *Danny Blanchflower, Spurs and Northern Ireland*

Charles William Paynter was brought to London when his family moved to the capital. They settled in Blanche Street, Plaistow, a street off Hermit Road, Canning Town. The son of Welsh parents from Pontypool, Charlie was born in Swindon on 29 July 1879. The Paynters had been in baking for generations prior to making their way to Wiltshire in the early 1860s, where the family changed direction and became ironworkers with the Great Western Railway.

Charlie's aunt Sarah married William Absalom and it seems he was the first member of the family to work for Thames Ironworks (he was a labourer). Charlie's uncle, Fred Paynter, was soon after taken on at the Canning Town works (situated close to where Canning Town DLR station now stands). Ultimately Charlie's dad (also Charlie) was also employed by the ironworks.

Young Charlie went to Grange Road School, a short walk from the family home, and by the age of 12 he was a fully fledged

East Ender. From an early age Charlie was an all-round sportsman, and when the home of Thames Ironworks FC (the side that would evolve into West Ham United), the Memorial Grounds, was opened in 1897, practically on the Paynters' doorstep, he began to spend most of his free time there, competing in athletic events and, after a time, coaching.

Charlie managed to get himself an apprenticeship as an electrician (with the City of London Electric Light Company), but it was not long before this was cancelled (something that for most families would have been close to a scandalous event at the time). Colloquially it has been claimed that the ending of his apprenticeship was directly related to him spending more time playing and watching sports than focusing on his work. But such an action was an effective dismissal from the company. With the family living in what was anything but a well-off area, the story of Charlie's departure from the LELC, which amounts to an amicable parting of the ways, feels an unlikely scenario, especially when he soon found employment as a casual labourer with the ironworks. Nevertheless it is indicated in much that has been written about Charlie that he did spend as much time as he could training athletes. It has to be said that, for most in the field, this wasn't a huge area of expertise at the time compared to contemporary coaching practice, but mostly comprised tips and passed-on folk knowledge.

CHARLIE AND THE FOOTBALL FACTORY

Charlie played his football with Old Castle Swifts, a club among the best in the then East London/West Essex district. Swifts eventually merged with Old St Luke's. The side, who were to become 'West Ham South', made their home ground close to the Paynter family home in Hermit Road.

In 1901 Charlie was working as a dock labourer. This made sense as, being casual work, it allowed him the flexibility to develop his career in sport. Inevitably, spending most of his spare time at the Memorial Ground, a huge sporting facility (probably the best in the country at that point) that boasted a cycle and cinder running track, tennis courts and the largest outdoor swimming pool in England, Charlie became involved with the Hammers, at first on a part-time basis, working with Abe Norris, the club's 'assistant' trainer, who was unpaid but got a fair bit of 'bunce'.

Not long after Thames Ironworks became West Ham United, on 5 November 1900, Charlie was signed as an amateur for the Hammers. The teenage left-winger did all right for a couple of seasons, but problems with a knee, an injury picked up in 1902 at Plumstead during a game *v.* Arsenal, became a limiting factor in his playing career, although there are scant reports of him having any particular prowess.

However, it seems that Paynter's principal enthusiasm had for some time been working with athletes and players as a trainer. His commitment had led him to build up some knowledge of what was then known more as 'physical therapy' ('coaching' had something of a different meaning in that era, and what Charlie did would have been understood as 'training'). Paynter appears to have used his links with the club to get a job as an assistant to the club trainer Jack Ratcliffe. He also worked under Bill Johnson before West Ham moved to Upton Park in 1904.

In 1902 Syd King was appointed West Ham United's secretary (a role that often from our current perspective might be understood as manager). King recommended Charlie to another new West Ham trainer, Tom Robinson. Paynter became the reserve team trainer and in 1912, when Robinson retired, he took over as club trainer with former West Ham player Frank Piercy as his assistant. Paynter would stay in that post for two decades, a role that included a scouting function.

In 1906 Charlie and Emily Ada Hadley were married in West Ham. Shortly after the marriage he was given a benefit match, fittingly perhaps *v.* Arsenal. This was the first time a benefit game had been organised for any West Ham employee. As one of the Second World War Hammers told me in the 1980s, 'Charlie was always well in! He knew how to grease up the board.'

Under King, West Ham rose to the top echelons of English football. In the Hammers' initial League season they finished in seventh place in Division Two; in their second term as a Football League club the Irons claimed fourth position in the Second Division, just 4 points short of a promotion place, and the third West Ham campaign concluded with the runners-up position achieved, finishing 2 points behind Notts County. In one eventful season, 1922/23, King took West Ham to their (and the) first Wembley Cup Final and broke into the elite division of the Football League.

It seems the local media in the Docklands area appreciated Paynter's contribution, especially after it was confirmed that West Ham had made it to the first Wembley Cup Final. A piece in the *East Ham Echo* of 27 April 1923 included something of Charlie's attitude as a manager:

> As Charlie Paynter, your trainer, says, 'Harmony, happiness, ability, and last but certainly not least, the spirit to fight and win' dominates West Ham United.

THE GO-BETWEEN

Charlie Paynter was something of go-between, mediating between the players and King; player issues and complaints were always, in the first instance, voiced to and filtered through Paynter. In this way, problems would only come to King's attention if Charlie thought it necessary.

In 1924 Charlie was appointed trainer to the England team for the first international to be played at Wembley (a 1–1 draw with Scotland; 5 minutes before half-time Edward Hallows Taylor put through his own net, but William Henry Walker put England level on the hour). This appointment was very likely connected with his experience of the Wembley turf, having taken West Ham to the first cup final there the previous year. Charlie, perhaps tellingly, was never to be asked to take such a role again.

Charlie did, however, allegedly build something of a reputation and other clubs, cricket teams and players, boxers and athletes, were said to have called on his services from time to time. Perhaps this was related to several of the players he worked with becoming internationals.

West Ham were relegated at the end of the 1931/32 term. King had let his side age without the introduction of sufficient new blood. This is indicated by studying the West Ham team defeated at Stamford Bridge in the final Division One match of the 1931/32 season. It included three members of the 1923 Wembley side. This was a failure of foresight but also probably involved a lack of scouting nouse, energy or will. Although his position was not under threat, during a board meeting that took place on 7 November 1932, when team matters were being discussed, King, in a drunken rant, insulted at least one director. It was recorded that:

> It was unanimously decided that until further notice, C. Paynter be given sole control of the players and that E.S. King be notified accordingly.

At an emergency board meeting convened the next evening it was agreed that:

> Mr King would be suspended for three calendar months from November 9 1932 without salary and further stipulate[d] that he shall not visit the ground during this period.

It was decided that if after this block of time the directors could be satisfied that King's behaviour had modified, he might be reinstated as secretary only (the status of manager-secretary being withdrawn) and that his salary would be reduced to £8 per week. Yet another meeting of the directors on 3 January 1933 decided that King should not be employed in any capacity. The board had also expressed concern about King's honesty in the day-to-day business of running the club. This marked the end for King at West Ham. His ostracism and humiliation were complete.

The new secretary, Alan Searles (himself sacked for nefarious practices in 1940), advised King of the decision and informed him of the board's offer of an ex-gratia payment of £3 per week 'as long as the company sees fit'. But less than a month later, the then most successful manager in the history of West Ham United and Thames Ironworks was dead. He had imbibed an alcoholic drink laced with 'corrosive liquid'. An inquest jury recorded the verdict that King had taken his own life 'whilst of unsound mind'. His son told them that the Hammers' former manager-secretary had been suffering from 'paranoia', but King the younger assured them that his father had been 'quite satisfied' with West Ham's offer of a £3 a week 'pension'. The latter contradicts the paranoia diagnosis somewhat; 'they are after me, but they are being reasonable about it'.

It was well known that King liked his ale and at the best of times would have had no trouble in finishing a crate a day. How much this had to do with his psychological condition or behaviour is debatable, but it seems that alcohol had played a part in King's demise and there were those associated with the club who thought that his death had been much more a mistake on his part than a considered attempt to take his own life.

In 1932, following King's tragic demise, Charlie Paynter was appointed manager of West Ham United. At first, there were some board members who did not want to see Paynter's appointment made permanent in the wake of King's suspension. However, given King's immediate legacy, few would have made Charlie overly culpable for West Ham's relegation to Division Two in May 1933, although it was reasonable to consider that he was also not without responsibility for the club's position. The club clearly saw Charlie as a pair of safe hands, and to mark his promotion gave him ten shares in the club and a pay rise (from £6 to £10) in 1933.

Almost immediately Paynter withdrew from training players, apparently having lost his love for the pursuit. First he brought in Sidney George 'Sid' Gibson, the former Nottingham Forest and Sheffield United outside-right, to do most of that work; and then in 1938, following Gibson's untimely death at the age of 39, Bob John from Arsenal.

Perhaps Charlie could have achieved that top-flight status had the war not intervened. In 1940, he saw the club win a Wembley Cup Final (the 'War Cup'), but by 1946, when League football resumed, too much had happened and the team that was brimming with potential in 1939 had broken up. Charlie, then 67, probably knew that he was unlikely to take the Irons back into the First Division and he told the board that he would soon be thinking of retirement. However, reading the history and talking to players who worked under Charlie, it is pretty palpable that he was very much seen as a 'yesterday man'; someone who had 'held the fort' until a younger man became available to take the club on. At the same time, he never seemed in any hurry to leave Upton Park, being around the place long after his role had been passed on to others. This does not seem like the behaviour of a man who wanted to leave the Boleyn Ground.

Paynter is widely credited for bringing Ted Fenton back to Upton Park in 1948. Although it is unlikely that he would have done anything but approve of this move in public, apocryphally it was the influential director and friend of the Cearns family,

Reg Pratt, who instigated this development. It seems that Charlie might not have been altogether pleased that Fenton was seen as the man to shape the club's future, having no great affection for Ted or his approach to the game.

Nevertheless, Fenton spent a couple of seasons alongside Paynter as his heir apparent before taking over when Charlie finally stood down in 1950. Charlie's testimonial game that same year brought Arsenal to Upton Park, yet again the Gunners playing a role in Paynter's life. It is perhaps telling that only 18,000 people (including Vera Lynn) turned up to watch West Ham play the then FA Cup holders when compared to the opening attendance of that season at the Boleyn Ground: 30,000 to watch a draw with Hull. The lowest home gate of the term was close to 13,000 – a defeat by Birmingham with nothing at all to play for at the end of April.

Charlie kept a presence at the club, outwardly stoically supporting Fenton, the talented striker who had been in Charlie's War Cup-winning side, right through the demanding decade that ended in 1960. While Charlie at times seemed to be, in the words of Malcolm Allison, 'wandering around Upton Park like a ghost', he witnessed the return of West Ham United to the First Division in 1958, something he had been unable to achieve given a much longer time than Fenton. It must have been a hard thing to watch and live through.

Charlie lived to be 91, passing away in 1971. He and Emily had three children – Charles Aubrey Llewellyn (born 1908), Winifred (1913) and Leslie (1916). Up to almost his last days he was still to be seen ambling around the club.

'THE PAST IS A FOREIGN COUNTRY: THEY DO THINGS DIFFERENTLY THERE'

So says L.P. Hartley on the first page of *The Go-Between*. It is a fact that Charlie Paynter, working in the shadow of King, was with West Ham over nine seasons when the side were amongst England's footballing elite. The Hammers had finished in sixth place in 1927/28, a feat not to be equalled for twenty-two years and not bettered until John Lyall led the Irons to fifth place at the end of the 1978/79 season. For all that, I have talked to around seventy players who worked under Paynter (see Belton 2013a, 2013b and 2006 for instance) and others who were at Upton Park while he continued to have an influence over the club and Ted Fenton, and it is hard to conclude that Paynter was more than a good-average Division Two manager. In terms of success his performance was better than mediocre. For nine Second Division seasons his sides finished twelfth or better. In 1934/35 he took West Ham to third place in Division Two. Bolton were runners-up to Brentford that term, bettering the Hammers on goal average, but bettering them substantially.

While this is not an altogether 'bad' record, one might be forgiven for asking if something had happened to the teenager who had, by his own determination, broken away from the background of hard factory work. He and West Ham had become, from a historic point of view, complacent. But it is difficult to understand Charlie as anything but complacent by nature. He had, after all, sat in the role of trainer for twenty years and had never shown any inclination or ambition to move on or up until fate, in the shape of King's demise, took a hand. Even then he was more placed in his role than making it his own.

While many players related to Charlie fondly as a 'good man', and the majority showed both loyalty and respect for him, few were able to elaborate on his particular skill set or approach, beyond a sort of fatherly attitude – the expression 'father figure' was often applied to Paynter. This overall response was no less than one might expect. These players were polite, generous and for the most part intelligent men. They were themselves mainly from respectable working-class families and of a generation where it would be 'bad form' to do down anyone but the worst of people. For many Charlie had opened a world of opportunity, effectively taking them away from the curse of drudgery and shift-work, to pay them for playing a game. At the same time, the 1940s and 1950s were not an era of widespread labour militancy in Britain, certainly not in football. Work, with a few exceptions, was subject to feudal regimes, none more so than football. It had a pecking order and a clear hierarchy that it was foolish to buck.

Many players become as good as institutionalised in the club system. Just one example of this is when one former player, who had been at Upton Park for many decades from the late 1920s, asked me if I knew the whereabouts of one of his colleagues from that era. I apologised because I didn't have the information. He looked at me blankly and said, 'The club'll know'. I answered that I doubted if they would, that West Ham appeared to have comparatively little information about, or were just unprepared to supply information relating to, former players. His expression was unchanged as he said, 'The club'll know where he is'. This utter and unquestioning faith in the power and the awareness of the club is something I have consistently come across when talking to players of or before the mid-1950s generation. There have been, of course, notable exceptions, although the most vocal of those were understood to be 'rebels', and were either admired, feared or openly disliked. Such is the situation of the contrarian (I write from experience, but if you are interested, take a look at Hitchens, 2002).

It is clear Charlie cared about the players he was responsible for; he was obviously a nice man. Together with his chairman (from 1935) W.J. Cearns, Charlie would personally deliver Christmas turkeys to players stationed outside London during the war years. This was no easy task in the winters of the early 1940s, and the cost of fuel to get to some outlandish spots in Essex and East Anglia would have been appreciable. However, according to one player I talked to about this, Charlie was pretty much the chauffeur on such trips.

I have not been able to find much indication, on a player/manager basis, that Charlie was a consistently able motivator or a particularly deep thinker. One or two players found the occasional pep talk helpful, but many more were met by something of a brick wall response, albeit a relatively amicable one. He'd provide a team talk before most home games, but this would often be repetitious and full of clichés like 'Do your best, no one can ask for more' or 'Watch the inside-right, he's no mug'. Sometimes he'd spend time expressing the chairman or board's pride or expectations. I have found no strong or consistent suggestion that Charlie, seemingly a master of the solicitous (or patronising) pat on the back, 'managed' the dressing room in any way. He seemed to be more in the Grace Brothers (*Are You Being Served?*) 'You've all done very well' mode. Most of the management, certainly in terms of tactics and the pastoral support of players, came from senior professionals. As Eddie Chapman, who had great respect and affection for Charlie, told me: 'The players sorted themselves out mostly.' It has to be said, this was nothing unusual in that era.

THE SEARLES AFFAIR

In the summer of 1940 Alan N. Searles, the club secretary, was fired following the discovery of some pretty obvious irregularities. On 2 July 1940, the chairman informed the board that Searles had been dismissed three days previously. Cearns was unable to locate an accountant willing to take on the job as secretary – not a great sign in itself. After nine days Charlie Paynter was given the role, initially on a provisional basis. The bank was informed that 'in the future cheques would be signed by two directors'.

The board was informed that the auditors had uncovered the means by which Searles had been swindling the club and that losses would be set aside as 'bad debt'. It was decided that the club would not take action against Searles, which again raises all sorts of questions and doubts.

The chairman's report to the 1940 AGM dealt with the matter of the balance sheet thus:

> My first duty is an unpleasant one and that is to explain to you that the amount shown in the revenue account as a 'Bad Debt' is a defalcation by the late secretary. The directors have considered the 19 years honest service given by him prior to this occurring and decided not to prosecute, and ask for your confirmation of their action in this matter. There is also an amount of approximately £100 since the end of the period under review and your board proposes to treat this amount in this year's account in a similar manner.

Following this, not another word was heard about Searles at Upton Park.

Paynter continued as 'manager-secretary' throughout the war years, but he had little interest in or ability for secretarial duties. Part-time clerical help was drafted in and members of the board assisted him quite a bit. Ultimately Eddie Chapman, then a 17-year-old, combined much of the secretary's role with his playing career. Chapman had picked up clerical and office skills from working close to Searles.

According to Chapman, 'Paynter wasn't cut out to be a secretary ... he did it, but never liked it.' It was Chapman's father who had negotiated him an office job rather than the usual ground staff position when his son signed for West Ham. Chapman senior wanted Eddie to be set up for 'respectable' employment on the conclusion of his playing career. On 17 August 1937, he and Nobby Strange were engaged for the ground and office staff at a wage of £1 and 5*s* (£1.25) a week.

It has often been written that, during the war years, Charlie more or less kept the Boleyn Ground going single-handed in terms of team preparation, player welfare and administration. However, given the presence of Chapman, the input of the board and the very active part the players took in training and the maintenance of the ground, this seems at least a slight exaggeration. Doubtless, at times his job was no cake walk, given that often just minutes before a match he was still putting a side together. Many programmes detail the line-up with two or three spots subject to an 'or' ('player A' or 'player B'), but West Ham was far from a one-man band.

At the end of 1946 the directors recognised that Paynter had never been up to both jobs and, keeping it in the family, Frank Cearns (the chairman's brother) took over as secretary in November on the tidy salary of £500 per annum. A couple of months later, Chapman became his assistant.

The publicly stated purpose of Frank Cearns taking the reins was to give Paynter more time with the players, but in truth Charlie was becoming increasingly remote from them. By the end of the 1940s Billy Moore was responsible for the pretty monotonous and undistinguished training the players were put through (mostly minus a ball). Almost unfailingly, Paynter would turn up at Upton Park dressed in a three-piece suit, shirt and tie, bearing no resemblance to the managers who followed him. But this was no exception to the rule of his era. The 'track-suit' manager was a phenomenon of the future.

In actuality the board had not fully trusted staff with the club accounts since Syd King was suspended in 1931. Thereafter no club employee would be allowed to spend appreciable funds without the counter-signature of the chairman or a designated board member. However, the board did use King's departure as an opportunity to take on someone to avoid the chairman having responsibility for the everyday workings of the club. At the same time, hiring a full-time secretary demonstrated that West Ham was a club of some standing and ambition. As a board member, Searles gained Will Cearns' confidence, showing he was able to operate without direct supervision of the chairman, and by 1934 he was overseeing the regular expenditure of the club. Every year he got a bonus of £50, half of what Paynter received. Searles had a solid position in 1939, when his wage was raised to £10 per week and his bonus went up to £75 (Charlie's bonus remained static).

During the late 1940s many players would only find themselves connecting with Paynter as a functionary (or, in their language, 'office monger'). He imposed dress codes on and off the field and a vague standard of behaviour. If there was a fine imposed, it would come from him; if a player was dropped without clear reason, it was his doing. There was talk of favoured players who were understood to influence his decisions.

TO THE MANOR BORN

Paynter himself appeared never to have made any major judgement, including about team affairs, off his own bat. Like a feudal overseer might relate to the lord of the manor, or a long-term family butler to the head of the household, he would defer to the board, taking only the action they dictated or underwrote.

Some have tried to portray or assess the Will Cearns/Paynter association as a friendship. But one has to wonder if this is not misunderstanding the nature of the divide betwixt board and staff that pertained from the point Paynter was hired by the club as manager, and which more or less sustained up to his retirement. Could such a situation include authentic *bon vivre* between the likes of Paynter and Cearns? While Cearns was more nouveau riche than landed gentry (the family wealth coming from the construction industry), there was a Cearns heritage at the club that went back to 1900 with James William Youngs Cearns (a stock taker at Thames Ironworks).

In 1924, the West Ham board co-opted two new members, W.J. Cearns and F.R. Pratt. Cearns was the son of J.W.Y. Cearns, and Frank Reginald Pratt, a local timber merchant, was his business associate and pal. Will Cearns was to serve on the board for twenty-six years until his passing; he was chairman between 1935 and 1950. Frank Pratt remained on the board until 1941 when he died (he was vice-chairman from 1935 to 1940). Frank was succeeded on the board by his son, Reginald H. Pratt. In 1948, Cearns's son Len joined the board. From 1924 up to the 'Icelandic farce', one or both of these families had a presence on the West Ham board: between 1935 and 1986 the chairman and the vice-chairman was either a Cearnses or a Pratts (let's avoid the obvious puns).

Will Cearns served on the board for a decade with his father. Cearns senior had been associated with the Castle Swifts, St Luke's and the Thames Ironworks football clubs, the three leading amateur teams in East London before the turn of the twentieth century. He had also been a founding member of West Ham and it was his company that constructed the first concrete stands at Upton Park and, a few years later, the 5,000-capacity double-decker grandstand.

Given this heritage, the butler/master relationship might bear closer comparison in terms of the association between Paynter and Cearns; not quite Wooster and Jeeves, but certainly not Charlie and Billy. Paynter would telephone Cearns to talk about players and the selection of sides prior to matches. He would also visit his chairman at his Wanstead home to provide physical therapy for him. Again, this very much echoes the ethos of the archetypal faithful family retainer; nothing was too much for Charlie where Cearns was concerned, always on call and ready to be summoned, to carry out instructions to the letter.

The system of patronage, although in demise with the coming of a Labour government in 1945, could still to be found in the mills, factories and offices of post-war Britain. It was a hangover from the past, a reflection of the servant/master nexus of the great households of the Victorian and Edwardian eras, the last stronghold of feudalism. Partly because of Paynter's wartime stewardship, this persisted at West Ham probably up to the point when Malcolm Allison began play his massively influential role in the club (see Belton 2013a). This was evident in a 1960 interview with Reg Pratt.

PRATT

Reginald Pratt took over as West Ham chairman after Will Cearns died in 1950. Typical of many men in his position, he came to football from what Karl Marx called a 'petit-bourgeois background' – he was born in West Ham (in September 1905), brought up around Upton Park, but owned a wood-yard in Wanstead, a business inherited from his father, Frank Reginald Pratt. Reg took over his father's place on the board in 1941.

A television interview took place at the Boleyn Ground in 1960 related to the abolition of the minimum wage in football. This was perhaps the last powerful vestige of the feudal character of the professional game. It was clear that Pratt was resistant to this. His accent, for the most part, was reminiscent of a 1930s Guards captain, but every now and then, the way he formed his words and sentences betrayed his more workaday roots. The interview was undertaken on the terraces with Reg leaning nonchalantly on a barrier, in a dark suit, shirt and tie. He wore the trilby hat without which he was hardly ever, in his adult life, seen in public.

As the chairman of a large London club what will the implications of it be?

Well, it's the most serious thing that's happened in this game. We are very concerned, of course, with the effect on public support, and we can only live by the public, and we feel it is a most untimely thing, something which could have probably been avoided, with a little more patience and understanding on both sides.

What about the new contract?

The main bone of contention, I think, with the players is the retain and transfer system. Well now, I think this must be said – the retain and transfer system has been the bedrock of the League structure. It was introduced seventy years ago to bring order out of chaos. And we must be very careful we don't return to chaos. I think it's sufficient to say that it has been copied by every other football competition of our kind in the world.

What does the retain and transfer system mean?

It means a club can be sure, from one season to another, of the players that it's going to have on its books.

The players argue that they're being kept, even though they're not playing and losing some of their vital working life as a player.

Well now, that is not general, of course. I feel that if there are cases of hardship, and I am yet to be convinced there is much hardship by this system, that it can easily be resolved by the appeals committee.

It is pretty clear where Pratt stood on the subject. The measure of humane and/or fair employment is that its rewards avoid 'hardship'; the employer does not need to be concerned with their workforce beyond that. As long as the employee 'gets by', then the employer's payment for their labour is deemed reasonable. There is no notion that the worker might thrive or grow more prosperous, reflecting their contribution to the business, which of course was invaluable because it was in fact the sum of the business.

Anything that departed from this contorted logic was, for Pratt, stepping into 'chaos'. Pratt portrayed the supporters as potentially being the main victims of players asking for what was, at that time, no more than fair wages and conditions. He makes no mention of the club's profits. This indicates that the directors were going to accept no detrimental effects on their pockets; additional costs would be passed on to those paying at the gate. This is the sensibility and rationality of second-generation wealth and people knowing and staying in their place: 'We've got it, because we deserve it, and we are going to keep it – why you haven't got it is because you don't deserve it, and we are not going to just give it to you' – any alternative analysis is understood as 'chaos'.

However, much of this attitude was the culture of the era rather than any personality defect on Pratt's part. It would have been close to impossible for him to have broken ranks with his peers at West Ham or the wider horizon of the football business at that time. In fairness, Reg, in later life, did much to modernise West Ham United and in practice moderated his perspective. As an employer of his time he was seen as 'fair' and even generous. His contribution had a much wider impact on football generally, playing an underestimated part in enabling English football to become dominant in the world game. He was perhaps one of the first truly innovative chairmen in football, but at the end of the 1950s he clearly articulated the traditional character and irrational rationality of the football industry, and of West Ham in particular. Reg retired as chairman in 1979, handing over to Len Cearns; he became club president. He died in Essex in 1984, aged 79, ending the Pratt family's sixty-year reign as directors of the club.

BROKEN TIME

Wartime football resuscitated issues from the game's pre-professional history in terms of grievances relating to coaching and broken-time payments. A divide opened between military and civilian players.

The former presented relatively few difficulties; their wages, modest as they were, were assured and they were paid each week. The football authorities understood that civilian players were pulling down a reasonable wage and that no payment for broken time was warranted. Payments for broken time were stringently prohibited and severe action was threatened if this rule was contravened.

That the authorities found a need to remind clubs of the rule is probably a strong indication that the regulations in this respect were being breached. There was an effort to sustain even-handedness between players and, perhaps more significantly, to shield clubs from richer clubs recruiting the best players by way of broken-time payments; this practice was likely to be aimed at players too young to join the Services and those in restricted occupations (war work). These groups in practice would be able to establish themselves as essentially free agents, waiting for requests to turn out for clubs. The potential of broken-time payments was to circumvent the maximum wage.

While the maximum wage was important to the footballing authorities, the inviolability of contract was their foundation. The transient lifestyles of many players in wartime demanded alterations in the requirements made of them by their contracts. It was irrational to expect a player to turn out only for the club that held his contract, given that it might not be feasible for him to make games because of wartime obligations or location. This is why players were allowed to perform for clubs on a game-by-game basis if necessary. But as this arrangement needed to be sanctioned by the clubs that players were registered with, throughout the war, there was a huge correspondence between clubs focused on arrangements for guest players.

It was in the interests of clubs to give permission for their players to guest in order to preserve or hone their skills, but also to ensure the return of the favour when required. However, perhaps more pertinently this was a way of keeping the game viable or even alive during hostilities. The structure worked because those controlling clubs (the likes of Pratt and Cearns) understood that it practically guaranteed that they, and not the players, maintained control of wages and playing conditions.

West Ham, alongside other clubs, made the system work; while Liverpool consented to allow West Ham to approach players stationed in Suffolk, West Ham came to an agreement with Mansfield Town that Cliff Hubbard could play for the Yellow, except when his services were required by West Ham. This was reaffirmation of the club's rights over its players.

So, Hubbard was allowed to play for Mansfield when Paynter found out that the train connections could not be relied on to get Hubbard to Upton Park for games, while Ted Fenton was not allowed to play for Reading, Fenton being stationed at Colchester, within comparatively easy reach of Upton Park.

However, the exigencies of wartime football gave rise to something much closer to freedom of contract than the players had ever experienced. The situation effectively paved the way for the fight to come and the type of resistance expressed by Reg Pratt in the interview at Upton Park in 1960. This was the final blow that ended the traditional way of things at clubs like West Ham. To his credit, Pratt recognised this and eventually did more than make the best of the circumstances.

THE WARRIORS OF '39

For all this, the West Ham side that readied itself for the 1939/40 season, although destined never to fight a full Football League campaign together, was impressive, with Len Goulden, Ted Fenton, Archie Macaulay, Charlie Bicknell, Joe Cockroft and the free-scoring George Foreman, as well as talented younger players like Ernie Gregory and Eddie Chapman coming through the ranks. This was a side worthy of the Second Division Championship and perhaps greater things thereafter. All this potential was brought together under the watch of Charlie Paynter. Retrospectively, this is perhaps his legacy, his stand-alone achievement. While it wasn't quite all downhill from then on, there were to be no great fireworks after the war until Ted Fenton took the reins.

If stasis is an achievement then Paynter was a success. In an era when we find ourselves congratulating coach-driver-like managers for a 'top half finish' or even managing to avoid relegation, perhaps this is correct. That said, on my death bed, I don't think I'll be talking to my grandchildren about the year West Ham finished with 'mid-table respectability' or even when we came fourth in the League; fourth is not glorious – it's 'ok', but do we watch sport, devote great chunks of our life and personal finance, in the hope of 'ok-ness'? I don't. I want to fight to win, even if it means potentially losing, and I want beauty. I want Bobby Moore's grace and Martin Peters' goals; I want players for whom the hammers over their hearts mean more than just another week's pay. I don't want stasis; I'd rather die with a sword in my hand than live on my knees – I want to go out all guns blazing; I want to 'sink the *Bismarck*' more than run away from it! I don't want a seat in the stands; I want a heart and a soul!

NEW CAMBRIDGE *V.* CLAPTON AND CAUSTIC CECIL

Why did tens of thousands of people turn out to watch West Ham and many other professional teams during the Second World War; right through the Blitz and some of the coldest winters of the twentieth century? Why do I, and probably you, make our way to Upton Park or other grounds dotted all over England, Europe and the world? Two of the passengers killed on the tragic 'Flight 17' shot down over the Ukraine at the time of writing were Newcastle United supporters on their way to watch the Toon in pre-season friendlies in New Zealand!

What draws us in this way, particularly if you are not part of a ghastly distortion like the 'Cockney Reds'; supporting one of the 'big' Premiership sides almost guaranteed glory? If you support West Ham or Wolves or Rotherham, you are guaranteed practically nothing, outside of consternation and the low-level agony and sometimes slight embarrassment of match days.

In the late 1970s I was a youth worker in Bethnal Green. This was a time when you still took kids out on Christmas Day to play football. This cold 25 December, I was due to take the New Cambridge Boys' Club under-11 side to Mabley Green on Hackney Marshes to play ... CLAPTON! The latter team was the Real Madrid of East London under-11 football. They were, as one of the lads said on the way there, 'shit hot'. New Cambridge Boys' Club under-11s were not 'shit hot'. At their very best they were 'assertive' (perhaps 'over-belligerent' at times) with a record we spent as little time as possible mulling over.

We started out from Colombia Road, in the ancient light-blue mini-bus, with the six kids who had turned up. We encouraged ourselves with the delusion that the rest of the team would be brought to Mabley Green by relations or friends who had nothing better to do on Christmas morning. Not surprisingly, we got to our destination to find not a soul there. We then speculated how we might claim the points if Clapton didn't turn up, but just as we were doing this Clapton turned up, at full strength. Happy Crimbo!

I turned to the 'magnificent half-dozen' and asked, 'Do you want to go on with this ... do you want to play?' It was the self-appointed skipper, Charlie Fait (aka Fred Cait ... don't ask!), who spoke immediately. 'Yes!' I had long before accepted that Charlie (Fred) was nuts, so I turned to the rest. By that I mean the handful of mini-Cockneys who, having got their kit on, suddenly seemed reminiscent of Christmas elves – especially 10-year-old Jake, wearing the massive woollen bobble-hat his nan had knitted for him – bright blue – to 'keep him warm'; if he'd have pulled it as far down as possible, it would have reached his ankles. The five elves responded, resoundingly, in the affirmative.

So, there we were. I watched these six little lads spread themselves out across Mabley Green on a freezingly grey Christmas morning. They were directing each other, clapping and praising each other. They lost 19–0. They remain the greatest football team I have ever seen. They shame the best of Brazil in my memory. I applauded them from the field, their only supporter; their fan. As Fred (Charlie) walked passed me, I said: 'Well done, Chas!' He climbed directly back on the mini-bus (the showers were not working, of course), but without raising his head or looking back, he said: 'Shit or bust, Belts. Shit or bust, mate!'

This memory continues to resonate with me because it seems the essence of being part of a sport, either as a participant or as a spectator. We see or look for something admirable. Within a simple game the indomitable human spirit can prevail despite all else. Defeat, at times, is a necessity in this victory of spirit. But I still want to win; I want to strive, if only to find the indomitability in myself or others.

FIVE

THE CUP OF WAR

> The war tested West Ham as it did other clubs. That the club came through as it did says a lot for the way the players committed themselves.
>
> *Eddie Chapman*

GETTING READY

Given Britain was at war, things seemed relatively quiet on the home front. There was lots of activity, but the massive aerial assault expected had yet to happen, although months previously, on 31 August 1939, Hitler's 'Directive No. 1' had made German intentions pretty clear:

> The Luftwaffe is, first of all, to prevent action by the French and English Air Forces against the German Army and German territory.
>
> In operations against England the task of the Air Force is to take measures to dislocate English imports, the armaments industry, and the transport of troops to France. Any favourable opportunity of an effective attack on concentrated units of the English Navy, particularly on battleships or aircraft carriers, will be exploited. The decision regarding attacks on London is reserved to me.

> Attacks on the English homeland are to be prepared, bearing in mind that inconclusive results with insufficient forces are to be avoided in all circumstances.

Before war was declared, the organisation of the London Fire Brigade area was preparing for the worst. Each station encompassed five satellites, U, V, W, X and Y, allocated with the number of the local station. So No. 28 Station Whitechapel's satellites were 28U, 28V, 28W, 28X and 28Y. This system was altered after the fire service was nationalised in 1942.

Every auxiliary fire station had a core of experienced firefighters, deployed to train auxiliary crews. Of course, no one knew at that point that it would be months before the first air attack and all laboured hard and long to be ready for the coming of the bombers.

You can see from this that the people of West Ham, like others all over Britain, were pretty much expected to look after themselves. This would be a war fought as much by civilians as by those in the services; this, in every sense, was total war.

TO THE BRIDGE

The last pre-war encounter between the Hammers and the Blues had been in the spring of 1932; this had been Irons' last First Division season, and the side was to finish at the very foot of the League that year. The 5-goal thriller had seen West Ham's Tommy Yews and Jim Barrett hit the rigging, but it was the West Londoners who had won the day with goals from Bill Russell, Billy Ferguson and George Pearson. In the Cup that same year (4 January), Chelsea had eliminated West Ham at Stamford Bridge, Tony Weldon scoring the East Enders' only goal in the 3–1 defeat; George Mills hit 2 of the Chelsea goals, Hugh Gallacher got the other. So on 27 April 1940 there was potential for a modicum of War Cup vengeance.

Charlie Paynter didn't need to change his first-leg side much. Although he was without Macaulay, Len Goulden was available so the Irons travelled with the confidence that they were probably as strong a side as they had been in the initial game of the tie.

West Ham: Harry Medhurst, Charlie Bicknell, Charlie Walker, Norman Corbett, Dick Walker, Joe Cockroft, Sam Small, Ted Fenton, George Foreman, Len Goulden, Stan Foxall.

Chelsea: John Jackson, Alex White, George Barber, David Alexander, Bob Griffiths, Sam Weaver, Dick Spence, Tom Kiernan, Joe Payne, Sid Foss, Alf Hanson.

Paynter also brought Harry Medhurst in as keeper. The only change in the Chelsea side was White coming in for O'Hare.

A measure of how the fixture list had fallen behind schedule was the second leg of the first round of the War Cup not being played until 27 April, the day the FA Cup Final would have been played had there not been war going on.

The slender 1-goal advantage from the Upton Park tie hardly seemed adequate in the spring of 1940, in front of a Stamford Bridge crowd of 14,897 (a very healthy wartime attendance). But Medhurst blocked his future side out and West Ham ran to a 2–0 victory, the goals coming from George Foreman and Sam Small. Revenge was indeed sweet; the proud West London Blues had been humbled, home and away.

BIGGIE SMALL

Samuel John Small played 172 wartime games for West Ham, scoring 80 goals. He was born in Birmingham on 15 May 1912. His peacetime appearances for the Hammers from 1937 to 1948 numbered 116, and he found the net 41 times.

In 1937 Small came to East London from the 'Second City' after playing just half-a-dozen games in his three years with the midlands' Blues (before they adopted the 'City' appendage). A centre forward with a magnanimous attitude in attack (although in his first 18 outings for West Ham he scored 11 goals), he was also an industrious defender for the Irons when need dictated. According to the club's handbook of 1939/40, Small was 'one of the nicest chaps in the game'.

In March 1948 Small moved on to Brighton and Hove Albion, turning out in 38 League games for the Goldstone Ground outfit. Small, who began his career with his local Bromsgrove Rovers club in the early 1930s, died on 19 December 1993.

GEORGE AND THE FOXES

West Ham were drawn away to Leicester City for the first leg of the second round. Like Chelsea, Leicester had been a top-flight outfit prior to the war (although they were due to be relegated after the 1938/39 season).

City had met Clapton Orient in the first round. Over the two legs they went through 5–4, losing 2–0 in the second leg at Brisbane Road (Harry Smith and Bob Shankly had scored Clapton's home goals; Smith had scored both of Orient's away goals). It seemed that the away leg was going to be the test for the travelling Irons.

As the Hammers anticipated the trip to take on the Foxes, Small and George Foreman were looking a more than promising attacking combination.Alexander (Alec) George Foreman was with Walthamstow Avenue as an amateur before signing for West Ham in Mach 1938. He gained an England amateur cap (*v.* Northern Ireland) in 1939, just before signing professional forms. Prior to joining the 'A's he was with Leyton FC in the Athenian League.

Foreman was born in West Ham (1 March 1914) and while he only made 6 League and 3 Cup appearances for the Hammers (scoring a couple of goals) as a peacetime player, he ran out for the Irons 228 times during the war, claiming 161 goals. During hostilities he represented the Essex County side on three occasions.

A hard-working and skilled centre forward, after the war Foreman joined Tottenham Hotspur. He had turned out for the Spurs in wartime games during 1945 and netted 15 times in 37 games for the North Londoners in the 1946/47 term. Foreman died on 19 June 1969.

TARGET WEST HAM

The 64 first-round matches of the War Cup had been pretty popular, pulling in more than half a million fans. However, retrospectively, a good crowd at Upton Park must have looked like a potentially damaging target in the face of Nazi bombing.

When war had been declared, AFS recruits had been told to be prepared to report to their nearest fire station for full enrolment. On 1 September 1939 the mobilisation order had gone out, summonsing thousands of men and women to their local fire stations.

It didn't take much foresight to predict that the Royal Docks would be a major target for the Luftwaffe. Just before the declaration of war, more than fifty vessels, from the *Mauritania II* (a 35,000-ton liner) to 7,000-ton tramp steamers, took up nearly all the berths in the 'Royals' – the Royal Albert, Queen Victoria and the King George V Docks. Laying stem to stern, ships were moored over 11 miles of quayage, while gangs of dockworkers unloaded and loaded cargo.

The adjacent warehouses were piled with food, raw materials and manufactured goods, bound to or from ports around the globe. The repair yards were alive with industry, while the couple of dry-docks were rarely empty. A military genius was not required to understand what a succulent objective this hive of activity would be for the Nazi bombers and how vulnerable the surrounding area, including Upton Park, was to purposeful or accidental destruction and carnage.

Built abutting the dockside, the warehouses presented a challenge in terms of their protection. A fire balloon blooming from a warehouse was likely to block the advance of land-based fire appliances. Understanding this, fire officers organised the mounting of four Dennis trailer fire pumps in the hold of a dumb barge – a long, hefty, typically flat-bottomed craft, used for the transport of freight such as coal. Generally designed without its own means of propulsion, the barge is towed or pushed by another vessel, such as a tug boat. Holes were cut in the coaming to allow a suction hose to be placed in the dock water.

This ad hoc 'fire float' was able to pump 2,000 gallons of water a minute, enough to supply sixteen healthy firefighting jets with the advantage of a virtually limitless supply of water, more dependable than even the Thames herself, because dock water level was 2ft 6in higher than the high watermark of London's river.

The biggest problem with this appliance was that a tug was needed to locate and manoeuvre the barge. This was potentially costly, but at the same time it would be hard to guarantee a tug would be available at a moment's notice (as would be necessary). The brilliance, experience and knowledge of firemen solved this issue. The back pressure of a fire jet could provide the thrust to propel the barge.

A tiller was fashioned and attached to the after deck, with two branches secured to a horizontal bar. These discharged water over the stern of the craft with adequate power to produce a speed of a steady 5 knots. The tiller enabled the jets to be deployed to steer. With a little practice the firefighter/helmsmen was able to achieve a decent level of control of the ungainly vessel.

Ultimately, four barges, *Monsoon*, *Fred*, *Sweden* and *Brampton* (not a bad forward line), were transformed into auxiliary fire floats, producing a valuable resource to fight fires in the docks.

This improvised armada saw action facing fires in buildings from the waterside. However, the priceless role played by the fire barges was the maintenance of water supplies to land-based pumps all the way through the Blitz.

SIX

THE CORBETTS

> My strength has now been reduced to the equivalent of 36 squadrons … we should be able to carry on the war single-handed for some time if not indefinitely.
>
> *Sir Hugh Dowding, RAF Fighter Command, May 1940*

Norman Corbett had played in both legs of the Football League War Cup first round. Alongside Charlie Bicknell, Joe Cockroft, Dick and Charlie Walker, he had effectively got the Irons through to the second round by shutting out the Chelsea attack at Stamford Bridge. Three Corbett brothers would play for West Ham over two decades from the 1930s. In the wartime game Norman and Willie represented the club consistently. Norman was around for every season of the conflict, while Willie was called on for three of the six wartime seasons. Willie and Norman appeared together 15 times in claret and blue. David made up the treble, although he wasn't to appear at Upton Park during the 1940s.

NORMAN GEORGE 'NORRIE' CORBETT

Norman George 'Norrie' Corbett was born in Camelon, Falkirk, Scotland on 23 June 1919. Possessed of an extraordinary long throw, he was probably robbed of the chance to play for his country by the war, although he did turn out for the Football Combination *v.* Belgium.

Although Norman didn't play in the Football League War Cup Final, like all the West Ham and Blackburn men who played in the earlier rounds but missed out on Wembley, he was awarded a medal because he had appeared in the first round tie *v.* Chelsea.

Before arriving at West Ham, Norrie had captained the Falkirk Boys team that won the Scottish Schools Trophy in 1933. While with the Musselburgh club, he played for Scotland Boys and Scotland Juniors. He then joined Dunipace Thistle and was with Maryhill Juniors, turning professional with Heart of Midlothian as a 15 year old (although he was never to play a first-team game for Hearts).

Coming to West Ham in 1936, Norman made his debut for the first team as a right half *v.* Sheffield United on 1 May 1937. That was the final game of the Division Two season, John Morton scoring the only goal of the game and sending the Hammers fans into the summer happy. Norrie was still a teenager and only managed 6 starts in the 1937/38 season but in all he would play 173 games for the Irons, hitting 3 goals. During the war, while serving with the Essex Regiment (as a physical training instructor, Norman was given the rank of sergeant-major), he played in 21 Cup games, scoring 2 goals; he was involved in 106 League games, contributing 3 goals. He also guested (8 games in all) for Leeds United (1943/44), York City (1941/42), Southampton (1943/44 and 1944/45) and Swansea (1945/46) during hostilities.

Norman was ever-present for the Irons during the 1947/48 season. He played his final League game for West Ham (a 1–0 defeat by Cardiff City at Upton Park) on 15 April 1950. He stayed at the Boleyn Ground for a while, towards the end of his career filling in for reserve games. Becoming an FA coach, Norman later joined Clapton. He died in 1990.

WILLIAM R. CORBETT

Another member of the Corbett family to serve West Ham during the war was Norman's youngest brother. William R. Corbett, also born in Falkirk, on 31 August 1922, joined Hearts as a youngster, but before getting a first-team game in 1941 he signed for Celtic (at the time he was working as a motor mechanic). He would make 99 appearances for the Bhoys in the first couple of post-war seasons, scoring 3 goals.

The 1947/48 term wasn't the greatest for Celtic. Modern football sensitivities are tweaked when learning that they were struggling close to the foot of the table, threatened, for the first time in their history, by the prospect of relegation. However, on 28 February an 89th-minute penalty, converted by Willie, provided the Hoops with the only goal of the game *v.* Falkirk and ultimately the Glasgow side finished in twelfth position in the sixteen-team League.

Willie moved to Preston North End on 7 May 1948 for a fee of £10,000, running out for the Lily Whites for 19 League matches prior to joining Leicester City for £7,000 at the start of the 1949/50 campaign, and playing 17 games for the Foxes.

Willie was with non-league Yeovil Town in 1950 before returning to Scotland in November 1951, signing for Dunfermline Athletic and making 24 appearances in the cause of the Pars. His next stop was Morton, playing 11 League matches during the 1952/53 season.

Willie passed away at a nursing home in Bonnybridge, Falkirk, on Sunday, 31 July 2011. He suffered with dementia, but the condition was alleviated by the 'Football Memories Project', pioneered by Michael White after he discovered a group of men with dementia living close to his hometown club of Falkirk, out of which the project was born, involving Alzheimer Scotland and the Scottish Football Museum. As Tony Jameson-Allen reported in the *Sabotage Times* (6 December 2013) there are now sixteen groups working throughout Scotland, providing interesting activities that improve the well-being of those involved, often uncovering extraordinary stories.

A fine defender, calm under pressure, Willie served in the Royal Navy for four years from 1942. The centre half wore West Ham colours 33 times during the war years, but he also guested for Cardiff City, Swansea and Southampton as well as playing 39 wartime games for Celtic.

Bill (as he was known later in life), remembering his arrival at the Boleyn Ground, told Jameson-Allen, 'My brother Norman played for West Ham. Their manager was a right Cockney and he told me anytime I was near London, just come along and I'll get you a game.'

On 10 October 1942, Bill was selected to play against England in front of a crowd of 75,000 at Wembley. This was a game dominated by the respective defences. England did twice get the ball in the net, but on both occasions the offside rule pertained. The crowd were not best pleased with the second call, after Denis Compton had sped on to an intelligent pass by Stanley Matthews, which went beyond the Scottish defenders. W.F. Smith reported in the *Daily Herald*:

> With Lawton and Dodds – two of the most dangerous centre forwards of modern times – on either side, it seems incredible that no goals were scored.

But both these prolific goal-getters were blotted out by the brilliance of the centre-halves playing that day – in particular, making an impressive debut for his nation, the young Willie Corbett. As Smith wrote:

> Could Lawton only have received the ball on the ground a reasonable number of times one felt England would have got goals ... but in heading the ball Corbett was as good as Lawton.

This was praise indeed, as no striker was more highly thought of than Tommy Lawton in that era.

Dodds (who also appeared for West Ham in the war years along with Lawton) had achieved a hat-trick in the 5–4 Scottish victory at Hampden in April, but he was also marked out of the Wembley game by Stan Cullis, who for Smith 'gave as perfect a centre half display as I ever expect to see'.

In the second half Walker gave Hapgood a worrying time, while Matthews was subdued by the attentions of Beattie and Matthews' nemesis, Matt Busby.

Reading the match reports of the time, it is hard to argue that Bill was anything less than the man of the match. One impressed hack commented: 'I have never seen a Scottish centre half play Lawton as well as young Corbett did this afternoon.' The press rang the praises of the 20-year-old, waxing lyrical about his future potential as the rock at the heart of Scotland's defence.

Smith pointed out at the end of his report for the *Daily Herald*:

> ... I doubt if either side would make more than one change if they were to meet again next Saturday.

This would certainly have been the case in terms of the Scottish side. As Bill was to proudly comment on looking at the Scotland team detailed in the programme for the game – particularly the rank of Shankly, Corbett and Busby – 'Not a bad half-back line, eh son?'

England: George Marks (Arsenal), Joe Bacuzzi (Fulham), Edris Hapgood [c] (Arsenal), Cliff Britton (Everton), Stan Cullis (Wolverhampton Wanderers), Joe Mercer (Everton), Stanley Matthews (Stoke City), Maurice Edelston (Reading), Tommy Lawton (Everton), James Hagan (Sheffield United), Denis Compton (Arsenal).

Scotland: James Dawson (Rangers), James Carabine (Third Lanark), Andrew Beattie (Preston North End), William Shankly (Preston North End), William R. Corbett (Celtic), Matt Busby (Everton), William Waddell (Rangers), Thomas Walker (Heart of Midlothian), Jock Dodds (Blackpool), Gordon Hutton Bremner (Arsenal), William Liddell (Liverpool).

Referee: Stevens (England)

DAVID JOHN CORBETT

David John was the oldest of the Corbett brothers to play for West Ham, although unlike his siblings he wasn't in the ranks of the Hammers during wartime. He too was born in Camelon, on 1 February 1910. He was employed by a string of clubs before turning up at Upton Park: Old Plean Amateurs, Linlithgow Rose, Hearts, Camelon Juniors, Ayr United and Dundee United. Like his brothers it seems he never got a first-team game at Tynecastle, but he played First Division football with Ayr, making half-a-dozen League appearances in 1932/33.

Dave found more regular first-team football with Dundee United in the Scottish Division Two, making 32 League appearances and being ever-present during the 1933/34 term, but he suffered a serious knee injury in November 1935 before joining the Irons in 1936. At Upton Park he managed just 4 League games at right half before making the move to Southport in 1938. He made the Soundgrounders first-team just the once.

Managing only half-a-dozen games at right-back for Dumbarton during their wartime schedule of 1941/42, Dave returned to Dundee United for a single Southern League match in October 1945. It seems his footballing life was over as the war years came to an end. He died in 1995.

SEVEN

FENTON

Born on 7 November 1914, not too far from West Ham's Upton Park home, as a boy Ted Fenton had been a prolific scorer for the Odessa Road School side (the Fenton family lived at No. 87 Odessa Road). He could box, winning schoolboy medals in the sport, and might have made his way as a professional pugilist. Edward, his grandfather, had gained some distinction as bare-knuckle fighter and Ted had come close to joining West Ham Boxing Club before the Irons took an interest in him.

A KID WITH PROMISE

When called up by West Ham Boys, Ted continued to hit the back of the net. He was denied an England Schoolboy cap when, Ted having been selected to face Scotland, the match was called off due to an outbreak of smallpox. However, in 1929 he played in his country's forward line at this level, facing the Scots at Ibrox Park. But in his early years Fenton was something of an all-rounder, also representing West Ham Borough in cricket and athletics – there is no record of a child before Ted achieving similar feats.

Edward Benjamin Ambrose Fenton came to the Boleyn Ground as a youngster. He had left school at 14 and was pushing a cart for a living. For around year he worked in an off-licence, not far from Upton Park, until he got the chance to play for West Ham. This came in 1931 when, on 13 March, former Hammer Dick Leafe put a postcard, from manager Syd King, through the Fentons' letterbox, asking Ted to bring his boots a week later, and turn out in a trial match for West Ham *v.* Queens Park Rangers. The young Ted scored both goals in the Irons' 2–0 victory.

Ted was, he said, 'amazed' to be offered a contract. When he got his expenses (10*s*, or 50p) for appearing in the trial, he remembered thinking, 'I would have paid them to let me play'. It had taken him ages to save up for his playing boots by way of a paper round; now he would be able to buy a new pair and have money to spare.

The young Ted Fenton had dreamed of being in the West Ham team, but had not thought of football as a profession. As such, when travelling to matches, Ted got a tremendous thrill from showing off the shiny leather bag with 'West Ham United' emblazoned on it.

Ted was the first youth to be signed as a ground-staff boy by West Ham. As well as playing for the 'A' side at the club, he needed to clock on at 7.30 a.m. every morning for work around the ground, although he was expected to be at the Boleyn Ground well before that time and didn't go home until he was told he could. His strongest memories were the 'flair' with which Syd King seemed to do everything, the army-style inspections of trainer Frank Piercy (another former player employed by the club), and Charlie Paynter being a ubiquitous presence around the club. There were the repeated trips to the Boleyn pub to buy cases of beer for King, an errand that carried a 10*s* tip from the manager; more than a day's wage for many. He recalled that there seemed to be the constant cry of 'Go and get Fenton' to undertake a whole range of tasks. Everybody ranked over him and they could all find jobs for him to do.

On his seventeenth birthday Ted signed professional terms, spending a spell on loan to Colchester Town, playing for the Oysters on Saturdays, and in midweek running out for the

Hammers. He had to wait until 7 September 1932 to make his debut for West Ham. It was the game against Bradford City at Valley Parade. This was the fourth match in West Ham's first Division Two season for the best part of a decade. Ted took the field as centre half. Although the immortal Vic Watson scored for West Ham, the East Londoners were thrashed 5–1. Ted was to be on the losing side five times in his first six outings that season. However, in his dozen games during the spring of 1934, Ted was on the winning side six times and got a hat-trick against Bury in a 3–1 victory at Upton Park.

Establishing himself at right half, filling the number 4 shirt that had been the property of Jim Collins before his injury at Barnsley in 1935, Ted, having made 18 league appearances over the previous couple of seasons, was on the Hammers first team sheet on 32 occasions.

Up to the outbreak of the Second World War, between 1932 and 1939, Ted made 176 appearances for West Ham, scoring 18 goals. His last peacetime appearance was in the final Division Two game of the Hammers' 1938/39 season, a 2–1 Upton Park victory over Manchester City on 6 May 1939 (Len Goulden and Cliff Hubbard providing the home side's answer to Jimmy Heale's single for City). At this point Ted and his wife Irene (Len Goulden had been Ted's best man at his wedding) were living at No. 27 Mighell Avenue, off Roding Lane, Ilford, having moved from No. 141 Sheringham Avenue, Manor Park, where he had made his home since 1937. The couple had met as 12 year olds at Odessa Road School. They were to have three children, Brenda, Alan and Simon.

Until the war, Ted had been running a building and decorating business for about ten years. The conflict put an end to this, but there were compensations. In 1940 Ted won a Football League War Cup winners' medal and played 5 times for England in wartime internationals, between serving as a PT instructor (a post that carried the rank of sergeant major) with the army in North Africa and Burma. He was later sent to work on commando training at Colchester. In 1945 Ted organised a game involving the Colchester Garrison and the Combined Services. The match raised £600 for charity.

Ted played 211 wartime games for West Ham, many in defence, but managed to net 43 times during this phase of his career.

MANAGER TED

Like Ernie Gregory and so many other promising West Ham players, the war robbed Ted Fenton of the chance to fulfil his true potential as a player. If it had not been for the intervention of Nazi ambitions, Ted might have established himself as an international, although he was never in the class of other pre-war West Ham and England men like Len Goulden and Vic Watson. He left Upton Park for the first time in the summer of 1946, to become player-manager of Southern League Colchester United, a club which at that time had little more than a decade of history. He guided the Essex club to the fifth round of the FA Cup in 1947/48, bringing them national fame.

A number of managerial opportunities were to arise in the light of this success, including, it was rumoured, the vacant job at West Bromwich Albion, following the retirement of Fred Everiss. Some writers have argued that this would have meant Ted moving straight into a 'top' First Division job, and that this is why he didn't take the offer, not wanting the pressure or responsibility of running a club at that level. However, these authors appear to forget that West Brom did not win the Second Division Championship until 1949, following eleven years in the wilderness. At that point Jack Smith had been manager since Everiss left the Hawthorns in 1948. Smith was with West Brom up to April 1952, when Jessie Carver took over. During this period the Throstles had never been out of the bottom half of

Division One. One has to look a little more closely at Albion's intentions in 1948 to get a clue as to why Ted might have turned them down. That said, other than during his time in the forces, Ted was very much a southern-based man; it is debatable how much he might have wanted to head north beyond his East London/West Essex homeland.

Ted also seemed destined to return to his former club. The story was that his success at Colchester did not create the opening for him, but it accelerated an offer that might otherwise have been a few years in coming. According to Ted, he immediately contacted Paynter for advice about how to handle the offer from West Brom – Paynter, having been Ted's manager, the man who had worked to develop him from a novice into a veteran player. Ted claimed that Paynter had advised him to decline the offer from the Baggies and come back to West Ham on the understanding that he would take over when Paynter retired. In effect Ted was assured that he would start as assistant manager in what had become a rather mediocre Second Division outfit.

Ted's starting wage at Colchester had been £15 a week. By 1948 this had risen slightly. He would have looked for an increase in his salary at West Brom. His starting salary at West Ham was £15. This, in itself, was peculiar because Fenton was known to 'watch the pennies' (see Belton 2013a); after all, he had not been brought up in a family where money came easy. Given Ted's seeming proclivity for care in matters financial, why did he move to West Ham?

According to Ted, following the telephoned counselling from Paynter, he got a call from Will Cearns offering him an assistant manager's position at Upton Park, although for £5 a week less than he had been offered at the Hawthorns. However, at this point, while Cearns would have understood that the West Ham manager was contemplating retirement, for some time there had been talk that the board intended to bring Ted back to Upton Park.

A change was clearly needed. Hardly anyone – supporter, player or board member – would have seen Paynter as the man to take the Hammers into the second half of the twentieth century, and Ted knew the club well. He'd be a new broom but he would not be making any clean sweeps; he knew how the hierarchy of the club worked and wouldn't be making ripples any time soon. Another question was who would replace Paynter if not Ted Fenton; the 'people's choice would have been Dick Walker, but a player's player and something of a loose cannon, Walker was never going to sit in the manager's seat at the Boleyn Ground.

However, looking at the politics of the club at the time, it seems that Reg Pratt, a consistent and growing influence on the board, was the man who rang the managerial changes at Upton Park. To suggest that Paynter was the mover and shaker in it all is to see football then as it is often misunderstood now. Charlie hadn't moved or shaken anything much during his time as manager, and for some this was part of the problem. According to Malcolm Allison (it has to be remembered that he was a harsh critic of both Fenton and Paynter), he had done little more than cause the club to 'stay in the same place it had been in for years'. Pratt was the only rational means to real and lasting change for West Ham United; the only person able to envisage the nature of the football future, while holding on to something of the club tradition in terms of its power structures, exerting an authentic level of authority and influence. Paynter had no sway above the level of the playing staff, while Will Cearns, although a long-time and stoical custodian of the club, was a man of the past at this point.

Due to the Blitz damage at Upton Park, Ted was based in Boleyn Castle. But this was indicative of the mess West Ham were in when he returned to the club. By the end of the 1949/50 season, relegation was barely averted and it was becoming clear why Pratt had apparently seen Paynter as something of a relic.

The change from Paynter to Fenton thus, from a distance, seemed a fairly smooth process, but as long-time West Ham defender John Bond confirmed, the two men didn't get on as well as legend has it (see Belton 2013b). Nevertheless, Fenton suited West Ham. He wasn't an outsider. He was used to the way the club operated, its traditions (or foibles). He would not need to be inducted, and if any insurance were needed, his period 'in waiting' would provide this.

Ted Fenton's willingness to become Prince of Wales at West Ham was not altogether surprising. He had been part of the club for most of his life; he was a local boy made good. Ted was a sort of embodiment of the club, its values and conventions.

One of eight children (the oldest of four boys), Ted's father was a Forest Gate policeman, who would often take his boys to Upton Park. For Fenton, 'West Ham was our club, East London's club ... I'm a Cockney, not a proper one, but still a Cockney, and that's what West Ham is.' Here it seems he wanted to say that because he was from the East End, and of the Hammers, he would fit into the Upton Park culture. Moreover, going back to West Ham, to stand in the shoes of Charlie Paynter, had many more possibilities than might have been forthcoming at the Hawthorns. The offer to move back to West Ham could be understood as providing Fenton with straightforward security and a move up. On the other hand, the board of West Bromwich Albion had, on the retirement of Everiss, decided to split the coaching and administrative roles. Smith, in all but name, and later Carver, by contract, were chief coaches.

The conclusion that Ted was swayed in his job choice by the relative influence involved in the posts on offer seems to be based on a deal of conjecture. This can't be denied, or avoided, given the character of the club and Ted himself. However, it is not until one studies Ted's eventual dismissal that the probability that his ambitions lay beyond the control of matters on the field of play is confirmed. Maybe Ted wasn't so much avoiding responsibility involved in a bigger club as looking to maximise his influence in helping a more modest club grow. Certainly there was more potential for growth in London than West Bromwich. In this respect it seems that many of his critics may not have done him justice. But all this retrospective, amateur psychology could well belie the simplicity of the man. The explanation given for Ted's choice by one of the players who worked with him seems to hold more than a drop of water: 'West Brom didn't offer him enough money.'

Fenton, from the outset, threw himself into the task of changing the profile of the club. Straight away he made every effort to alter West Ham's reputation as an unfashionable, middle-of-the-table Second Division side (largely, in practice if not purpose, cultivated by Paynter), lacking ambition and desiring only security. He and Reg Pratt were faced with a vicious circle: West Ham's inferiority complex, which promoted a lack of ambition within the club, which in turn generated a general belief among the supporters that the Hammers wanted to avoid the perils of success and top-quality football.

Fenton used West Ham's return to the First Division as a means to develop his public persona. In 1960 he published a book, *At Home with the Hammers*, part autobiography, part West Ham folklore. The book was an example of the school of what the great American sportswriter Red Smith called 'gee-whiz' sports writing (the sort of template most authors involving themselves with West Ham seem to have followed). It did not include a single negative word about anyone or anything; in short, this type of book would save everyone's time if it said no more than 'Everything is just great!' However, Fenton's tome did have prophetic elements. He tried to convince his readers that the Hammers were on a par with the big English clubs. Fenton wrote of his admiration for Paynter, and how he owed so much to this, his mentor. For all that, he had much more in common with Paynter's predecessor, the showman Syd King.

In his book Fenton wrote that King was 'Personality plus and adored by the players. He was the Herbert Chapman of his time.' Chapman, the legendary manager of Arsenal, was in charge of probably the biggest football club in the world in the pre-war period; he revolutionised the game. King, on the other hand, was a moderately successful manager of a relatively small club. He did not claim any special prowess, and certainly was not gifted in the technical aspects of the game (most of which had not been thought of in King's time). What then was Fenton getting at? Perhaps it was that King had wanted to get West Ham noticed. Chapman had done this for the Highbury club; he had built a tradition that sustained the Gunners even when results were not all they might have been. Fenton, along with many of those who played for him, saw Arsenal as the big London club, and he wanted to emulate them. The North Londoners were the standard to aim for.

Every spring Fenton would approach the board with a list of possible tours in Europe and matches that could be arranged with sides visiting England. He made contacts and organised fixtures. He pushed hard to enlarge and improve the Boleyn Ground, saying that it would both increase attendances and improve the performance of the team. In his book he wrote about 'our plans for Upton Park', wanting 'to make West Ham a glamour club and Upton Park London's jewel of the east'. He wanted 'to make us so ritzy that we will get the kind of reputation Arsenal had in the 1930s'.

Ted believed he could change West Ham and the role of manager at Upton Park; he supposed that the function of manager at West Ham would enable him to do this. A limited coaching job at the Hawthorns did not offer this kind of potential. And if you wanted a stage with a frisson of glitz then 1950s London was the place to have it rather than a rather non-descript location between Birmingham and Wolverhampton. Reading between the lines, while deciphering his activity and approach, Fenton seems to have perceived a power-vacuum at Upton Park that he could take advantage of, riding West Ham like a great big claret-and-blue surfboard into the modern world.

Ted Fenton's decade as West Ham manager would be successful. He produced a team that represented the standards of the board and won matches. The club gained promotion in 1958, along with a reputation for playing good football. The foundations of a youth policy were laid. Fenton's role in the development was both critical and equivocal; it might be seen as passive encouragement in that he reflected the most conservative traditions of the board and the club, but there seemed to be more to it than that.

Reg Pratt, meanwhile, was a force for change, perhaps *the* force for change in the club, and he was known not to like losing. In 1950 he led the smallest and youngest board in the game, made up of himself, the 36-year-old vice-chairman Len Cearns (son of W.J.), his eldest brother the 38-year-old Will Cearns and Dr Oliver Thomas.

Pratt administered the development of the youth teams and training methods that gave rise to 'The Academy of Football' and the building of training facilities at Chadwell Heath, Essex, after seeing the impoverished nature of player training on Wanstead flats. Pratt presided over the purchase of the freehold of the Boleyn Ground in May 1959, paying the Roman Catholic Archdiocese of Westminster £30,000, and he later appointed the far-sighted and innovatory Arsenal and England Under-23 coach Ron Greenwood. During 1980 Pratt told how the signing of Phil Parkes was among the accomplishments that he took most pride in. The board had been split and it was Pratt's vote that decided the issue, triggering the club paying what was then a world-record fee for a goalkeeper to bring Parkes to Upton Park.

This might account for Fenton's willingness to allow the team to take chances, even when it appeared that how the side played and organised itself slipped out of the control of the manager (see Belton 2013a). Many of the players agree that Pratt made a difference; he gave the impression that he cared about what was happening, both to the club and to the players.

One consistent feature about West Ham has been the way in which the board and chairmen have desisted from taking actions that would give the impression that they knew more about football than the manager or the players. Contemporaneously they have, however, been more involved in implimenting change when it is deemed necessary. This approach has changed over recent decades, firstly under the watch of Terry Brown and certainly since Davids Gold and Sullivan have been overseeing the direction of the club.

As the 1950s dawned it is not surprising that Fenton, the manager raised within the West Ham system, might have been understood to have acted almost passively in a situation where his players were doing part of his job for him, and probably doing it better than he could have (see Belton 2013a).

But the changes at West Ham depended on the unique personalities and talents of its young playing staff. In Malcolm Allison they had a leader who had no interest in coming close either to the manager or to the board, a man who left no doubt that he was concerned only for his fellow players. They had a manager who was secure enough in his job to let the players go their own way. They had a chairman who would not sabotage team development. They were playing for a club that could afford to be different because West Ham had very little to lose.

After 1950, West Ham achieved some significant changes on and off the field. The future Second Division Championship was the end point of a steady line of development started by Fenton under the guardianship of Pratt. The process included changes in personnel and tactics, the improvement of players' conditions, and the introduction of skill-oriented training, together with a youth scheme that fed players into the first team. Ted Fenton was involved in all of these innovations, if only (at times) by giving his approval.

FENTON OUT!

By the end of the 1960/61 season, Ted Fenton had left West Ham, only three years after the high point in his managerial career. It is true that after 1959 the team seemed to be going backwards, but there had been no serious complaints from within the club or from the press. The media had little to say about the details, a surprising fact given that Ted had been quite publicity oriented and had a relatively affable relationship with the press.

The timing of Fenton's resignation and the probable cause are the most dramatic evidence of how West Ham directors ran the club. Over the years questions have abounded about Fenton's managerial career at West Ham, and his departure in particular. Nothing in Ted Fenton's career as a manager of West Ham United is as significant in terms of analysing the nature of the club as the way he left; how and why it happened and its immediate consequences.

On 19 March 1961, the first sign of anything happening came by way of a report in the *Ilford Recorder*, which told of how Fenton had disappeared from Upton Park, and explained that no one at the club was saying anything more than the prepared statement to the Press Association, delivered on 16 March 1961, to which the board had given its approval. The statement by the chairman read: 'For some time, Mr Fenton had been working under quite a strain and it was agreed that he should go on sick leave. For the time being, we shall carry on by making certain adjustments in our internal administration.'

The *Recorder* concluded its article by reminding readers: 'The Upton Park club are proud of their tradition of never having sacked a manager. The present position gives a distinct and undeniable impression that a compromise has been attempted to preserve that tradition.'

The sports editor of the *Recorder*, Trevor Smith, was right when he pointed out that West Ham had traditions to look after, but not necessarily those he had highlighted. What was at stake was not the idea that an Upton Park manager had never been dismissed, but whether Ted was acting in line with other West Ham traditions. The board was working in something of the same way it had in 1932 with Syd King. King had been 'moved on' for reasons that had little connection with how the team were doing. He just didn't behave in a way the board saw as appropriate. His suicide prevented most people from remembering the fact that King was sacked. It is difficult not to conclude that in 1961, sick leave was used, as it had been in 1932, to divert attention until things could be sorted out in a manner that would enable both sides to avoid publicity and give the impression of an amicable, mutual decision. Analysis of the situation indicates that the board was interested in achieving a couple of objectives: it wanted Fenton to go, and it wanted to keep the knowledge of what had caused the break 'in the family' to itself.

Fenton did have interests outside football, including a sports shop, and it was said that he kept a low profile on his departure from the club. The board and its ex-employee were in agreement on at least one thing: what happened would be kept confidential – what happened at Upton Park would stay at Upton Park.

If the board gave any protracted consideration to their decision about Fenton, it was kept quiet. There were no published rumours about Fenton's impending departure; nor were there any comments in the board minutes about the subject having been discussed. This may have been a purposeful attempt to keep things off the record, but a more realistic conclusion, premised on what the club actually did, is that the decision was made swiftly and was made by the chairman off his own bat.

Until the board meeting that sent Fenton on sick leave, the manager had attended such gatherings regularly. Five weeks before the fateful day, Fenton had submitted the 'retain and transfer list' to the board. In early February he was instructed to make arrangements for a visit to the ground by Inter Milan and for a proposed tour of Israel.

As a result, when the West Ham manager went on sick leave, everyone outside and most inside the club claimed to have been taken completely by surprise. The majority of the board did not know that there were reasons to consider dismissing Fenton until the weekend before the Monday board meeting. The players at the time seemed genuinely shocked by Fenton's dismissal and unaware of the reasons for it. Most then and later did no more than guess at the possible rationale for the decision. They did not talk about it to the press after it happened. The public were also clueless. Even writers who had established close connections with the club had written nothing about a possible change.

After Fenton's departure the gossip was understandably rife. There was some talk that he had being upset about the sale of John Smith to Spurs, or the whole affair being a backlash in response to the allegations about 'fixing' a game against Newcastle United at Upton Park.

Fenton's staff were left to make guesses about what had happened, or draw what conclusions they could from the rumours. For all this, it is clear that Fenton was, at the time, not always valued by the professionals (see Belton 2013a).

About a year before Ted Fenton's demise, the *Ilford Recorder* had approached him to write an article about why West Ham had dropped so quickly from first to ninth position in the table. Fenton had told the paper that he 'was too busy to give the matter his attention'. The newspaper was to reiterate a familiar theme: how could West Ham succeed on a shoe-string? The writer asked, 'Are West Ham seeking men of established repute, or are they persisting with the "empty-kitty" policy? Only one man knows the answer AND THE MAN ON THE SPOT JUST NOW IS TED FENTON.'

Debate about Fenton evaporated over the following months while the newspapers concentrated on which players might be coming or going. By January 1961, the club was rooted to the lower reaches of the table, but there was no public talk about Fenton leaving Upton Park. The big rumours were that John Bond might be on his way, or maybe even Phil Woosnam, the Welsh international who had been West Ham's most expensive purchase, might take over.

After Fenton left Upton Park, within a week Reg Pratt issued another statement to the press in which he said that the board had no plans to name a new manager and that no one was being considered at that time. West Ham would be 'managed by the board' with the help of trainer Albert Walker and skipper Phil Woosnam. This statement was not wholly correct. The board was not talking to anyone specific, but Pratt and others had begun to make enquiries about possible replacements for Fenton. It was near the end of the season and West Ham were in no danger of relegation, so there was no immediate urgency. Fenton had produced the transfer–retain list, so the incoming manager would, in the first instance, just need to think about who he wanted to bring to the club, not that the board anticipated splashing out straight away.

When Fenton left, it was under two weeks before the AGM of the shareholders and, consequently, no manager was in attendance at the meeting. Fifteen shareholders turned up, which was about normal. Following the financial report, the chairman briefly reviewed the season and gave the usual thanks to staff and players. Not a word was uttered about the managerial situation; nothing about Fenton, possible successors or how the board was currently running the club. No questions were raised from the floor. It was almost as if nothing had happened.

The manner in which the board restructured the manager's role following Fenton's departure provides some clues about his effective disappearance. On 13 April, Ron Greenwood was named manager. The board told the press that Greenwood's work would be 'concerned solely with the coaching and training'. All administrative jobs would be delegated to Eddie Chapman, the club secretary, and his staff. Eddie would also take care of all West Ham's public relations. The split mirrored the division of labour which Fenton had seemingly rejected when in negotiation for the job at West Bromwich Albion before he returned to Upton Park. This suggests that the board wanted the club to be run at two distinct levels, without the connections between players and the day-to-day running of West Ham developed under Fenton. In effect, throughout most of the 1950s, there was a two-way conduit between the field and the board. This new regime sought, as far as possible, to make the links between the players and the club's administration a 'one-way street', using Chapman and Greenwood as circuit breakers. This also meant that the manager's plans for the Boleyn Ground set-up would be restricted to the field of play – initially, it seemed, not including the negotiation of transfers – rather than involving the club as a whole. The latter had been Fenton's focus, as he openly admitted in his book. Syd King, West Ham's first manager, had had ambitions of similar amplitude.

Ted did manage again at Southend, leading the club to victory in the Essex Professional Cup in 1962 and 1965, but in his four years with the Shrimpers he never took them any higher than eighth in the old Third Division. Thereafter he went into the pub trade. After retirement he passed on his sports shop to his son, Alan, who also played for West Ham, in the 'A' team, during the 1950s. Ted went to live in Gloucestershire, where he was able to play a good deal of golf. He died in July 1992, aged 77, after a car crash near Peterborough.

Everything I have experienced, relating to or found out about Ted Fenton leaves me in no doubt that he was a kind, talented, intelligent and often funny man, with a good memory. With the backing of Reg Pratt, Fenton was the man responsible for bringing most of the great West Ham players of the 1960s to Upton Park. In his eleven years as manager of the Irons, he had presided over the birth of a small revolution in British football at the Boleyn Ground (although it has to be said that much of this was instigated by the young Malcolm Allison). At the same time, he was one of the 'old school'. He was a white-collar leader, for the most part wielding a pipe rather than wearing a track suit (although unlike Paynter he wasn't above getting his kit on). He called a great deal on his military training and it stood him in relatively good stead. Perhaps in the end he knew what was needed and understood that he was not the man for the job. He was not by nature or inclination a Brazilian, although he was not the diametric opposite in some respects; he brought something of the modern world to the club, particularly in terms of his relationship with the press and the fans. To his credit he was able to make use of the knowledge and influence of the likes of Allison, which in modern management could well be seen as a strength; it is unlikely to have been something that, say, Ron Greenwood would have had the personality or fortitude to achieve in his early career. Nevertheless, Fenton was a man made in the English Second Division game of the 1930s and 1940s.

Fenton's departure from Upton Park was part of the ushering in of the future. He had opened the door to development, but the testimony of many of the players who worked with and under him in the late 1940s and early 1950s, those who broached the subject of his attitude, suggests that he ultimately resisted progress. Perhaps if he had embraced change, things would have been different. As it was, the need for the new was obvious.

Ted Fenton was in many ways made by and in the war, and that is why considering his destiny here is instructive. That he became a person who wanted change, but also seemingly retreated to the security of what he knew best, is hardly surprising given his developmental years in the game. Reg Pratt, in his actions, made it clear that while Fenton was manager, he was 'his' manager and not ultimately 'the boss' (Greenwood was never to question this exact same place he was given in the West Ham hierarchy). This, alongside the latitude the likes of Allison had been given, or taken, likely sealed Fenton's fate irredeemably.

EIGHT

'CAN ANYONE GIVE HIM A LIFT TO LEICESTER?'

(1940 WAR CUP – SECOND ROUND, FIRST LEG)

Minister of Transport appeal to motorists (according to Eric Idle)

Most players put their whole selves into any game they played; first-team or reserves. I don't know if that was more or less so during the war. I know I worked as hard in wartime games as at any other time. No one wanted to lose.

Harry Kinsell (West Bromwich Albion and West Ham)

On 4 May 1940 West Ham were at Filbert Street for their third game of War Cup football. The middle section of the Main Stand of the home of Leicester City suffered bomb damage in that year, and further damaged was sustained by a serious fire later. By 1949, the stand had been rebuilt, much of the labour being supplied by German POWs from a local camp.

The second round of the Football League War Cup was another two-legged, home-and-away tie, to be completed over successive weekends.

West Ham travelled to the midlands with Charlie Paynter finding himself with much the same group of players he had called upon in the last round.

'HAMMERS' CUP CHANCE'

The above newspaper headline told a somewhat concise tale of the opening tie of West Ham's second round. As you can see, the attendance wasn't entirely agreed.

> Leicester City 1, West Ham 1
>
> West Ham should feel satisfied with their performance in the first leg of their cup-tie at Leicester and when the teams meet again on Saturday at Upton Park they should be able to progress to the next round. They were without Fenton at Leicester, but Macaulay, who deputized for him, scored the Hammers goal through Small in the presence of just under 7,000 spectators. The game was closely contested as the score suggests, and the result was a fair one. Att: 6,320
>
> The team:
> Herman Conway, Charlie Bicknell, Charlie Walker, Norman Corbett, Dick Walker, Joe Cockroft, Sam Small, Archie Macaulay, George Forman, Jackie Wood, Stan Foxall

In truth the tie had been saved for the Irons by their defence and there was no more stoical defending partnership than West Ham's 'two Charlies', Bicknell and Walker.

Bicknell, a powerful defender, had started his football career in the non-league game, among other sides turning out for New Tupton Ivanhoe. Bicknell moved to the Football League in October 1927 with Chesterfield (where he revelled in the nickname 'Wag'), making 85 League and Cup appearances between 1928 and 1930 before, in May of the latter year, moving to Bradford City for £600. He was to make 244 successive appearances for the Bantams before signing for the Hammers in March 1936. After making his debut for the Irons in November of that year, he held on to his place for 96 consecutive matches. His 'ever-present' record before the outbreak of war was spoilt by missing one (at Prenton Park, 28 January 1939), at which point he was club captain.

During wartime Bicknell served as a Special Constable. Over that period he appeared for West Ham just over 200 times, scoring 9 goals.

Bicknell turned out in 19 Second Division games following the resumption of customary League activity in 1946/47, after which he was given a free transfer and became manager of Bedford Town in the Southern League.

Born in Pye Bridge, Chesterfield, on 6 November 1905, he grew up in Tupton, Derbyshire. Before breaking into football he had worked as a miner. A keen gardener and talented musician, Charlie Bicknell died in Cambridgeshire on 6 September 1994, aged 88. He had made 137 League and a dozen Cup appearances for West Ham in peacetime and overall more than 450 appearances in the Football League.

Charlie Walker, although growing up in Sheffield, was born in Nottingham on 14 May 1911. He played 118 games for West Ham in the peacetime seasons between 1936 and 1939, and ran out for the Irons on 77 occasions during wartime football.

According to the club handbook of 1938/39, Walker was said to be amongst the best left-backs ever to don the claret and blue in East London. He came to Upton Park from Highbury in 1936, having found his chances at Arsenal restricted by the Gunners having England skipper Eddie Hapgood in their ranks (he never got a first-team game with the North London side).

At the Boleyn Ground, in partnership with Charlie Bicknell, Walker became a stalwart in the West Ham defence; between them the pair were absent for just two matches in the final pre-war season.

At the start of the war Walker had joined the police force, but when some of his close friends joined the armed forces he signed up for the RAF. While serving on the Burma border in India, close to the conclusion of the hostilities, Walker turned out for an England XI *v.* a Scottish XI and in several Services matches he played as part of an 'All India' tour.

After serving in the Far East, Walker returned to Upton Park for the first part of the 1945/46 season. However, in April 1946 he took up the post of secretary/manager at Margate Town when the club re-formed for the 1946/47 season.

Walker had started his footballing life with Manchester United but had, early in 1935, joined Margate on loan (a side that had an informal 'nursery' arrangement with both West Ham and Arsenal). During his one season as a player at Margate he made 66 appearances, scoring 4 times. His starting salary at Upton Park was £7 per week. The move was made on the understanding that he could play for 'The Gate' as long as his League rights were retained by West Ham.

Walker's second stint with Margate lasted a couple of seasons, winning the Kent League twice (1946/47 and 1947/48) in that time. He often played centre-back, usually marking the opposition centre forward out of the match, having retained his strength in aerial combat.

In May 1948 Walker was a member of the Margate side that defeated Ramsgate 2–1 to win the Kent League Cup Final and in the same month he played at centre-back in the team that beat Gravesend and Northfleet to claim the Kent Senior Shield, completing a three-trophy haul for the term. It was his last game for the club; the following month Walker was sacked, the club's management committee believing that his acquisition of a grocery shop in Canterbury Road, Westbrook, would distract him from his footballing duties. A special meeting of club members followed, the aim of which was to reinstate Walker, but it came to nothing and, having played 78 games for Margate, Walker moved to Ashford United as player/coach (under the marvellously named manager Joe Fag – who must have been quite a draw and the butt of a few jokes). He led 'The Nuts and Bolts' to the Kent League Championship (1949) in the first of his three seasons at Essella Park; thus Walker had won three championships in his first three seasons with an 'off-field' brief.

Charlie Walker remained with Ashford up to May 1951 when Ken Horrigan left Margate to take over. Walker became Ramsgate's part-time manager for a couple of years as he continued to follow his own business interests. However, in 1961, at the age of 50, he emigrated to Plainfield, New Jersey, USA, working as a mechanical engineer, and for two years coached a local Irish side. Moving to Florida, Walker coached his grand-daughter's high school team, a side that had only just got started when he arrived, but which under his guidance won two local league titles.

Reflecting on his career during a short visit to Britain in September 1988, Walker said, 'I was never a great player, but I was strong and reliable.' Looking back on his sacking at Margate, he told how, 'It came as a complete surprise. I was never given a reason and to this day I do not know what I did wrong. I was not so much bitter as puzzled.'

Just a few days short of his 79th birthday, on 7 May 1990, Charlie passed away in Jacksonville, Florida.

NINE

FOOTBALL AND WAR

At the Football League's AGM of 29 July 1940, the clubs rejected a no-pay proposal. Instead it was decided to keep the player pay rate the same as 1939/40. Referees would receive 10*s* 6*d* (52p) for every game they officiated, while local linesmen were seen to be worth 5*s* (25p) each with additional travelling expenses.

Two regional groups (north and south) were proposed, with fixtures being worked out by the participating clubs. As clubs would not be playing a standard number of games, it was decided that no points should be awarded, but positions were to be worked out by way of goal average (dividing goals for by goals against). The plan was for peacetime Division One and Two clubs to play at least two clubs from the Third Division. It was envisaged that every club would contest at least 20 games. No matches were to be rearranged; if games were abandoned, scores at the time of abandonment would stand. No medals or trophies would be awarded. Tellingly, showing the level of fear of invasion, it was agreed that fixtures would only be planned up to the end of 1940. The idea apparently was not to disappoint people more than was necessary by having to put up with the cancellation of a football match as well as storm troopers goose-stepping down the high street.

For the coming season, clubs were not obliged to play one another both home and away. Travel was to cause problems. West Ham cancelled a game *v.* Luton, but who can blame them for that?

BOMBING

German aerial attacks on Britain started in earnest in August 1940, after air raids on convoys and other shipping in the Channel and Dover Harbour. Initial targets were aerodromes and dockyards, giving the fire service a taste of what was to follow in the near future.

London's experience of bombing came later that month, with bombs falling in the south-eastern suburbs. Eltham and Woolwich were the first of the London boroughs to feel the wrath of the Luftwaffe, which caused fires and inflicted casualties.

On 13 August 1940, Hermann Goering let loose his 'Eagle Day' plan that involved 1,485 sorties against Britain. The Luftwaffe lost forty-five aircraft, the RAF thirteen. A couple of days later the most intensive air attack on Great Britain ever was launched; some 1,790 sorties. The RAF lost thirty-four aircraft but destroyed seventy-five Luftwaffe planes.

The day of 15 August was a hot one in Kent. My grandmother and my father were hop picking in the county. This had been traditional 'holiday' for my family for generations. In peacetime most of the men would come down from the East End at weekends, while wives and kids worked in the fields for a little pay the week through for the final months of the summer. This time few men would be making the Saturday/Sunday trip.

With the rest of the people in the garden, it was the noise of the German attack that first drew their attention to the almost cloudless skies. The engines of the Nazi planes had a distinctive sound, a sort of 'rumm, rumm, rumm' with an almost discernible pause between 'rumms'. With the other pickers my dad and grandmother ran to the trenches that surrounded the hop garden, dug in preparation for such circumstances. When I was a boy my dad told me how it became almost dark as the great cloud of bombers gradually blotted out the sun. It also got noticeably cooler. The angel of death was flying above and the flapping of his wings could be heard.

Dad knew where this great menacing shadow was headed: London, the docks, his home. It seemed everyone in the trench was paralysed in fear and awe; what resistance was possible? A feeling of tangible hopelessness pervaded the small crowd of Cockneys cowering in the dirt.

Then, as the gloom was almost total, something roared overhead, towing a low, powerfully constant, thunderous buzz. Dad watched as the Spitfire, seemingly just above the hop vines, banked perhaps a mile away to his left, and as it did so another rushed by in the opposite direction. The two fighters turned in unison at opposite ends of the prospect and started to fly back towards each other; there was something joyful, playful in this; they were revving each other up!

The two planes crossed as they passed over the hop garden, both throwing in victory rolls as they soared upward into the blackness above, disappearing into the inky storm. Suddenly it seemed that hope had returned once more.

Everyone in the trenches surrounding the garden was standing up cheering. Far away a big black cross, streaming smoke, tumbled and spun from the sky. It exploded somewhere between the hop garden and the horizon before the cheering started again, louder and more frantic than before. Dad told me, 'That was at least one of the bastards that wouldn't get to drop its load.'

With the Blitz biting, the Hammers' records were the first casualty of war at Upton Park. The West Stand had to be evacuated along with what remained of the club administration, and offices were set up in Green Street House, known colloquially as 'Boleyn Castle' (the folly looked like the turret of a castle). The South Bank was also badly damaged.

The Boleyn Castle, which stood to the left (as you enter) of the current Upton Park main gates, was not actually a castle at all; it looked a bit like what a kid, who had never seen an actual castle, might have imagined a castle to look like. When the West Ham board leased it from the Archdiocese of Westminster, the structure was a local landmark. For over half a century the club tried to find a use for the building beyond its symbolic, sentimental worth, but it was never much more than an irritation in terms of the club administration; it had always presented difficulties, for example, in improving access to the ground. At the start of the Great War, the castle housed a social club called the 'Boleyn Club', which had no affiliation with West Ham United. By this time the social club held sway over what happened to the building. During the 1930s the social club approached West Ham's directors for assistance with the upkeep of the castle, predictably without success, as the only help they might have been willing to give was in its demolition.

A lightning attack on the city, made on 25 August, demonstrated the potential chaos that incendiary bombs might wreak in the congested areas of the capital's commercial centre.

PLAY THE GAME ... OR NOT

As the sky over East London and southern England began to be one of the most crucial battlefields in history, the dissatisfaction of the southern clubs was reaching its zenith.

The War Cup competition would be played on a home and away footing, and regionalised into north and south up to the last four. This effectively created a guaranteed north *v.* south Wembley final. A London Cup was also proposed, which caused further disgruntlement on the part of some southern clubs left out of this supplementary competition. They came up with an alternative arrangement that would encompass them, but the London clubs dismissed the idea and went ahead with their own cup competition. Seemingly in response, Bournemouth, Brighton, Portsmouth, Southampton, Southend United and Watford got together in a South Regional League of their own. Luton Town and Norwich City were pulled into this fold after arguing that the competition should not include the word 'south' in its title until they were part of it; 'Cry "Havoc!" said he who fought chaos with chaos and let slip the dogs of war.'

The Home Office stipulated that play should be halted when the air-raid alert sounded. Hoping to get round this, clubs made the case for 'spotters' – people placed on the roofs of stadiums. The spotters would literally watch the skies and bring an end to play via signals only when enemy planes were seen, despite the alert having been sounded previously. Initially this was seen as too hazardous by the authorities, but the first official spotters were in action by 21 September 1940 at London grounds. This avoided the automatic suspension of matches as the sirens sounded.

However, throughout 1940 and into 1941, games continued to be interrupted, not unusually for more than an hour. Players played cards, bingo (then known as 'housey, housey') and had sing-songs while waiting for the 'all clear', but it wasn't unusual for some to give up and go home or, if serving in the forces, return to their base. As a result, it was not uncommon for the referee, having attempted to get all the players back out on the field, to find a clutch of them were absent. This would lead to the abandonment of the game because of lack of players; the score at the point of the players leaving the field then stood as a result. If you were 6–0 down with half an hour to play, or all you needed was the draw you had with only the first half played, there wasn't much incentive to hang about. Consequently, not a few supporters were turned off attending games, having spent most of their Saturday in an air-raid shelter waiting for a game to restart, only to find their wait had been in vain.

The season opened well for the Hammers with a 3–2 Upton Park victory over Spurs. Jim Barrett and a Ted Fenton double did the business for the Hammers. But the away fixture against the North Londoners the following week was less than exhilarating; despite a Len Goulden goal, West Ham lost 4–1.

That night the Woolwich ferries were involved in their customary backward and forwarding, but on this occasion they weren't moving the usual passengers and vehicles but evacuating the people of Silvertown from the blazing Essex shore, with oil burning on the river.

Throughout the war years the ferry continued a twenty-four-hour service whenever necessary. For a time, during the blackout, they were not allowed to use any navigation lights. Steering was made even more problematical because the wheelhouses were covered with concrete blocks to protect the crew from shrapnel. On one occasion a bomb exploded beneath the stern of one of the ferries, although the damage was not enough to put the craft out of service. A V1 rocket also just missed the bridge of a ferry, burying itself in the opposite riverbank.

The rocket (its official name was the 'Fieseler FZG-76') first hit London in the summer of 1944; sixty-eight fell on the Borough of West Ham. You knew it was coming on hearing its droning engine. When this ceased it was descending towards its target and for a moment all that had heard it held their breath. For some of those listeners, that noise would the last thing they heard.

On 19 September the FA relaxed its ban on Sunday football, granting permission for works teams to play on the Sabbath.

As if there wasn't enough fighting going on, at the end of September, following a disputed penalty, Millwall players became embroiled in a punch-up with the Selhurst Park crowd (the attendance was 2,500). The referee had to evacuate the field for a six-minute cool-off period. Palace won 2–1 to go top of the Southern League.

The government introduced a new entertainment tax on 12 October and put up admission prices to 1*s* 1*d* (just under 6p). At the same time, the FA ordered that during air-raid alerts all matches should be halted.

The couple of games following the defeat by Tottenham produced a win and a draw, so it wasn't a great start for the Hammers, which didn't do much to make anyone think they were in for a glorious campaign at the Boleyn Ground. Football notwithstanding, Hitler ordered a colossal bombing operation concentrated on London and other big cities in October. The aim was to break civilian morale and persuade the government to pursue an armistice. In the face of appreciable casualties, loss of life and extensive destruction, London and Britain's population remained steadfast and defiant. In fact, London's resolve and Londoners' determination to resist and even fight back from the ground probably lifted the country's fortitude, creating a sense of solidarity. Edward R. Murrow, an American journalist working in London, famously told the world: 'Not once have I heard a man, woman, or child suggest that Britain should throw her hand.'

At the end of the month, the home secretary banned the 'spotter' system at football grounds during air raids.

The season was around two months old when Southend United found their way to the Boleyn Ground. The press report made the most of a phenomenal score-line that would constitute the Irons' biggest winning margin of the war years:

> West Ham's forwards were in deadly shooting form, and they were by far the more accomplished side, but Southend were not inferior to the extent of 11 clear goals. As a matter of fact their forwards at times contributed some quite attractive football, and there were occasions when they would have scored had the ball run more kindly for them. In addition, Conway, in the Hammers' goal, brought off a few remarkably fine saves, which frustrated their efforts. On the other hand, however, it must be said that the home forwards missed several 'sitters' which should have added to their tally.

Southend had to call upon West Ham to provide a player to complete their team and Chalkley, originally down to play for the Hammers, turned out at the back for them. He and Phyfers, the other back, and Turton at centre half, made a brave show but, with wing halves who could not combat the cleverness of the opposing forwards, they had a hopeless task, and the Southend goal had succumbed eight times before the interval arrived. Macaulay, making his first appearance for West Ham for some time, was in great form, and so was Goulden in the other inside position. They got a goal apiece, and were in the thick of the fray in making chances for others. Foreman and Foxall were in fine shooting form. The Hammers' defenders had a comparatively easy time against forwards who promised a lot in midfield, but often petered out before they reached shooting distance, although on several occasions they were out of luck. F. Jones and Bell were the best of them.

Rapid Scoring

Both Foreman and Foxall allowed openings to slip by during the first few minutes, but Foreman made amends after 8 minutes, when he ran through the middle and scored with a shot that passed over the goalkeeper's head as he came out. Some 4 minutes later Goulden shot against an upright, and Small, capturing it from the rebound, centred for Barrett to head through. Conway then made two grand saves in quick succession, from F. Jones and Walton, before West Ham returned to the attack, Ricketts bringing off a splendid save from Macaulay, who was clean through the defence.

For a time the Southend defence made a fight of it, but then they conceded four further goals in the space of 12 minutes. A neat pass from Foreman gave Foxall the chance to net the first of these at the end of 20 minutes play, and 5 minutes later Fenton headed through from a corner kick by Foxall. In the next minute Foreman ran through on his own to record the fifth goal of the match, and 6 minutes after, following neat passing by Macaulay and Small, Foxall added the sixth. Two more goals fell to the Hammers before half-time. Foreman netting one with a splendid effort, and Goulden forcing his way through to score the other and bring the total to eight.

Out of Luck

Southend were certainly out of luck just after the interval, when Conway managed to get in the way of a shot by Edwards, and then while he was away from his goal, R. Walker saved on the goal-line from Bell. Later, shots by F. Jones and Burley struck defenders standing in front of goal. At the other end, in a series of West Ham attacks, Ricketts made good saves from Foxall, Fenton and Barrett.

Twenty minutes of the second half elapsed before West Ham added to their score, and then Macaulay dribbled through single-handed to net a deserved goal. Foreman missed two easy chances before Foxall brought the score to double figures, and Foreman rounded off a good afternoon's shooting by scoring his fourth goal and making the total 11.

West Ham United: Herman Conway, Robert Edward 'Ted' Savage, Charlie Walker, Ted Fenton, Dick Walker, Jim Barrett, Sam Small, Archie Macaulay, George Foreman, Len Goulden, Stan Foxall.

West Ham had been 8 goals up at half-time against the embattled Shrimpers, but only 500 people watched the game. The return game, at Chelmsford City's New Writtle Street, took place the following week, on 2 November. The Estuary boys were obliged to play at that venue as the previous season they had been evicted from their home ground by the army (the club was located in a restricted area). In July 1940 they had approached West Ham, asking to share Upton Park, but the Hammers board concluded that such a venture would disrupt plans for the development of a junior side. Southend and Chelmsford became more or less a combined team during wartime.

West Ham made their way to Chelmsford with every reason to expect that they would be the authors of another annihilation of the battered, bruised and beleaguered Southend. But the result belied recent history. There was no hint that the host side was the same team that had previously (certainly in the first 45 minutes) allowed virtually every Hammers sortie into their half to conclude in a goal.

The visitors started with pretty much the same forward line that had done so much damage at Upton Park, but this time round they appeared to have lost their ability to penetrate their opponent's defence. Maybe their heaviest recorded defeat effected a sense of stoicism and/or determination in the ranks of the Essex Blues. Certainly, scoring the first goal of the game in the first half seemed to restore their belief in themselves. Retrospectively, this strike by Burley turned out to be crucial. The hosts were 2 up at half-time, and although West Ham got 1 back, and for a time threatened to draw level, Southend held out and ultimately secured a result that, with Brighton losing 5–1 at Aldershot and Swansea getting beaten 4–1 on the road to Bristol City, pulled them off the bottom of the league.

Southend had retained less than a third of the side that had faltered so badly in East London. The pitch was heavier, which did not favour the probably more skilful visitors. But really, just as everything had gone wrong for Southend the last time the two teams had met, on the first Saturday in November most of the home side's efforts were rewarded, producing what many saw as their best performance of the season.

Even though conditions were slippery, Southend displayed some good passing skills and teamwork that West Ham, considered among the best teams in the league, were unable match in this game. F. Jones, whose form for most of the season had been under par, pulled out a classy touch that had, for much of his time with the club, been typical of him, to notch up the home side's second goal.

The sturdy defensive pairing of Turton and Sliman thrived in the conditions; the latter had rarely been seen to perform better in a Southend shirt. Although Foreman worked hard, he seemed to get no change at all from this strapping opponent. Leighton had been brought in at right half and the comparatively slow pace of the match suited him well. He fed the attack almost faultlessly, but overall his passing was a telling factor in the game.

Playing out of position at left-back, Gunner Fuller, seemingly bringing some artillery with him that day, filled Calland's boots more than adequately (the Blues' usual defender was unable to arrange leave from his unit). His aerial presence was a boon to the home team; indeed, it was his head that prevented a goal when keeper Ricketts was left helpless.

Bell and Burley provided good service on the flank, but the Chelmsford pitch was not kind in terms of a short passing game, although Southend seemed quicker to adapt. Parry toiled tirelessly at left half, although his passing was not up to the standards set by Leighton.

The Macaulay/Foreman/Goulden attack squad that had been so destructive at the Boleyn Ground and – by a combination of the conditions and the Southend defence – had cut down the space available to them, were all but becalmed, crowded out by passion, physical effort and psychological determination. Sliman was particularly effective in this respect.

West Ham's wingers were pinned down, while the supply from their fighting half-backs was cut off. At the same time, with their tails up, the enthusiastic Southend attack, clearly with everything to prove, kept the Hammers on the back foot for long periods. Chalkley, assigned to mark Burley, was hard pushed to stay with his man, while at the same time Barrett was finding it much more difficult to turn as swiftly as he had been able to at Upton Park.

The opening goal of the game was the result of a centre from L. Jones, following a smart move between Fieldus and Leighton. As Conway came to gather the ball, F. Jones got his head to it and Burley was there to fire it into the net.

Southend's second came after Barrett shouldered F. Jones off the ball, but the Shrimper recovered swiftly, to accelerate beyond the West Ham defence, and with good finishing skill, beat the advancing Conway.

Stan Foxall scored for West Ham after Ricketts parried a stinging Chapman drive. Following this the visitors took control for a good slice of the second half, but the Southend defence stood firm.

Burley effectively killed the game with a rapidly executed header from a Fieldus corner. Savage got to the ball, but as his header skid, slopped, slipped, slid and bounced across the goal-mouth, Burley darted in to nut it beyond the floundering Conway.

Southend's enthusiasm, teamwork and individual effort, on a demanding surface, had restored their dignity at least to some extent, and although only 400 spectators had shown faith in them following their humiliation of the previous week, the home side had given the match a cup-tie feel and shown that they had something about them.

Southend: Ricketts; Turton and Gunner C. Fuller; Leighton, Sliman and Parry; Fieldus, Jones (L.), Jones (F.), Bell and Burley.

> West Ham: Conway; Chalkley and Savage; Fenton, Barrett and Lewis; Chapman, Macaulay, Foreman, Goulden and Foxall.

Heading toward the middle of November, West Ham had recorded just five wins, but the loss against Southend was only their second defeat. So prior to the meeting with Charlton at Upton Park on 23 November, it was hard to gauge how well (or badly) the Irons were doing, although things seemed clearer following newspaper reports of the latter game:

> Although they often found it difficult to circumvent the off-side traps set by their opponents, West Ham United won their game with Charlton Athletic at Boleyn ground on Saturday by a convincing score.
>
> On one occasion there was a break owing to the sounding of an alert, but the referee, after consulting the police, allowed play to proceed after a few minutes, much to the delight of a large section of the crowd who were obviously oblivious of the opinion that the only excuse for interrupting the game would be the dropping of bombs actually on the pitch.
>
> Bicknell's Return
>
> For the first time since last season's cup final, Bicknell appeared at right-back. Having undergone removal of a cartilage, this fine player was accorded a warm welcome on his return, and, while he was not yet completely regained of his confidence, this will not be long in coming. Most of the attacking on both sides was initiated by the left wings – in the case of the Hammers by Goulden and Foxall; and by Lancelot and Hobbs for Charlton. Two clever centre forwards in Foreman (West Ham) and Kurz (Charlton)

were doing duty, with the former being more successful in his efforts to find the net.

Combined with a slight superiority in pressing home attacks, the Hammers' defence was a little more compact and less liable to become spread-eagled than their opponents, whose efforts to throw the opposition forwards offside were sometimes their own undoing.

There had been near misses at both ends before Foreman opened the Hammers account. Receiving from Goulden, Foxall took time to steady himself and his accurately placed centre was met by Foreman, who rushed in and headed into the net. This was at the end of 12 minutes, and the success encouraged the Hammers to further endeavours. Once Foreman almost beat Hobbins again with a quick turn and shot from a pass by Goulden. After Lancelot had tested Conway with a ground shot, there was a hectic time for the home defenders, and it was the goalkeeper who extricated them from their difficulties. From a forward pass Foreman found the net again, but the point was disallowed, as Foxall was adjudged to be offside.

Foreman's Second

Pressure was then exerted by the visitors, during which both Kurz and Dryden came near the mark, and clever headers by Chalkley and Barrett staved off disaster. A hard drive by Hobbs caused Conway to concede a corner, which was cleared. Foreman's second goal came a few minutes before half-time, and resulted from a smart movement started by Goulden. Actually Foreman's shot struck Green, who was challenging him, and was deflected by the defender into the net.

Good work was performed by Conway in stopping a free kick from just outside the penalty area. The Hammers

> subsequently became very aggressive and, after Foreman had run through and narrowly missed, Fenton obtained a third goal for his side, surprising the goalkeeper by back-heeling into the net. By then the game had been won and lost, and the sporadic attacks by the visitors never seemed capable of stemming the tide. From a well-judged pass by Foreman, Foxall ran on to score the fourth for West Ham.
>
> There were interesting exchanges later, but nothing to shake West Ham and although Hobbs sent in a magnificent shot, which Conway saved well, there never appeared much likelihood of the visitors reducing the leeway.
>
> West Ham: Conway; Bicknell, Chalkley; Sergt-Instr. Savage, Barrett, Lewis; Chapman, Sergt-Instr. Fenton, Foreman, Goulden, Foxall.
>
> Charlton: Hobbs; Joblin, Sergt. Green; Reveil, Hammond, Whittaker, Dryden, Robinson, Kurz, Lancelot, Hobbs.

West Ham were doubly glad to see Charlie Bicknell, the side's skipper, make his return as they had lost the services of Charlie Walker, the regular at left-back in the Hammers side, Walker having been called up for service with the RAF.

At the end of November the FA sent out a circular to London clubs supporting a scheme under the auspicious of B.P. Miklos to share grounds and pool expenses. B.P.'s other plans included staging two matches for the price of one. Bola Miklos would be one of those killed in the tragic 1958 Munich plane crash that took such a huge toll on Manchester United.

In December the Football League decided that referees could wear glasses while officiating Regional League games. Thus at a stroke a million pleas for the referee to put his glasses on were made possible.

The success *v.* Charlton was the second of seven straight Hammers victories going through to Christmas Day. Certainly one of the highlights of this run was a 6–2 triumph over Chelsea in the East End but, on reading match reports, perhaps a better performance came the following week, on 14 December, when Clapton Orient came to Upton Park:

> The Orient had their young goalkeeper, Spears, to thank for the fact that they were not more heavily beaten at Upton Park on Saturday, and to a lesser degree they owed it to defections by Hammers' forwards when in good scoring positions. There was no doubt about the superiority of West Ham in attack and defence, but in both departments they were inclined to treat their task in light manner. The forwards were particularly at fault, and indulged in far too much fancy play. When they went straight ahead for goal they were a much more powerful force, and proved too speedy and clever for the Orient defenders. Montgomery, at back, was the best of the latter, except for Spears, who made a number of excellent saves, and a particularly fine one from a fierce drive by Barrett. The Hammers keep their position at the top of the Southern Section.
>
> The team: Conway, Bicknell, Chalkley, Savage, Barrett, Corbett, Small, Fenton, Foreman, Goulden, Foxall.
>
> Att: 1,200
>
> Scorers: Fenton, Foreman (3), Goulden

A couple of days after this match the League Management Committee looked into the complaints of southern clubs effectively excluded from the London Cup. They came up with the idea of creating two sections, one comprising the out-of-London clubs. But the London sides rejected the idea on 22 December, declaring their intention to introduce their own competition.

With the war now intensifying and the daily bombing a constant menace, the availability of players became increasingly unpredictable. In December, West Ham arrived at Craven

Cottage a man short. A centre forward from Romford, one J. Osborne, was due to make his debut for Fulham, but ended up playing for the Hammers, partnering Eddie Chapman on the right wing. Apparently he acquitted himself well, scoring the winning goal in the Irons' 2–1 win (George Foreman got the other goal for the visitors; Ronnie Rooke was on the mark for the Cottagers).

As the game's politics rumbled on in the background, along with the bomb blasts from Hitler's consistent bombardment of the country, on Friday, 27 December 1940 the local press reported West Ham's continuing march and their Christmas Day game:

> It was like old times at Upton Park on Xmas Day to see something resembling a big crowd at a football match and the 9,000 or so spectators saw something worth while. There was almost a cup-tie spirit about the play, and the desire to win displayed by both sides was there for all to see. Midway through the first half it looked like Arsenal's match for then they had a 2 goals lead and were playing better and more constructive football than the Hammers, who, however, were labouring under the disadvantage of having Foreman injured and transferred to the wing.
>
> The Hammers, however, pulled the game off and by so doing maintained their place at the head of the Southern Section of the Football League competition, which they appear certain to win. Their path to such a revival was made easier by a slip on the part of the Arsenal goalkeeper which gave them their first goal, and they were a fortunate side to be on equal terms at 2 all when the interval arrived, but there was no denying their quality in the second half. It was a good match to win, but it was not accomplished until nearing the end. Then 2 goals in successive minutes did the trick.

Barrett in Form

The Arsenal, with D. Compton and Kirchen on the wings, as the principal danger to the home defence, played some grand football in attack in the first half. They were quicker on the ball and took up position much better than the West Ham men, but the latter turned the tables in this respect after the interval. A lot of the credit for keeping the Arsenal's score down to 2 goals went to veteran Jim Barrett, at centre half, playing as well as ever, and to young Gregory, now a gunner, who kept a grand goal and brought off several saves of the first-class variety.

West Ham's defence was surprised by the speed of Arsenal's attack in the first few minutes, and it led to a goal. Kirchen careered in from the wing and crashed in a great shot. Gregory could do no more than parry the ball, and Bicknell tried to head it away, but Kirchen had followed up and was successful with his second effort. Before the Arsenal scored their other goal Gregory had punched away a full-blooded drive by Compton, and Hapgood had kicked off the goal-line from Fenton. Curtis, who has been seen in West Ham's colours during wartime football, got the Arsenal's second point, when he smartly slipped the ball into the net from Kirchen's centre.

Goalkeeper's Slip

Foxall obtained the Hammers' first goal with a single-handed effort after he had taken over the centre forward position from the injured Foreman. Challenged by three opponents, Foxall got in a swift low shot which Rigg allowed to slip under his body. The equalizer came from Foreman on the wing. There did not appear much chance of a second when he took a pass from Goulden but manoeuvring into position, he shot a grand goal from 25 yards out.

Gregory saved West Ham from dropping behind again when he pushed a fierce shot from Kirchen over the crossbar, but the most exciting incidents after the interval occurred at the Arsenal end, where the defence was subjected to heavy pressure from forwards who moved faster and with more precision than in the first half. Foreman was again in the centre, Rigg was fortunate to scramble away a shot from Yorston, but he made a splendid save from Corbett.

It was getting near the finish when West Ham got in front, and 2 quick goals gave them the victory. The first of them followed a free kick, when Foreman challenged Rigg, who had fallen with the ball, and forced it into the net. A minute later Foreman was again in the picture when he beat Scott for possession out on the left and put across a centre for E. Chapman to head through.

West Ham: Gregory; Bicknell, Chalkley, Fenton, Barrett, Corbett, E. Chapman, Yorston, Foreman, Goulden, Foxall.

Arsenal: Rigg; Scott, Hapgood, Bastin, Collett, Henley, Kirchen, Nelson, Drake, Curtis, D. Compton.

As the second half of the football season gained momentum, clothes rationing was introduced in Britain. The rules applied to everyone and therefore the government would not allow football clubs to replace kit without coupons. It is amazing that many supporters were prepared to donate their precious coupons. The rationing of clothes was just another item in a catalogue of bleak war news. Heavy bombing continued night after night as the Luftwaffe pounded all the nation's big industrial centres as well as the capital.

On 11 January 1941, Portsmouth, Bournemouth, Brighton, Watford, Southend and Southampton started a Regional South competition, later augmented by Luton and Norwich. The whiff of schisms smelt at the start of the season was rising to something of a stench.

On 4 January, the breakaway London War Cup got under way. There were two sections ('A' and 'B') with six teams in each, playing 10 qualifying games. The top two clubs in each of the sections played each other in the semi-finals on 31 May. Bill Voisey, the 50-year-old manager of Millwall, selected himself to play outside right in a match *v.* West Ham. Voisey had played in the Millwall half-back line from 1908 to 1923. During the First World War, as a sergeant in the Royal Artillery, his bravery under fire on the Western Front had earned him the Military and Distinguished Conduct Medals as well as the Croix de Guerre – 'Cross of War' – a French military decoration created in 1915, commonly conferred on foreign forces allied to France, for acts of heroism involving combat in the face of the enemy.

Voisey's decision was forced on him by the fact that he only had ten men available for the game against the Hammers. He had tried up to that point in the war to manage with local players rather than enlist guests, unlike his successor, the marvellously named Jack Cock, who – maybe wanting to introduce more penetration to the side – was only too ready to call upon strangers after his appointment as Millwall's manager in November 1944.

TEN

ONWARD!

(1940 WAR CUP – SECOND ROUND, SECOND LEG)

> I played for West Ham during 1944/45 and 1945/46. It was marvellous really, how the players were all together and the way the fans turned up to cheer us on. We didn't spend a lot of time on working out that we'd do this or that before a game, more worked it out as you were playing. In that way it was a joy … fun.
>
> *Ken Bainbridge*

A week after the first leg of the inaugural Football League War Cup (4 May 1940), the Irons were facing Leicester City at Upton Park in the second leg. Starting all square gave West Ham the opportunity to go out and express themselves. Charlie Paynter, as so often in this era, was again able to call on the considerably able services of Joe Cockroft, one of his most reliable troops.

NO ORDINARY JOE

Cockroft was a remarkably dependable wing half, ever-present in the Hammers' Division Two team over four successive terms between 1933 and 1937. As a lad he was in the same Barnsley school team as the pre-war Spurs forward George Hunt and Arthur Hydes of Leeds United. Many supporters who saw him play would argue that he was amongst the best uncapped players of his era.

Having started his footballing life with Yorkshire Paper Mills, Barnsley Old Boys, Ardsley Athletic and Wombwell (the town where he was born, on 20 June 1911), his first professional club was Rotherham United, but he was not highly rated by 'The Merry Millers'; between 1931 and 1932 Crockroft played just 3 games for the Millmoor men, scoring 1 goal.

Cockroft arrived at Upton Park, initially on a four-week trial, in the latter part of the 1932/33 season from Gainsborough Trinity. The Midland League club seemed to be something of a feeder club for West Ham before the Second World War.

With hardly time to catch his breath, let alone adapt from Lincolnshire town to big city life, Cockroft found himself, on Good Friday 1933, after just 4 reserve matches, drafted into the Irons' League side at left half, following the injury of first Albert Cadwell and then Joe Musgrave. Chesterfield won the match on the Saltergate Recreation Ground (1–0), but Cockroft did well enough to hold on to his place in the first XI, and to be on the winning side in the following 4 games, a run that helped the Irons steer clear of relegation to the third level of the English football (a single point saved West Ham from the drop that would probably have changed the entire history of the game).

Cockroft was absent from the West Ham League line-up on just three occasions before the outbreak of war. He had the dubious honour of being the first player at Upton Park to have his home blown away in the Blitz. Then, early on in the hostilities, direction of labour regulation dictated Cockroft's return north to Sheffield; as part of the war effort, he was required take up employment at Edgar Allen's Steelworks. However, making the best of the situation, he guested for Sheffield Wednesday, the club he would move to after the war, following a spell with Dartford; he would make a total of 96 appearances in all competitions for the Hillsborough club.

During 1949, at the age of 37 and for a fee of £4,000, Cockroft made the short journey from Wednesday to Sheffield United. The Blades were to be the only top-flight club he played for. At that point he was the oldest debutant the First Division had ever seen. A year on, he took up the post of player-manager at Wisbech Town. He spent three years with the Fenmen of Cambridgeshire before retiring from football.

Cockroft became a pub landlord and then got into the printing trade. He was an enthusiastic golfer and swimmer. He passed away in February 1994 (aged 82) in King's Lynn, Norfolk. He had played 251 peacetime games for West Ham and during wartime he took part in 29 matches under the Hammers flag.

He was an extremely versatile player, blessed with insight and skill, arguably the finest West Ham players of his day. At Upton Park, Cockroft would often switch roles with Len Goulden during a match (as would Stan Foxall). This would invariably confuse the opposition. Up to the 1938/39 term he made 263 appearances for West Ham. He scored 3 times for the Hammers, all in the Second Division. The first came in a 6–0 home win against Bury in February 1936. The next was probably his most important, the second in a 3–3 draw at Norwich in October of the same year. His final claret-and-blue peacetime goal came in a 6–1 Upton Park win over Tranmere Rovers.

In 1940, the press were becoming increasingly interested in the War Cup and the Hammers' progress:

Hammers' Cup Win – Leicester's Weak Shooting

West Ham United 3, Leicester City 0

Having drawn with a goal all at Leicester, this match at Upton Park on Saturday was the decider as to which team should enter the next round of the War Cup, and although up to a point it was either side's game, in the end there was no doubt about the virtue of West Ham's victory. They owed their success not to the fact that they played better football than their opponents, but because there was more tenacity about their forward play. As a matter of fact, if points were awarded for prettiness of movements, the spoils would have gone to Leicester but their nice passing got them nowhere and their finishing was lamentably poor. They lacked that extra bit of dash that West Ham had in their attack, the difference that meant goals. Although they did not deserve it, Leicester might have been beaten by a more substantial margin but for a couple of fortunate saves on the goal line by their right-back.

There was no doubt about West Ham's superiority in finish, but it took them a long time to make certain of the game. They could claim only a goal advantage at the interval scored by Foreman in the first minute, although they had the assistance of a strong breeze, but they played better against the wind than they did with it, and a couple of goals by Foxall and Foreman in that order gave them a comfortable victory.

The team: Conway, Bicknell, C. Walker, Barrett, R. Walker, Cockroft, Small, Fenton, Foreman, Foxall, Chapman.

Att: 15,500

EDDIE CHAPMAN

Foreman's brace, alongside the contribution of Stan 'the Lincolnshire Poacher' Foxall, demonstrated that West Ham were now a team to fear in the competition. A 16-year-old Eddie Chapman turned out for the Irons that day, feeling quite flush with his 30*s* (£1.50) match fee. His wartime experience was typical of many young players in the professional ranks at the time:

> I was called up in 1942 and went to the Isle of Wight for six weeks training. I couldn't even pump-up a bike tyre at the time. After the test they gave you, to see which part of the service you were best suited for, I came out as a Royal Engineer, although I'd wanted to be in the Royal Artillery. I went to Chatham and became a field works instructor in a few months. I was teaching after that. I was determined to try to get on a bit in the services. After a while I saw the sergeant-major and asked to go on a PT course. I did a three-week course in Aldershot. I came out and got my cross-swords, then I carried on at Chatham. After a couple of years I was posted to Longmoor Camp, in the Portsmouth area. It was sport all the time. I virtually slept in the gymnasium.

Eddie, who was something of a child phenomenon in terms of his footballing talent, signed a professional contract at Upton Park in September 1942 and made a total of 26 wartime appearances for West Ham, scoring 8 goals. He also played for the Royal Engineers All-England XI.

> I was stationed at Chatham. Gillingham Football Club wasn't too far away, so I played for them. Football League regulations had it that you couldn't earn more than 30 shillings a game, but Gillingham were in the Kent League at that time and I got a fiver a match from them. So sometimes I used to say to Charlie Paynter, 'Can't make it this week, Charlie, playing for Gillingham.'

While at Gillingham, Chapman scored 9 goals in one week against Chelsea, and then 7 the next against the RAF.

The 16 ties of the second round of the War Cup had pulled in 140,000 spectators. The third round draw, oddly, was carried out in Glasgow following the England *v.* Scotland game;

the Lord Provost of Glasgow, ball bag in hand, drew the spheres that fated West Ham to meet with Huddersfield Town, a team with a massively distinguished footballing pedigree. Having produced a string of internationals for all the home nations, the Terriers had been League Champions for three years running over 1923/24, 1924/25 and 1925/26, and runners-up in 1926/27, 1927/28 and 1933/34. The club had claimed third place in 1922/23 and 1935/36. The Leeds Road side were also Cup fighters of renown, having won the FA Cup in 1922 and got to the final in 1920, 1928, 1930 and 1938; they were semi-finalists in 1929 and 1939.

Consequently, with the Football League War Cup reverting to sudden-death, one-match knockout ties in its third round (one replay was allowed if needed) and for the rest of the competition, the combative Irons looked to have a mountain to climb. This task was made more onerous by West Ham being obliged to travel to Yorkshire to face this north *v.* south battle (venues for ties were decided through the draw).

Upton Park faithful.

Recruits being trained to operate the searchlights that would probe the night sky for Nazi raiders.

West Ham Air-Raid Precautions Dare-Devil Messengers.

London's burning –
the Blitz.

The East London Docks –
Britain's lifeline.

West Ham *v.* Chelsea – the War Cup.

Ron Greenwood – a new direction.

Dick Walker introduces himself to Dave Corbett.

Len Goulden.

1958 promotion – the legacy of war.

Hyde Park armed – anti-aircraft guns protecting London.

John Charles lifts the FA Youth Cup in 1963; first fruit of West Ham's youth policy developed by Ted Fenton.

Charlie Bicknell.

Stan (Joe) Foxall.

The legendary Jimmy Ruffell.

Albert Morris: prisoner of war.

Bunking in.

Firefighters/home front warriors: my grandfather, George Morris, is standing on the far left – the squad included two of his daughters and a son-in-law.

Charlie Bicknell collects the FA War Cup.

The deadly V2.

Legends reassemble – wartime Hammers heroes, including Len Goulden (fourth left, front row) and Ernie Gregory, come back to Upton Park for a peacetime friendly.

Blackburn's Bill Rogers.

The immaculate Vic Watson.

ELEVEN

SOCIAL SOLIDARITY AND POLITICAL FOOTBALL

> We played for each other, looked after one another. No one person was better than another.
>
> *Almeric Hall (West Ham United)*

At the start of 1941 it was announced that the War Cup victors would receive four National Saving Certificates (worth £3) and the losers one less (value around £2.10).

In February 1941 Len Goulden was called up for England duty. In the autumn of 1939 the mood was such that international football seemed doomed, as it had been during the First World War. But the pull and distraction of the game became its own justification as the Second World War moved out of its initial stages. Two matches against Wales were played in November 1939, but with the underlying conviction that these would be the last representative games of their type. After some debate it was agreed to play a match with Scotland at Newcastle in aid of wartime charities. The game, in December, was won by England 2–1 and aroused so much enthusiasm in the north-east that the authorities decided to continue to play home internationals 'when circumstances permitted' for their value in raising civilian morale.

However, there was more to it than this. Football is and was the product of an industry and, like all commercial products, when people learn to live without them, they lose their attraction. But the game is also set in the British consciousness and so its parameters exceed those of fiscal enterprise. Football embodies symbolic identity and cultural meaning at local, regional, national and international levels; it makes a basic statement, from the viewpoint of those who watch and support 'their' team – 'this is us'. Clubs peddle sentiment; they sell a means to fulfil a need to express loyalty and solidarity, a 'we-ness'. 'International' football turns up the volume in this respect, but at the same time embeds the tribal character of the game.

Now, I'm not saying this sort of analysis was understood in 1940 in the way I have just articulated it, but a general awareness of the way the game permeates the reality of our lives clearly provided the impetus for state and commercial interests to cooperate in generating an ethos and motivation to do whatever was practicable or possible to 'life-support' football.

At the same time, the authorities (the military and government), albeit at times grudgingly in some sectors, obviously grasped football's ability to stoke the nationalist agenda – an 'us' against 'them' mentality – in a way that other sports did not. The sense of general camaraderie that is engendered behind an idea of identity (enforced by symbols such as club colours, badges and iconic figures; managers, players, etc.) is relatively harmless in terms of the prevailing order in a way that other incarnations of unity, commonality and shared activity, such as trade unions, are, at least potentially, not.

Arnold Hills, the owner of Thames Ironworks, brought his football team, the side that would become West Ham United, into being (as part of a whole range of other sporting, social and cultural works-based activities) during an era haunted by historically recent and intense working-class organisation and political belligerence. Looking at his *Thames Ironworks Gazette*, it becomes obvious that this was an attempt to create a sense of loyalty to, and identity with, the company among its workforce (see Belton 2003). This was certainly informed by Hills's own experience of public school and university; promoting a sense of cohesion synonymous with the 'old school' tradition – a social fraternity more than advanced ideas about political solidarity. It offered an alternative to affiliation via patronage to the 'brotherhood' of the growing trade unions. The latter were perceived by the establishment, of which the Hills family was a part, as a real and venomous threat, not only to industry, but to the social order and persistence of the Empire.

It's not too much of a leap to understand the effective propagation and nurturing of football at a regional and national level during the Second World War as a reiteration and reincarnation of the type of effectively depoliticising social and economic project that Hills fostered, as chronicled in the *Ironworks Gazette*.

That football might be made to work was evident by way of an examination of the circumstances of the international game scheduled for May 1940 in Glasgow. The environment could hardly have been worse. The seemingly bad start to the war, with Britain on the back foot, put the game in doubt right up to the kick-off. Lord Haw-Haw, the German radio propagandist, had threatened that Nazi bombers would not permit the match to extend beyond half-time.

However, the day before the game the local chief constable promised: 'Unless something terrible happens overnight, the game will go on.' In the event only 6,000 who had bought tickets allowed themselves to be deterred from attending and 75,000 watched the game.

Team problems were also overcome. Goalkeeper Bartram had been refused leave by the RAF and because England's only reserve was amateur forward J.L. Lewis, Vic Woodley of Chelsea was asked to catch the sleeper to Glasgow to take over. Not until their train steamed into Glasgow was it certain that Stan Cullis, Joe Mercer, Bert Sproston and Don Welsh had been given leave by the army.

Between the outbreak of hostilities and the final melodrama of a Berlin bunker, England and Scotland met in 16 international matches that produced some absorbing encounters between some of most gifted players of the era. Yet none of these games counts as 'official'; most record books ignore even the fact of their happening. Caps were not awarded to the players; nor were the victories and defeats credited to their accounts. This is a monstrous injustice. Those too young or too preoccupied with surviving battles and the Blitz to have seen football at that time have only the haziest notion that international games were played, and as such are obliged to accept officialdom's valuation that it was all utterly meaningless. Scratch teams, playing hastily arranged fixtures, before small and untypical crowds, seems to be the lasting impression of the period provided for those who were absent. That picture, however, is utterly false.

Although international football between the nations seemed only a remote possibility late in 1939, it became an established pattern and procedure that allows it in retrospect to stand as valid. To ignore or dismiss the wartime matches – international or at club level – is an injustice, especially to the players who took part. The years between 1939 and 1946 took great bites out of the career-span of some of the greatest players Britain has ever produced; the conflict should not deprive them of their credit – for it did not disguise the evidence of their talent.

In the late 1930s a great England team was emerging and this, together with the passion and at times ferocity of the wartime games, particularly on the international stage, demonstrated that this was not 'phoney football', but a real test of personal, club and international merit. Butter may have been rationed, bombs may have rained, but the quality and desire of Britain's football would have stood as high, war or no war. To reject the wartime matches as something less than 'full' games/internationals it would be necessary also to declare that the likes of Goulden, Swift, Cullis,

Macaulay, Mercer, Matthews, Carter, Lawton, Busby, Shankly and Compton would not find places in the first XI of their clubs or be selected for 'full' international teams at any other time. It would be necessary to claim that Hampden Park with 130,000 fans, or Wembley with 75,000 inside, were not the true settings and true audiences for 'full' international matches.

After missing out on England's 1–1 draw with Scotland in Glasgow in May 1940, Len Goulden was back in the side for the game at St James' Park, Newcastle, on 8 February 1941.

The 21-year-old Wilf Mannion, with his wizardry on the ball, introduced a new and venomous threat to the England strike force ... Mannion connected with Len Goulden to create what looked like a promising new partnership in the England ranks.

Clyde's Doug Wallace hit England twice; his second was an 18-yard rocket. Scotland's other goal came late on from Joe Bacuzzi after the Fulham defender misplaced his back header.

Everton man Tom Lawton scored his side's second goal after creating its first, scored by Ralph Birkett of Newcastle United.

While many thought the half-time 2–2 scoreline would have been a more accurate result in terms of the performance of both teams, Scotland's 3–2 win had provided an exciting game for the 25,000 who turned out to cheer the teams on. Scotland had started 1941 with what would be their last victory for two years (4 matches) and the world had a shufti of the astonishingly blond genius that was Wilf Mannion, who had been rescued from the beaches of Dunkirk just twelve months earlier.

TWELVE

TACKLING THE TERRIERS

(1940 WAR CUP – THIRD ROUND)

In terms of the Richter scale this was a force 8 gale.

John Lyall (West Ham)

On 18 May 1940 Charlie Paynter found himself needing to juggle his side for the trip to Huddersfield for the third round of the Football League War Cup. Both Eddie Chapman and Ted Fenton were unavailable, but if anything, with Archie Macaulay and Len Goulden being drafted in, the Hammers were a better side than the one that had beaten Leicester at the Boleyn Ground.

Huddersfield Town had beaten Chesterfield 3–2 over the two legs of the first round. Their second round experience brought a 2–1 aggregate victory over Hull. Town had won the North East Division convincingly (there were 10 points between them and runners-up Newcastle United). In the Terriers the Irons also faced yet another pre-war top-flight side and so a hard-fought draw with the sides producing half-a-dozen goals between them at Leeds Road was a more than creditable performance for the East Enders.

The team: Herman Conway, Charlie Bicknell, Charlie Walker, Jim Barrett, Dick Walker, Joe Cockroft, Sam Small, Archie Macaulay, George Foreman, Len Goulden, Stan Foxall.

The crowd of 7,750 were treated to a 6-goal thriller of a draw. The game remained deadlocked at 3–3 so the sides were obliged to go to extra time. However, the teams played two 10-minute halves, not the stipulated 15 minutes. The decision to flout League rules was made to allow the Hammers to catch their train back to London. Nevertheless, goals from George Foreman, Archie Macaulay and Stan Foxall gave West Ham a second bite at the cherry.

STAN FOXALL

Joseph Stanley Foxall made 111 peacetime appearances for West Ham, scoring 42 goals. Born in Crowle, Lincolnshire, on 8 October 2014, he turned out for the Hammers 145 times during the war years, scoring on 61 occasions; an admirable total for a winger.

Known both as 'Stan' and 'Joe' during his time in football, Foxall was one of many players to make the trip from Gainsborough Trinity to Upton Park. Alongside John Morton in the latter's debut game for Lincoln St Andrews, Foxall stayed with that side for three seasons.

At times, because of his unconventional tactics, Foxall was given the epithet the 'Mystery Man'. Although an accomplished player, he often bewildered his teammates as much as the defenders he tortured.

Ostensibly a winger, Foxall was able to take any forward role. His first representative honour came in November 1936 when he was selected for the London Combination side that met the Central League team. This was the year that Foxall established himself as a Hammers regular. By the 1937/38 season he was joint top scorer with Archie Macaulay.

The season before the outbreak of the Second World War, Foxall began to play a more direct role, closer to the offensive centre of the Hammers side, while Sam Small shifted on to the wing. This reshuffle, worked out by the players themselves and put into action as and when needed, proved a great success. During that 1938/39 term Foxall became a feared weapon, certainly by London adversaries Tottenham Hotspur. Over four encounters with the men from White Hart Lane, starting with a League game on 29 October at Upton Park, Foxall claimed a handful of goals. *The Times* explains how one of these was scored and gives a flavour of Foxall's skill and attitude:

> ... a combination of swerve and speed took him right through the defenders until he had only Hooper to beat and he equalised.

Although the home side claimed a 2–1 victory on that occasion, *The Times* provided a vista on a better result for the Irons in the fourth round of the FA Cup:

> On a pitch that was so generously covered in sand as to suggest spades and donkey rides rather than football, not only did Foxall score 2 brilliant goals but his mere presence in the centre – after a somewhat unprofitable time on the right wing until West Ham were 2 down – seemed to revitalise the team. Almost immediately he scored a magnificent goal after a long dribble, and when he did very much the same sort of thing again 10 minutes from the end, West Ham drew level.

Back at the Boleyn Ground for the replay, Foxall and Sam Small once more exchanged tasks. Following a penalty miss by Archie Macaulay, the visitors took a 29th-minute lead. But less than 5 minutes on, for the third time in a trio of games, the 'Fox' pulled his side level, so dragging the North Londoners to Highbury for a second replay.

A turnout of over 50,000 saw Spurs once more take the lead on 3 February 1939. However, 5 minutes off the hour, Foxall, almost predictably, became the bane of Peter McWilliam's boys. Picking up a long clearance, he bounced through the efforts of two defenders, and from outside the penalty area let off a vicious, low drive that left Percy Hooper with no chance. Archie Macaulay's strike saw the collective heart of the Spurs break and they were a beaten team.

Although Foxall joined the then Southern League side Colchester United in August 1948, it was in September 1944, a decade after joining the Hammers, during a game *v.* QPR (a single goal from Len Goulden defeated the Hoops at Loftus Road) that Foxall picked up the knee injury that would ultimately close the curtains on his career.

However, Foxall was able to help the Us to promotion to the Football League in 1950 as runners up to the Southern Football League Champions that season, Merthyr Tydfil; the Martyrs' goal average was 0.17 better than Colchester's. That same term Foxall and the Essex men won the Southern Football League Cup (they had been in the runner-up spot in 1947/48 and 1948/49).

The first of Foxall's 86 League appearances for Colchester came on 21 August 1948 away to Cheltenham Town. He was to score 16 League goals before his last game for the club on 6 April 1950. He died at the age of 76 on 12 August 1991.

DUTCH COURAGE

With the draw in the third round tie of the War Cup, West Ham caused Huddersfield to undertake the sapping schlep down to London. However, from before the second leg of the second round until a few days before the Hammers' draw with the Terriers, the battle for Holland had been fought. Matters had all but been resolved over a five-day period. Following the failure of Nazi paratroopers to capture the government precinct in The Hague on the morning of 10 May 1940, assaults from the air followed. It took the German invaders just hours to take the Dutch Northern provinces. Taking up defensive positions in the hills of Utrecht province, close to Grebbeberg and at Kornwerderzand, at the tip of the Afsluitdijk in Friesland, the Dutch put up a stoic defence and the fighting was intense. However, on 13 May Grebbeline fell and the next day the centre of Rotterdam was smashed by concentrated aerial assault. Surrender was the inevitable consequence. During May 1940, approximately 2,200 Dutch servicemen died in defence of their homeland, while there were 2,700 causalities. About 2,000 civilians were killed or injured.

During the war the Dutch people mounted a continuous and brave non-violent campaign of resistance. However, alongside Australian forces, the Free Dutch were actively involved in a range of warfare, including guerrilla campaigns.

THIRTEEN

ALL IN THE GAME

Discipline strengthens the mind so that it becomes impervious to the corroding influence of fear.

Field Marshall Bernard Law Montgomery
(elected president of Portsmouth FC in 1943)

In early February 1941, Les Compton of Arsenal scored 10 goals in the Gunners' 15–2 thumping of Clapton Orient, while Jock Dodds hit 8 in Blackpool's 9–2 destruction of Rochdale. The Scottish international had a chance to make it 9 but missed the penalty (hitting the post).

Later that same month West Ham had begun their defence of the Football League War Cup with a convincing 5–3 aggregate victory over Norwich City. Although losing 2–1 in East Anglia, 2 goals from George Foreman led the way for a 4–1 win at Upton Park. This opened the way for a trip into deepest Essex on the first day of March and a meeting with Southend United. But the travelling Hammers were not at their best, leaving with a 2–1 defeat to contemplate.

However, a week later, at Upton Park, a Sam Small hat-trick in the 3–1 result put the Hammers through (4–3 on aggregate) to the third round and the juicy prospect of a meeting with Arsenal, with the first leg at the Boleyn Ground. However, a strike from

Les Compton was enough to beat West Ham at Upton Park. The older brother of Denis struck again in the return leg in front of nearly 13,000 and, with an Alf Kirchen goal and a single reply from George Foreman, the Gunners advanced with a 3–1 aggregate score.

Arsenal went on to beat Tottenham in the fourth round and Leicester in the semi-finals, to meet Preston on 10 May at Wembley. The 1–1 result meant a hard-fought replay at Ewood Park three weeks later that North End won 2–1. Retrospectively, West Ham had done well, beaten only by very worthy finalists.

The FA on 5 April declared that the season would be extended to 7 June. With two relatively important cup tournaments, the London and the national, there was a lot to fit in. The national competition was made up of northern and southern sections up to the semi-finals.

Early in April the FA called a ban on Good Friday games. It was thought that they might pull people away from war work. Also in April, Charlie Bicknell had played for the 'Police Pros' *v.* The Irish League, and Len Goulden turned out for the latter side (gor-blimey and begorrah!) – the game was goalless. Goulden was in an FA XI *v.* the Army in May, a match that the FA won 4–2 at St James' Park.

In the London Cup the Hammers just missed out on the semi-finals. Reading beat Brentford 3–2 at Stamford Bridge in a final watched by a comparatively disappointing crowd of 9,000. The surprise winners had convincingly beaten West Ham 4–1 at Elm Park and grabbed a point in the return at the Boleyn Ground. Arsenal had been the thorn in West Ham's side in both cup tournaments. Although obliged to play their home games at White Hart Lane, they had 'done-the-double' over the Irons twice in these competitions. But despite their ascendancy over Paynter's men, the North Londoners won nothing in the 1940/41 season.

London War Cup 'B' Division, 1940/41							
	Played	Won	Drawn	Lost	For	Against	Points
Reading	10	6	4	0	29	8	16
Tottenham Hotspur	10	5	3	2	32	13	13
West Ham United	10	6	1	3	23	19	13
Arsenal	10	5	2	3	38	18	12
Millwall	10	2	1	7	13	25	5
Clapton Orient	10	0	1	9	9	59	1

A fortnight before the Irons' final game of the London competition (a 3–0 loss to Arsenal – 2 goals from Ted Drake and a penalty from Les Compton did for the Hammers' chances of making the semi-finals), Len Goulden was once more called to the England cause and Hampden Park. Twenty-five minutes into the second half, Goulden's header from a Mannion cross put England in front, after Don Welsh had equalised Alex Venters' opener.

The last of the heavy air raids on Britain took place on 10 May 1941. This wasn't the end of the aerial war, but importantly for football, the daylight bombing raids were over: the Battle of Britain had been won.

The bombing and the effort to construct wartime football practically from scratch had made the 1940/41 term the most demanding of seasons during the years of hostility.

Playing out the somewhat awkward Southern Regional schedule, West Ham achieved a notable performance over the whole season. However, it is understandable why the clubs rejected the goal-average system, expressed via varied numbers of games played. It clearly skewed comparative, relative performance and as such was unsatisfactory. However, as can be seen on page 164, I have added a 'win percentage' column which demonstrates more accurately the relative success of West Ham's season, but also how hard done by Aldershot were.

South Regional, 1940/41								
	Played	Won	Drawn	Lost	For	Against	Goal average	Win %
Crystal Palace	27	16	4	7	86	44	1.954	59.3
West Ham United	25	14	6	5	70	39	1.794	56.0
Coventry City	10	5	3	2	28	16	1.750	50.0
Arsenal	19	10	5	4	66	38	1.736	52.6
Cardiff City	24	12	5	7	75	50	1.500	50.0
Reading	26	14	5	7	73	51	1.431	53.8
Norwich City	19	9	2	8	73	55	1.327	47.4
Watford	35	15	6	14	96	73	1.315	42.9
Portsmouth	31	16	2	13	92	71	1.296	51.6
Tottenham Hotspur	23	9	5	9	53	41	1.292	39.1
Millwall	31	16	5	10	73	57	1.280	51.6
Walsall	32	14	7	11	100	80	1.250	43.8
WBA	28	13	5	10	83	69	1.202	46.4
Leicester City	33	17	5	11	87	73	1.191	51.5
Northampton Town	30	14	3	13	84	71	1.183	46.7
Bristol City	20	10	2	8	55	48	1.145	50.0
Mansfield Town	29	12	6	11	77	68	1.132	41.4
Charlton Athletic	19	7	4	8	37	34	1.088	36.8
Aldershot	24	14	2	8	73	68	1.073	58.3
Brentford	23	9	3	11	51	51	1.000	39.1
Chelsea	23	10	4	9	57	58	0.981	43.5
Birmingham	16	7	1	8	38	43	0.883	43.8
Fulham	30	10	7	13	62	73	0.849	33.3
Luton Town	35	11	7	17	82	100	0.820	31.4
Stoke City	36	9	9	18	76	96	0.791	25.0
QPR	23	8	3	12	47	60	0.783	34.8
Brighton and Hove Albion	25	8	7	10	51	75	0.680	32.0
Nottingham Forest	25	7	3	15	50	77	0.649	28.0
Bournemouth	27	9	3	15	59	92	0.641	33.3
Notts County	21	8	3	10	42	66	0.636	38.1
Southend United	29	12	4	13	64	101	0.633	41.4
Southampton	31	4	4	23	53	111	0.477	12.9
Swansea Town	10	2	1	7	12	33	0.363	20.0
Clapton Orient	15	1	3	11	19	66	0.287	7.0

West Ham contested 8 games against clubs from a lower division and were beaten just twice. The Irons failed to score in only 2 games. A club that the Hammers did not meet, Crystal Palace, finished in first place. However, the overall objective, to keep clubs active, had been accomplished. If this involved getting beaten by Arsenal with a relatively big crowd in attendance, while smacking about the likes of Southend 10–0 in front of a few hundred, that was wartime football life. This was the balance the League was pursuing via its insistence that smaller clubs got at least a proverbial slice of the metaphoric cake.

However, the appeal of cup football, game for game, for the most part, appeared to dwarf what the Regional League South had on offer.

West Ham called on a number of guest players: from Charlton Athletic George Green and Harold Hobbis, South African Berry Nieuwenhuys from Liverpool (who interestingly played and scored in an 'All British' side that were beaten in the Football League 5–3 in January 1941), Middleborough's Benny Yorston, and Bernard Joy, Arsenal's talented amateur centre half (Bernard would become the football correspondent for the *London Evening Star* in peacetime).

Stan Foxall led the field with 41 Cup and League outings. George Foreman for the second season in succession was the leading goal scorer with 34.

At the start of June it was announced that clubs involved in the War Cup (68 teams) would receive £170 each. However, the FA reported a loss for the 1940/41 term of £9,287 while the Football League made a grand profit of £16.

FOURTEEN

INSTANT REPLAY

(1940 WAR CUP – THIRD ROUND REPLAY)

Great leaders don't focus on trying to get people to do something. They focus on trying to get people to be something. Imagine how much more productive you would be if your superior was constantly helping you become more than you thought you could be. This is a stark contrast to the way most 'bosses' operate.

Deputy Fire Chief Frank Viscuso

Just three days after the drawn third round tie of the Football League War Cup at Leeds Road, on 22 May 1940, given the demands of the war and the toll on his players, Charlie Paynter would have been pushed to keep his side together. The loss of Charlie Walker was certainly a blow as Huddersfield came to Upton Park looking to put an end to any hopes of wartime footballing glory their hosts might be contemplating. Reports of events show the contrary:

Hammers Win Replay – More Forceful Attack

West Ham United 3, Huddersfield Town 1

More than 20,000 spectators saw West Ham win the replay in the third round of the Football League Cup at Upton Park on Wednesday evening. The match produced some excellent football by both teams but West Ham's attack had more penetrative power, and that accounted for their success. So good was each defence that nearly half an hour had elapsed before anything in the nature of a good shot was delivered at goal, but even if nothing tangible accrued, a lot of the approach work by both sets of forwards was admirable.

The respective centre half-backs, Walker (West Ham) and Young (Huddersfield) were outstanding figures in defence, but the Hammers had the more forceful wing half-backs in Fenton and Cockroft, who were continually in support of their forwards. Both goals had narrow escapes from downfall before West Ham took the lead after 35 minutes when Macaulay forced the ball through in a fierce scrimmage which followed a corner kick. Just before half-time West Ham consolidated their position with a second goal, resulting from a grand movement in which Small and Macaulay took part before Foreman slipped the ball into the net.

Huddersfield should have made use of two good openings soon after the interval, but Beasley shot across the goal with a clear 3 yards and Brook hooked the ball over from 3 yards with Conway out of goal. Strong defences kept the forwards at bay for a long period, but after half an hour Foxall surprised the Huddersfield goalkeeper with a great drive which found its billet from 20 yards range. With the match well won, West Ham rested somewhat, and 7 minutes from the end Hagan took advantage of a defensive slip to shoot past Conway.

West Ham: Conway; Bicknell, Scott, Fenton, Walker (R.), Cockroft, Small, Macaulay, Foreman, Goulden, Foxall.

Huddersfield: Hesford; Hayes, Mountford, Baird, Young, Boot, Beasley, Barclay, Brook, Hagan Jullinssen.

Att: 20,000

The same three players who had scored in Yorkshire (Foreman, Foxall and Macaulay) had sent the Tykes away disappointed.

Charlie Bicknell picked up an injury in the last few minutes of the match. Worryingly, given the fourth round draw *v.* Birmingham, to be played just three days later, one of the Irons' key defenders would be out of the game for a fortnight.

MIGHTY MAC

By now you may have gathered that Archibald 'Archie' Renwick Macaulay was the pumping heart of the Hammers War Cup side. Signed from Glasgow Rangers by Charlie Paynter, the flame-haired capricious Caledonian came into this world in Falkirk, Scotland, on 30 July 1915. Making his debut in the Second Division Hammers side *v.* Aston Villa on 28 August 1937 (a 2–0 defeat in Birmingham on the opening day of the season), he would make 90 League appearances for West Ham in peacetime games from 1937 to 1946, scoring 31 goals. He wore the Irons badge 93 times during the war and while hostilities raged Macaulay was selected to represent Scotland on 5 occasions in wartime internationals.

In his first season at Upton Park, Macaulay finished joint top-scorer (with Stan Foxall) with 10 goals under his belt, having run out for 39 games. He also concluded the 1938/39 term as top-marksman, claiming 16 nets in 36 matches.

Before coming south in 1937 for a fee of £6,000, Macaulay became a regular with the Glasgow Blues (by the age of 18), playing as an inside right; that was remarkable for the era. The Gers won the Scottish Cup three times between 1934 and 1936 and the Scottish League Championship four times between 1934 and 1937. The young Macaulay won a Scottish Cup winner's medal in 1935/36 and the following season a Scottish League Championship gong.

Prior to his time at Ibrox, Macaulay played for a number of Scottish junior sides, including Comely Park FC, Lauriston Villa, Camelon Juniors and Sawyer.

Macaulay could hold his own in almost any position on the park and for Scotland he would take the roles of both left half and inside forward. He was able to make and get goals. He scored 16 times during the 1938/39 term, including a remarkable hat-trick in the Hammers' 6–1 win over Tranmere Rovers at Upton Park.

During the war Macaulay served with the Essex Regiment Territorials (based largely at Aldershot), rising to sergeant-major PTI (physical training instructor). After hostilities ceased, in October 1946 he was transferred to Brentford in the top flight of football for a fee of £7,500. Having converted to a right wing half, he played 26 games for the Bees, scoring 2 goals, and was selected for his first 'official' international after the war on 12 April 1947 (*v.* England at Wembley). The following month he was chosen to play right half for Great Britain *v.* the Rest of Europe at Hampden Park.

Macaulay's departure from Upton Park was not the most amicable of breaks. West Ham had sent letters to him while he was stationed in Scotland, and to Falkirk FC, reminding Macaulay and the Bairns that West Ham's permission for Macaulay to guest at Brockville Park ceased 'automatically with his release from the forces'. The Hammers board was prepared to allow the arrangement to continue for three weeks until the end of 1945.

Macaulay came back to the Boleyn Ground with little appetite to continue his career with the Irons and soon requested a transfer, which was pretty swiftly refused. However, very exceptionally, he was granted a meeting with the board, and 'following kindly further advice from the board', seemed more comfortable, but in November 1946 the Scot once more asked for a transfer. This time the board granted him his wish.

Slightly spoiled for choice, Macaulay met with officials from Sheffield Wednesday and Arsenal prior to signing for Brentford. Part of the deal was an assurance by Brentford that they would buy the West Ham property that Macaulay had rented from the club 'if they did not find him suitable accommodation within three months'. West Ham couldn't grumble; they made a good profit on a player that had given invaluable service to the club.

However, Brentford were relegated to the Second Division in 1947 and in July of that year Archie moved to Highbury for £10,000.

He appeared alongside Stanley Matthews as right half in the Great Britain side which met the Rest of Europe in May 1947 (Great Britain won 6–1 at Hampden).

The Arsenal manager, Tom Whittaker, had attempted to sign Archie when he was at Upton Park. Whittaker was to recall:

> Macaulay, a brilliant ball player and magnificently balanced, had the reputation of a temper in keeping with his red hair, but while he was at Highbury he was a loyal club servant and a fine footballer.

Making his debut as a Gunner against Sunderland on 23 August 1947 (a 3–1 Highbury victory for the North Londoners, with goals from Ian McPherson, Jimmy Logie and Ronnie Rooke), Macaulay played 40 League matches and won a League Championship medal with the North Londoners in his initial season. He was also in the team that defeated Manchester United in the Charity Shield the following season. Six more Scottish caps followed and although he was rarely out of the Arsenal side for the next couple of seasons, he did miss the Gunners' 1950 FA Cup victory, manager Tom Whittaker preferring his compatriot Alex Forbes for the final *v.* Liverpool.

In his book *Forward Arsenal*, Bernard Joy wrote of the similarity between Forbes and Macaulay:

> Apart from the striking physical likeness, he had the same vigour, traditional Scottish skill at ballwork and fine distribution … He had the same weakness, a sharp temper and an inclination to over-elaborate when the situation called for a quick pass.
>
> *Joy, 1952*

Donning the red and white 108 times during his three seasons under Tom Whittaker (scoring just 1 goal), Macaulay finished his footballing career at Craven Cottage, chalking up 49 appearances and 4 goals in three seasons from 1950.

In 1953 Macaulay moved to Guildford City as player-manager. He stayed with the Essex Clarets for four years, but also took on a trainer-coach role with Dundee between December 1955 and April 1957. However, during the latter year he accepted a management role with Norwich City, succeeding former Arsenal player Tom Parker. In 1959 Macaulay led the Canaries to the last four of the FA Cup while the East Anglians were still a Third Division club. Promotion to the Second Division followed a season later.

Macaulay's record as Norwich manager:

Played	Won	Drawn	Lost	Win %
223	103	60	60	46.19

Macaulay was a pioneer in terms of deploying the 4-3-3 formation and was, in the late 1950s, understood to be something of an innovator tactically. Following a relatively unsuccessful spell with West Bromwich Albion (between 1961 and 1963 he presided over just 26 wins in 67 games), Macaulay took the reins at Brighton and Hove Albion (1963–68), leading the Seagulls to promotion as Champions from the Fourth Division in 1965.

Macaulay then moved back to Scotland, joining Dundee in the First Division, taking on administrative duties. However, at the start of the 1970s he also had ties with Liverpool.

Macaulay finally turned his back on football to find work as a traffic warden in the Chelsea area. He died on 10 June 1993, aged 77. Bernard Joy had it that '[Joe] Mercer and Macaulay were the best club pair of wing-halves in the country' (1954, p. 168). For Charlie Paynter, 'There was no more reliable maker of goals than Archie. We were a lesser team without him.'

EMERGENCY POWERS

As West Ham and Huddersfield were deciding things, the Emergency Powers (Defence) Act was passed, giving the government authority over persons and property for the duration of the war.

While Allied forces in Belgium were busy fighting a retreat, the armed British merchant vessel *Dunster Grange*, en route from La Plata, Montevideo and Cape Verde Islands to Liverpool, repulsed a surface attack by a U-37 off Land's End. A seasoned war veteran – a year earlier she had dodged the massive *Graf Spee* coming out of Montevideo – *Dunster Grange* deployed her deck gun after the U-boat had missed her with four torpedoes.

At least 35,000 merchant seamen lost their lives during the Second World War. Close to 2,500 British registered ships were lost, with a tonnage of over 11 million. But *Dunster Grange* got her crew home. She arrived safely in Liverpool on 24 May – cargo intact.

Born on the Clyde in 1927, a child of Fairfield Govan shipyard, the brave motor merchant, 'Fighting' *Dunster Grange*, was scrapped in 1974.

FIFTEEN

WAR WITHIN A WAR

> Singapore … could only be taken after a siege by an army of at least 50,000 men … it's not considered possible that the Japanese … would embark on such a mad enterprise.
>
> *Winston Churchill, 1940*

> My attack on Singapore was a bluff, a bluff that worked … I was very frightened that all the time the British would discover our numerical weakness and lack of supplies and force me into disastrous street fighting.
>
> *General Yamashita, 1942*

> The only words I spoke to the British commander in the negotiations for the surrender of Singapore were, 'All I want to hear from you is yes or no'. I expected to put the same question to MacArthur.
>
> *General Yamashita, Manila, 10 October 1944*

On 7 June 1941 at Ninian Park, Cardiff, a crowd of 20,000 watched England beat a determined Welsh side 3–2. John Mapson was originally selected to play in goal for the visitors, but withdrew in order to turn out for Reading in the London War Cup Final.

Len Goulden was included in the English line-up. At half-time the hosts trailed 2–1, and it looked to be a game winnable by either side. The Welsh genius Vivian Woodward was on target for the hosts, as was Bill James. But Jimmy Hagan's brace and a single from Don Welsh finally overcame the brave Welsh fighters.

The Football League announced the schedules for 1941/42 (returning to the orthodox points system), only for them to be rejected by the eleven London clubs. At that point the Cockney sides were not persuaded that trips to Luton, Swansea and Norwich would do more for them than potential derby games amongst themselves. The consequence was that the clubs who would make up that season's 'London League' were effectively disqualified from the Football League programme. Portsmouth, Watford, Aldershot, Brighton and Reading were embraced by the London clubs, having their own beef with the League.

The government appeared to back up the London teams, given the need to avoid unnecessary journeys. This was confirmed by a written reply put to a question to Sir Arthur Salter, the minister of war and transport.

A week later, on 18 August 1941, a meeting looking to find some sort of compromise took place between the Football League and the manager of Arsenal, George Allison, the chairman of the London League. However, the Football League, having amended its schedules in the light of the London club's actions, refused to alter them for a second time. In response the Londoners stood firm and went ahead with their own sixteen-team tournament. This effectively placed the participating clubs under the threat of expulsion from the Football League. Indeed, in September the Football League let Portsmouth (still the holders of the FA Cup that they had won by beating Wolves in 1939) know that by joining the

London League, they were no longer members of the Football League and consequently their share had been cancelled.

At this distance in time it is difficult to fathom why the London teams thought it was all right to travel to Portsmouth but not Luton, although it was likely that Pompey would be a more 'happening' place than the Bedfordshire hat capital at that time, or maybe it was just that West Ham had an 'irrational hatred' of Luton (à la Robert Banks). However, the rebel clubs did their own thing, apparently cocking the proverbial snook at the rest of football.

All this didn't seem to bode well for the peacetime game. Football was at war on two fronts in practice. However, perhaps fearing the ultimate consequences, the Football League, in their own version of the Pythonesque 'dead parrot', decided it had not *really* excluded, debarred or otherwise expelled the rebel sides; they had expelled themselves!

The League's vacillation did nothing to stop the breakaway clubs from kicking off on 30 August in glorious weather.

Despite Stan Foxall opening his termly account, West Ham lost 3–1 to Portsmouth in their opening match at Upton Park. Three days prior to the Hammers' humbling by the travelling Pompey players, Britain and Russia invaded Iran under the auspices of Operation Countenance. Like its neighbour Turkey, Iran was a neutral country, but the British government, now led by Winston Churchill, was concerned about oil supplies and providing the USSR with the means to continue its fight against Germany through Iran. Largely repeating what had happened in the First World War, Soviet troops moved against Iran from the north while British-Indian divisions approached, in the main, from the south. The Iranians had surrendered by the final whistle of the West Ham *v.* Portsmouth game. The Shah was deposed and exiled in 1941, while his son, Mohammed Reza Pahlavi, was crowned as the country's new ruler and the stage was set for the conflict that burns on today.

England beat the Scots 2–0 (Don Welsh and Jimmy Hagan doing the honours) at Wembley in October 1941. Wilf Mannion again, and Stanley Matthews were the stars of a match fought out as Spitfires droned an unceasing patrol high over Wembley's famous towers.

On the first day of November, at Elm Park, half-back Harold Cothliff (who in peacetime had been with Torquay United) put Reading ahead in under 10 seconds. Although Charlie Bicknell scored a rare goal, which Archie Macaulay added to, the Hammers went home losers by the odd goal of 5.

West Ham's 1–1 result *v.* Spurs on 6 December was only the second time the Hammers had been held to a draw in 1941. Stan Foxall had been on target for the visitors. This was the Irons' fifteenth match of the League schedule and with just four losses the side seemed to have created something of a foundation for a final run at top spot in the second half of the campaign.

The next day, Japanese aircraft carriers launched 360 fighters, bombers and torpedo planes in a surprise attack on the American Pacific Fleet at Pearl Harbor, Hawaii. This action finally brought the USA into the war. The Japanese succeeded in sinking or damaging five battleships and fourteen other vessels, as well as destroying over 200 aircraft. Luckily for the Americans (and the Allies), most of their aircraft carriers were safely at sea, and these were to form the nucleus of their naval warfare over the next few years. Japanese forces also struck at Malaya and Hong Kong, and a few days later opened a full-scale assault on all Britain's colonial possessions in the Far East, forcing Western nations out of the region.

While the raid on Pearl Harbor is held up as an example of infamy, given it was undertaken without a declaration of war, its inspiration was the British naval action against Italy in the Battle of Taranto (11–12 November 1940). This was the first all-aircraft, ship-to-ship naval attack in history, directed at the battle fleet of the Regia Marina, at anchor in the port of Taranto, deploying aerial torpedoes.

With the issues with the Football League on-going, the sixteen London clubs played their own cup tournament, with sixteen teams divided into four groups, the winners of each group making up one-tie semi-finals. West Ham were unlucky to lose out to Arsenal for a place in the last four on goal average alone. Although it's clear the North Londoners defended better in Group 1, the Irons beat the Gunners 4–1 in the away leg, with Len Goulden being twice on target. Sam Small and Ted Fenton also hit home for the Hammers, while Denis Compton gave the home side some consolation. A crowd of 22,000 watched this game at White Hart Lane; it seemed the authorities were not enforcing their restrictions on crowd numbers as rigorously as their rhetoric sometimes suggested.

However, the Hammers' hopes were dashed at Upton Park after Ted Drake, Dave Nelson, Cliff Bastin and Alf Kirchen received no reply from the home side.

London Cup, 1941/42: Group 1							
	Played	Won	Lost	Drawn	For	Against	Points
Arsenal	6	5	1	0	19	7	10
West Ham United	6	5	1	0	18	11	10
Clapton Orient	6	1	5	0	10	19	2
Brighton and Hove Albion	6	1	5	0	11	21	2

It was at the Upton Park London League game *v.* Arsenal on 24 January 1942 that the 'Internationale' was played for the first time on a football ground in Great Britain. A collection from the 19,000 crowd was taken for Clementine Churchill's 'Aid to Russia Fund'.

In February, West Ham lost 2–1 in a friendly at Fratton Park. At this time there were shortages of nearly everything, which had a profound effect on football and everything else. Transport was a constant problem, petrol being scarce. In February 1942 the fall of Singapore and the Malayan peninsula hit the supply of football bladders (this was amongst the first non-essential processes to be restricted) – rubber controls limiting the manufacture of football bladders to a quarter of pre-war production. The general malady with regard to 'ball bladders' (sounds painful, doesn't it?) was added to by the fact that leather supplies were also restricted; consequently, footballs had to be used for more than one game (previously each first-class game had been started with a new ball). Goal nets had been in short supply for some time.

Ground admission charges were raised by 3*d* (just over 1p) to 1*s* 4*d* (7p), passing on increases in the entertainments tax to supporters. The amount was subsequently reduced by 1*d* and there was some conjecture about a further reduction, bringing the price down below the taxation level. This was not just to encourage more people to come to matches, but to increase income (making plant maximise its yield). However, this effective tax dodge was never pushed through.

At Derby, Archie Macaulay played for the Anti-Aircraft Command *v.* an Army XI at the end of March 1942 (the Pongos won 4–0) and just under a fortnight later Len Goulden scored the FA XI's goal in their 2–1 defeat at New Cross *v.* the Metropolitan Police.

E Command, with Ted Fenton in their ranks, were beaten by London Command 3–1 at Watford in mid-April 1942, and at the end of that month Charlie Bicknell got himself selected for the National Police *v.* the RAF, a side that included Bill Shankly and Eddie Hapgood; Bicknell's side won 2–0 at Derby. But early in May the 'Brylcreem boys' got their revenge at Wembley in front of a crowd of 10,000, defeating Bicknell and his Metropolitan Police comrades 6–3; Ted Drake and Ronnie Rooke both scored a hat-trick. After this last match, incidentally, the pitch was readied for another international between Holland and Belgium that kicked off a few days later, the sides selected from escaped soldiers. Every kick was broadcast to Nazi-occupied Europe.

At Upton Park on 9 May, Fulham were beaten 4–2, a week later Chelsea went down 5–2 and on the 23rd of the same month Millwall were pounded 6–2.

In June it was agreed that the London clubs might be welcomed back to the bosom of the League if they said they were sorry (in writing), accepting a titular fine of £10 per club. However, it continues to be something of a puzzle what the clubs had to apologise or pay a fine for, if the consequence of whatever they had done had been self-expulsion. It seems the whole affair had been more a matter of relative pride and having the final word. In the last analysis this would have mattered not a jot to the clubs because their primary purpose, as commercial enterprises, was to make money. Relatively low-cost games (in terms of travel, player sustenance, etc.) with the added spice of local rivalry and bragging rights were simply more lucrative than comparatively pointless sojourns to outlandish coastal towns or the wilds of Glamorganshire.

It wasn't just the cost of travel that made long journeys unattractive. Transport timetables were subject to change at short notice and there was no first-class travel in segregated compartments; no special privileges of any kind. This didn't impacted so much on players as on the upper echelon of clubs, board members, etc. However, it meant that players and support staff travelled in the same crowded trains as everyone else, not unusually finding nowhere to sit but on their kit-bags in the corridor, many sustained by what might be begged or stolen from the NAFI.

The Football League had deemed that it would allow the guest player system to continue, although if it hadn't, one might assume this would have been of little import in terms of what the London clubs actually did. However, players had been at liberty to continue to move freely between the London tournaments and the competitions staying loyal to the League (Leagues North and South).

It was another bad winter, which obliged the English season to be extended yet again – this time to the end of May.

George Foreman, with 36 games played in West Ham colours, appeared more than any other player, although Fenton, Goulden, Foxall and Small pushed him for consistency. But with 27 goals he was way out in front of any other player.

London League, 1941/42							
	Played	Won	Drawn	Lost	For	Against	Points
Arsenal	30	23	2	5	108	43	48
Portsmouth	30	20	2	8	105	59	42
West Ham United	30	17	5	8	81	44	39
Aldershot	30	17	5	8	85	56	39
Tottenham Hotspur	30	15	8	7	61	41	38
Crystal Palace	30	14	6	10	70	53	34
Reading	30	13	8	9	76	58	34
Charlton Athletic	30	14	5	11	72	64	33
Brentford	30	14	2	14	80	76	30
QPR	30	11	3	16	52	59	25
Fulham	30	10	4	16	79	99	24
Brighton and Hove Albion	30	9	4	17	71	108	22
Chelsea	30	8	4	18	56	88	20
Millwall	30	7	5	18	53	82	19
Clapton Orient	30	5	7	18	42	94	17
Watford	30	6	4	20	47	114	16

Perhaps the standout game of the Hammers' season was a 8–4 victory at Stamford Bridge at the start of September, which included the first of three hat-tricks that Foreman would score that term. He claimed his second later in the month at Vicarage Road in a 8–0 crushing of Watford. Foreman got his last triple of the season at the Boleyn Ground *v.* Brighton and Hove Albion in the London War Cup (Group One) encounter on 4 April, in West Ham's exciting 6–2 triumph over the Seagulls. It has to be said that none of these sides had much of a season, so perhaps George's best game of the schedule was against Arsenal at Upton Park. His 2 goals, alongside Len Goulden's contribution, sent the champions back to North London on the end of a 3–0 whacking.

Although West Ham were not as free scoring as some of their London League competitors, 13 goals were hit *v.* Chelsea while Watford took 12 from the Hammers; Brentford leaked 7 in the face of the West Ham strikers. A week after the Hammers cracked 5 without reply at Griffin Park, Crystal Palace came to the Boleyn Ground and did the same thing to the Irons, although it has to be said that the home side had been obliged to put Jim Barrett in goal because of the lack of a specialist for selection.

While George Foreman was streets ahead in the goal-scoring stakes, in terms of goals per game Eddie Chapman was 'the man', with half-a-dozen goals in 7 outings, although the goals came by way of hat-tricks in two games: *v.* Aldershot at the Recreation Ground at the start of 1941 and in the 3–1 victory at Brisbane Road.

Harold Ricketts (a more unfortunate name for a goalkeeper seems unlikely) played his only League game as a guest for West Ham in this match (he turned out for another in the London War Cup *v.* Brighton at Upton Park in that same season). Registered with Southend United, Harold had faced the Football Association's disciplinary committee in recent times. The previous term, in goal for the Shrimpers *v.* Crystal Palace, he got into a bull and cow with the referee about an offside decision that went against the visitors from estuary Essex. Ricketts marched off the Selhurst Park pitch in protest and would not return, despite the pleas of his teammates and the orders of the match official. After 10 minutes the game continued without him. Ricketts was suspended for a month for improper conduct, plus leaving the field of play without the referee's permission; Southend United lost the game 7–0. So while he made his point, there was not much point to his point; we've all been there. However, both his games for West Ham were on the winning side, so Harold will for ever remain a good egg in the eyes of the Hammers faithful.

At the end of October 1941 Charlie Bicknell had turned out for the War Reserve Police *v.* the Metropolitan Police, his side winning 2–1 at Imber Court, East Molesey. He was in the same side that won (3–2) in Ipswich *v.* The Combined Services.

On the last day of the season Bicknell had clocked up 100 wartime appearances for West Ham. George Foreman had made 18 more, while Stan Foxall was just 2 behind Foreman.

SIXTEEN

SOME KIND OF HARMONY

This is where you define yourself.
This is where you remove the 'I can't'
This is where you laugh, cry, sweat and breath,
This …
Is where you find brothers.

Kim Fitzsimmons, firefighter

The split between the League and the London clubs and their southern allies was healed in a typically British compromise. The rebel clubs were allowed to continue with their own competition (although, as the League had been able to do little about them continuing on their own steam through 1941/42, how they might have been able to do anything different the following season is a mystery), but under the patronage of the Football League. However, the league would be known as the 'League South' rather than the 'London League'. The mutinous clubs embraced Luton Town and Southampton, although with eighteen clubs and only 28 match days, not every team was able to meet all others home and away; for instance, West Ham didn't play Arsenal, Southampton or Reading. The aim was to complete all fixtures by 27 February, after which there would be a qualifying competition of four mini leagues, the winners of which would provide the semi-finalists for the League South Cup.

A North section and a smaller Western section were also created. Admission charges for League South fixtures were raised by 3*d* to 1*s* 6*d*. There were no increases elsewhere.

The changing trajectory of the war was reflected in the mood and direction of the Football League's AGM in June 1942. For the first time the development of a committee to consider post-war organisation was mentioned. There were later discussions about post-war issues and perhaps most tellingly a Victory Cup was purchased for £36.

A number of other trophies were bought, but notably, given the history of hostility between the London clubs and the League, none for the League South. Retrospectively, this feels like a public school snipe at the part of the game dominated by working-class culture. It is doubtful, however, if this counted for anything at all for the likes of West Ham, a club that the previous term had pulled 20,000 into Upton Park to watch the home side defeat Arsenal 3–0.

The opening schedule of matches controlled by the Football League was watched by 150,000 people.

As the sun rose over the new wartime season, the news broke that Charlie Bicknell would not be available for the first couple of games as he was getting over surgery to his nose. So, together with Eddie Chapman being occupied with military service, Charlie Paynter's options were narrowing from the start of the term. But the Hammers manager did manage to bring Norrie Corbett's brother Willie to Upton Park to strengthen the claret-and-blue ranks.

West Ham's first game of the campaign started a streak of 5 matches without a loss, including 4 wins. That opening sortie was an away victory at Portsmouth, an exciting 9-goal affair in which Sam Small hit a pair, while Foreman, Foxall and Goulden made it 5 for the Hammers. That opening game was Len Goulden's century of appearances for wartime West Ham. However, three successive reversals followed, setting in train a fruitless search for consistency that went on for the rest of the season.

Paynter seemed to be having a bigger headache than in previous wartime seasons getting eleven players on the field. Looking at reports of the time, there are regular references to his life being something of a continuous trudge around the country to the doors of commanding officers, negotiating the use of, or leave for, men to put on West Ham's colours. He informed a local pressman that he could see no light at the end of the tunnel in this respect, particularly as he was confined to public transport and Shanks's pony, having recently lost access to a car.

Too often amateur football historians rely on local newspaper reports as gospel commentaries of facts. They are anything but. Often several hacks would rely on a report by someone they had chipped in to watch a game while they sat in the warm. It wasn't unusual even for the surrogate themselves to turn up at a pub after a game and merely question those who had been to the match, so saving his entrance fee. Reports got repeated by the same and fellow reporters, and collectively facts are distorted, but one is tempted to ask whether Paynter's consistent complaint about his roamings was a case of 'thou doth protest too much'. It seems that clubs were more likely to get players coming to them looking for games than managers had the need to go out and lasso them. With Upton Park being pretty much at the hub of wartime troop movements, and central with respect to leave taking, this might have been more the case with regard to West Ham than other relatively geographically remote clubs. While on the day of games, players were sometimes unable to make the kick-off, which might have caused a degree of angst, a couple of players of the time I spoke with felt that their peers were sometimes more concerned that they'd lose their place in the side if an international turned up during the week looking for a match. This seems to have happened to George Foreman when Jock Dodds made himself available to West Ham during 1944/45.

On 17 October, at the Recreation Ground, the travelling Hammers were socked 5–1. Jimmy Hagan, guesting for the Shots (from Sheffield United), scored 4 and had two other efforts disallowed. Sam Small provided little in the way of solace for Hammers supporters.

Charlie Bicknell was on duty for the Civil Defence side beaten 8–2 by the Army in October 1942 at the Den. A week later Len Goulden scored in an FA XI victory over the RAF (4–3 at Stoke).

Another high-scoring game was West Ham's away fixture with Luton. Goals from Stan Foxall and Jackie Wood could not stop the 3-goal Hatters from taking the points. On that 5 December day a record 222 goals were scored in the 39 League matches (averaging half-a-dozen a game). Prior to the war years, the best total had been achieved on 2 June 1932 – 209 over 43 encounters.

The homecoming evacuees and the concentration of troops in London provided the capital's clubs an extended and growing (what today might be called) 'fan base'. In December 1942 the Army Sport Control Board gave the OK for serving professionals to be paid a match fee in approved games against civilian professional teams. This gave another boost to clubs close to where troops were stationed, although many servicemen had received both formal and informal 'expenses' for playing games since the first months of the war.

On 2 January 1943, Bicknell played for the Metropolitan Police *v.* the Army at Aldershot in a thrilling 10-goal draw, and eighteen days on, playing alongside fellow Hammer Jackie Wood, he retained his place in the 'Old Bill' defence for a game *v.* a Stan Cullis XI at Chichester (the Stan's side won 5–1). In the latter part of the month Charlie was back in the line for the National Police Force *v.* the RAF; an Upton Park crowd of 6,200 saw the airmen win 2–0. Also at the end of January, Aldershot brought a side made up of guest players only to Upton Park. West Ham won the game 6–3; the Hammers' half-dozen was made up of a Dick Dunn hat-trick, 2 goals from Sam Small and 1 from Len Goulden. The visitors included England internationals Cliff Britton and Tommy Lawton (Everton), Stan Cullis (Wolves) and Jimmy Hagan (Sheffield United).

The League South continued into February. Cup ties played on Boxing Day saw improved attendances; a total of 323,000.

In January 1943 the League gave attention to the idea of a transitional season to the normal peacetime game following the conclusion of hostilities. The 'no trophy' policy for the League South was to be maintained, but savings certificates would be given to those taking part in cup ties.

At the start of March, Charlie Bicknell was in the Police and Civil Defence team beaten 4–2 at Deepdale by the RAF. Ted Drake and Raich Carter (2) along with Peter Doherty beat up the rozzers and their allies.

On 24 April the Hammers went to Elm Park to play a friendly game, losing 3–0. A couple of days later a 6–0 defeat of Southampton at Upton Park compensated somewhat. However, fourty-eight hours on the St Mary's crew got their own back with a 5–1 victory over the visiting Irons.

Charlie Bicknell tried again with the National Police in May, but once more the RAF came off better at Wembley, where 15,000 saw the 4–3 result.

On 17 June the League agreed that a £5 bonus could be paid for those involved in cup games. The same amount would be awarded to league winners; runners-up would get £3. With regard to league games, player remuneration would rise to £2, but this level of payment would be limited to fourteen players per club. Also in June the FA held a full-blown meeting to discuss a broad range of issues with the post-war period in mind. The lowest admission charge to games would be 1*s* 6*d* (although the League South sides were looking for 3*d* more). This was probably in response to the Treasury letting it be known earlier in the month that football should have a higher entertainment tax burden. Tranmere Rovers countered by declaring it would bring a test case as football was theatre and not mere entertainment, and so needed to be assessed at a lower rate of taxation.

In July the FA laid out new regulations with regard to guest players. Unless their posting made it otherwise impossible to find a game, players in the armed forces were disallowed from playing for clubs outside their own association.

Just before the start of the new season, the chairman of Chester expressed his hope that, following the war, at least Division Three football would be made up of teams fielding amateurs and part-time professionals, saying he did not believe 'that after the war the country would be able to afford to let all her fittest and best citizens go into what was after all a blind-alley occupation'. It is hard to say who would have taken any notice of this statement; it seems reminiscent of the attitude that pervaded the First World War (see Belton, 2014). Things would be in a sorry state indeed if about 300 Third Division players constituted a sizable proportion of Britain's 'fittest and best citizens'; talk about small worlds!

Once more a 75,000 limit was in place at Wembley in October for the England *v.* Scotland game. The match ended without a goal scored. Every man in the England team was now a serving soldier, although the Scots still drew some of their players from men working in the vital industries along the Clyde.

By 1943 perhaps England's greatest team in history that far had found its inexorable pulse. The result of this over the next half-dozen matches was some big winning margins. In April, England won 4–0 at Hampden, when again the police restricted the crowd to 75,000 but 30,000 Scots had other ideas, storming the gates. In consequence, sixty-four people were injured in the crush.

On 14 April the Luftwaffe attacked Millwall's Den. At this point the 'nobody likes us' mantra of the Lions included Adolf Hitler and Herman Goering apparently. The North Terrace and the pitch were badly damaged. West Ham immediately offered the Boleyn Ground for Millwall's home games. The South-East Londoners were thankful but told their neighbours that they intended to build a temporary stand for the 1943/44 term. However, this could not be arranged and Millwall would be obliged to open what must have been an uncomfortable tenancy at The Valley (the Charlton reserve team played at The Den for the 1943/44 season). Things must have got difficult as the Lions found themselves also playing home games at Selhurst Park and Upton Park up to 24 February 1944. Apparently supporters preferred standing amid the ruins of The Den to being on the end of the kind of song a few West Ham fans chanted at one of their games at the Boleyn Ground:

If you got to Millwall
On your way to Kent
Tell the boys at Millwall
West Ham wants the rent

League South, 1942/43 – ending 27 February 1943							
	Played	Won	Drawn	Lost	For	Against	Points
Arsenal	28	21	1	6	102	40	43
Tottenham Hotspur	28	16	6	6	68	28	38
Queens Park Rangers	28	18	2	8	64	49	38
Portsmouth	28	16	3	9	66	52	35
Southampton	28	14	5	9	86	58	33
West Ham United	28	14	5	9	80	66	33
Chelsea	28	14	4	10	52	45	32
Aldershot	28	14	2	12	87	77	30
Brentford	28	12	5	11	64	63	29
Charlton Athletic	28	13	3	12	68	75	29
Clapton Orient	28	11	5	12	54	72	27
Brighton and Hove Albion	28	10	5	13	65	73	25
Reading	28	9	6	13	67	74	24
Fulham	28	10	2	16	69	78	22
Crystal Palace	28	7	5	16	49	75	19
Millwall	28	6	5	17	66	88	17
Watford	28	7	2	19	51	88	16
Luton Town	28	4	6	18	43	100	14

The season had not been the best for West Ham, although it's fair to say that they held their own. A 7–1 victory in East London over Brighton and Hove Albion in the League South Cup on 3 April 1943 perhaps warrants the accolade of being the most notable performance of the term, the centre piece of which was a Len Goulden hat-trick; George Foreman, Terry Woodgate and Dick Walker were all on target. An own goal added to the rout. George Foreman got his 100th wartime goal in this game.

However, in the same competition it was disappointing in the concluding game to go down 3–1 (Cliff Bastin, Denis Compton and Jimmy Briscoe being answered by only Sam Small) at White Hart Lane to Arsenal (more than 31,000 turned up for the encounter). This was especially the case as the Gunners had done for the Hammers by the same score at Upton Park on 20 March (Reg Lewis's brace and a net by Alf Kirchen overawed George Forman's offering).

None the less West Ham had been in with a shout right up to that final group game *v.* the Gunners. Before this reversal, letting Watford nick a point at Vicarage Road on 27 March had looked to prove decisive, but Arsenal also finished 'evens stevens' with the Hornets. So, the Irons journeyed to North London on 10 April hopeful of a gettable 2–0 result (at least) to make the last four. As detailed, they were to be disappointed.

The final league positions tell the tale. For all the above, Arsenal were easily the best side in the competition, beating QPR 4–1 in the semi-finals and Charlton 7–1 in the final.

The League South Cup, 1943 – Group 1

	Played	Won	Drawn	Lost	For	Against	Points
Arsenal	6	5	1	0	21	5	11
West Ham United	6	3	1	2	19	9	7
Watford	6	1	3	2	1	12	5
Brighton and Hove Albion	6	0	1	5	4	27	1

Annoyingly, Tottenham were equalled on aggregate by West Ham in the League South, although Spurs ended the campaign as runners-up to Arsenal, a side the Hammers didn't meet in the League because of the way the fixtures were organised (each team played fourteen of the eighteen competitors, home and away). The first encounter (at Upton Park) on 19 September was won 3–1 by the Irons; a single from Ted Fenton and George Foreman's brace sunk the visitors, the apparent unconditional surrender of the visitors emulating Italy's exit from the war the day before. However, six days before Christmas, West Ham went down 2–0 at White Hart Lane. On the same day, subsequent to a joint statement by the Allied governments on the persecution of the Jews across Europe, the Soviet Foreign Office published an extended announcement relating to the methodical extermination of Jews by gas, machine-guns and other means. However, the idea of this was so hideous that even in the Soviet Union many thought that more evidence was needed before it could be believed.

West Ham finished the season with a victory over Fulham, a defeat by QPR, a 6-goal draw with Millwall and a win against Brighton; the 5 points pushed them well into the top half of the League. The day before the 2–1 win over Fulham, the second meeting between Sugar Ray Robinson and Jake LaMotta took place at the Olympia Stadium in Detroit, Michigan, USA.

Robinson had defeated LaMotta in their first fight, in October 1942; however, this time, over ten rounds, in front of nearly 19,000 people, the unanimous decision went to LaMotta. This was Robinson's first loss in 40 professional contests. He had been a hot favourite to win the contest.

Robinson and LaMotta were to fight six times in all, of which Robinson won five. Jake later said, 'I fought Sugar Ray so often, I almost got diabetes.' The second fight was reported by the International News Service thus:

> A right to the body and a left to the head knocked Robinson through the ropes in the eighth round. Robinson lay sprawling outside the ring from a hard right to the body and a left to the head and the count was nine when the bell rang.

The INS went on:

> In a previous meeting, Robinson copped a 10-round decision from LaMotta. Robinson won that fight by steering clear of LaMotta's hard punches and sticking strictly to clever boxing. Friday night, however, he tried to slug it out with the bundle of dynamite from the Bronx and consequently had one of the most sensational winning streaks in the history of boxing rudely interrupted.

LaMotta's life was depicted in the film *Raging Bull* and a few years ago I was lucky enough to meet Jake. I have met Pele, Eusébio, Bobby Moore, Muhammad Ali, Malcolm Allison and many other famous sportspeople, but I have honestly never met anyone quite as eccentric as LaMotta. It might have been his age, he was well into his eighties at the time (but so is my mum and she is a sharp as a tack), but he seemed very much to exist in a place of his own.

For the fourth successive season George Foreman was the club's leading scorer with 30 goals. He also made the most appearances: 34. Len Goulden, who had missed 4 games, hit 17. Dick Dunn, in just 11 outings, had bagged 12 goals. These encompassed two hat-tricks; the initial triple was put together on 2 January during the 10–3 Upton Park mullering of Clapton Orient, while the second *v.* Aldershot came three weeks later as the future prison officer helped lock up the Shots 6–3 at the Boleyn Ground.

West Ham called on thirty-seven men aged over the 28 match League South schedule, including England wartime international Sam Bartram of Charlton Athletic, Cyril Trigg of Birmingham, who during the war served with the RAF in Burma and India, as well as Burnley and England amateur international and FA Cup Final player (1946/47) Peter Kippax.

It was at this point that professional football could afford the belief that it had survived and would be more or less able to take up where it had left off in 1939. But certainly the clubs, especially in London, had realised their ability to flex their muscles and consequently things would never be the same again. The London clubs would act as exemplars to others and consistently, if relatively politely, shake off the dominance of League and FA officialdom, using it rather than being used by it.

However, the players had also become more conscious that without them there would be no game, and over the next couple of decades or so it was this growing awareness that would cause the most seismic shifts in the game.

Before the Second World War, the commercial aristocracy of the game had largely replaced the old guard of football nobility, premised on class patronage and servitude. The latter had been mostly displaced during and after the First World War (see Belton 2014).

To an appreciable extent, the ruling elite of football between the wars had adopted many of their predecessors' forms of feudal control, while developing a much more assertive version of capitalist enterprise. The profit motive would be even more aggressively pursued after the Second World War across the prospect of the game, led by a darker group of football entrepreneurs, more a collection of cold diplomats supported by a range of business bureaucrats than the showmen and ringmasters of the earlier epoch. Comparing West Ham's directors to those controlling other clubs, despite reservations and limitations of the era and culture, one has to concede, comparatively, it was more the 'family club' it insisted itself to be than its contemporaries and peers. While 'characters' remained in football and would sustain into the 1980s, the age of the shadowy owners and directors was coming, seemingly informed by a particularly assassin-like brand of Machiavellianism. In contrast, whatever the 'West Ham way' might have been understood to be, it was something that at least kept some sense of duty to and affinity with its constituency of East London. West Ham was something more than a business organisation and the sum of its parts was a shared institution; it had its unique customs, values and collective beliefs. It was founded in its physical context and cultural traditions more than other more devoutly commercial clubs.

SEVENTEEN

RUNNERS-UP

> The function of football, soccer, basketball and other passion-sports in modern industrial society is the transference of boredom, frustration, anger and rage into socially acceptable forms of combat. A temporary substitute for war; for nationalism; identification with something bigger than the self.
>
> *Edward Abbey*

Over 200,000 saw the 1943/44 season kick off. West Ham were at Fratton Park, coming away on the end of a 2–0 defeat. While the government refused any movement on the entertainments tax, the Board of Trade released 40,000 clothing coupons to professional football clubs in the four home countries surrounding London.

The Players' Union began to press for a superannuation scheme and the abolition of the maximum wage or a substantial increase in the same. While there had been a more 'radical' element amongst the players for many years pressing for this sort of change, the discourse that arose in 1943 might be understood as the beginning of the end for the old master/servant relationship that had traditionally marked the association between players and the upper echelons of club administration, control and ownership.

In September, Scotland international and Liverpool player Matt Busby was featured in the *Sunday Empire News*. He was responding to accusations that international players were using their fame to keep themselves in relatively safe reserved occupations, and that many, even if they were in the forces, were acting as PTIs, a position that would, relatively, keep them out of harm's way. Busby was forceful in his response, arguing that most players had been placed in 'war work'; it had not been a choice. He went on to say that PTIs had a crucial role in readying men for battle, often finding themselves close to front-line positions, getting to the same via sea roots peppered with U-boats.

Arsenal's Alf Kirchen was badly injured in the 2–2 draw at Upton Park on 11 September. His knee ligaments were so seriously damaged that he was forced to announce his retirement after the end of the season.

Charlie Bicknell played for the Civil Defence *v.* an FA XI in November 1943. His side lost 5–4 at Luton. At Goodison Park, in front of a crowd of nearly 35,000, Archie Macaulay was in the Army Scotland team that drew 2–2 with Army England, while in Stoke, at the Victoria Ground, Irons Ron Cater, Jackie Wood and Terry Woodgate turned out for the Anti-Aircraft Command *v.* W. Command that had Hammer-to-be Harry Kinsell in their ranks. Wood scored a single in the 5–3 victory for the AAC.

The rise in football attendance was again continued over the festive period. Around 320,000 came out to watch Christmas Day matches; these included 16,000 at Stamford Bridge, who saw the home side share half-a-dozen goals with West Ham, a George Foreman single and a brace from Jackie 'Timber' Wood replying to a couple from Joe Payne and a Billy Sperrin goal. On Boxing Day 440,000 attended the opening Cup ties and League South games. Once more the Hammers missed out on a semi-final place in the Cup competition as group runners-up. Group winners Chelsea went on to contest the final after overcoming Reading in extra time. However, Charlton were the eventual tournament winners.

Watford were a thorn in West Ham's side in the competition. Both at Vicarage Road and at Upton Park 3 goals were scored, and both times the Hertfordshire men got 1 more than the East Londoners. A 4–0 stomping at Stamford Bridge didn't help either, but a 6–1 victory at Upon Park over the Blues was something to treasure, with Charlie Bicknell, Ted Fenton (2), Len Goulden and Sam Small inflicting pain on the visitors. Joe Payne managed to beat Harry Medhurst.

The League South Cup, 1944 – Group 2

	Played	Won	Drawn	Lost	For	Against	Points
Chelsea	6	4	1	1	17	10	9
West Ham United	6	3	0	3	15	11	6
Watford	6	2	1	3	7	13	5
Southampton	6	2	0	4	12	17	4

Nearly 41,000 saw Spurs get the better of West Ham by a single goal on New Year's Day in a League South table-top clash.

At the start of February, Harry Medhurst and Archie Macaulay were in the Army team that beat the Civil Defence at the Baseball Ground, Derby (16,000 watched the game). Ron Cater, Macaulay and Woodgate were joined by fellow Hammer Dick Dunn in the Anti-Aircraft Command *v.* Scotland Command in March 1944. The sides drew 2–2 at Greenock. A week later, on 11 March, Ted Fenton and his E. Command peers were thumped 5–0 by London District. Macaulay was in the Army ranks to face an FA XI at Stoke on the same day and 23,542 saw the Pongos' 5–2 win.

LIFE, DEATH AND FOOTBALL

Air raids became more concerted in London and the south than they had been for four years. In Custom House, where my dad's family lived, the effects seemed particularly profound, as the area immediately abutted the Victoria and Albert Docks. Their house was completely demolished. Ironically, it was situated in

Churchill Road, and for a while my dad wondered if Hitler had made a target of his home for this reason.

Fortunately, my dad and grandmother were in Kent at the time their home was destroyed. My grandfather was making his way back to East London on leave. It is odd to contemplate that if their home had been hit a day later, they might all have been killed.

As my grandmother and my dad walked down Churchill Road, having no knowledge of what had happened, they saw my grandfather, in his uniform and greatcoat, searching through the ruins of their home. The only object in one piece was a 78 record. Strange to think how such a brittle and delicate, shellac object might have survived. As my dad approached his father, Jim senior passed his son the disc; 'American Patrol' by Glenn Miller. He held on to that for the rest of his life; it still played pretty well when I was in my thirties. If you've heard it, you'll know that it probably summed up the American GI without one lyric; 'Fritz' had no answer to the swaggering, confident, well-equipped 'Joe'.

A few days later my granddad returned to his unit. The family had moved into an abandoned house in Sampson Street, Plaistow, a five-minute stroll down the Barking Road to Green Street and West Ham's Upton Park home. However, the family's support networks were a walk of half-an-hour away on the edge of the docks, so for a while my dad and his mum hiked backwards and forwards, up and down Prince Regents Lane. It was on this journey, starting back to Sampson Street, that mother and son had a close encounter with a Nazi dive-bomber.

Walking down Prince Regents Lane, away from the docks, the plane seemed to arrive from nowhere, just as the air-raid warning sounded. My dad heard the plane open fire and to his last years he told how he could see the pilot's begoggled face as the plane passed over them. Taking cover behind a low wall, mother and son heard the 'boom', 'boom', 'boom' of the ack-ack (anti-aircraft) guns as they targetted the enemy plane until the pilot apparently reviewing the situation and darted east and out of view.

Escape from and confrontation with death puts life into perspective perhaps; we walk a fragile path through this world with an inevitable end. As the *Tibetan Book of the Dead* tells us, the contemplation of death provides us with insight into the nature of life. Winning and losing are small tastes of life and death, and I believe this might go some way to explaining the attraction of sport. When sport is shared in what was once called 'spectatorship' and now 'support', the life ignited in victory is magnified in the sharing; the death of loss is consoled by the society of others. We become, in part, who we are and what we might want to be. In my life, perhaps yours, West Ham United, the gloriously fickle Hammers, the Irons of old, have been a means to such ends. When that team in claret and blue lose, I die just a tiny bit for a little while; when they win, I feel restored, reminded I am alive.

You can, of course, choose to support (or more realistically 'follow') Chelsea or Manchester City; sides that, for now, almost guarantee an absence of the death of defeat. But this is temporary and living in the clutches of one's own fantasy about living for ever. For all their faults, and there are many, West Ham are 'real'; you live, breathe, hurt, die and recover with them or finally go down at their side. Here is dimension, warp and weft, give and take, disappointment and elation, resentment and forgiving, love and longing … life.

Many years ago I was talking to a man in a bar in North Africa who had lived many years on the edge of the desert. During our conversation he said, 'Here we have heat, it is endlessly hot; the sun, it never ceases to shine. In England you have "weather"!' West Ham are hot and cold, rain and shine, snow, frost, ice, a chilly misty morning in early spring and sometimes the late evening sun. At the moment Manchester City is an expensive holiday resort where the heat never goes away, well not until the tsunami comes …

ALL IN THE GAME

As the respective squads were gathering for the England *v.* Scotland game at Wembley on 19 February 1944, the amazing 8–0 drubbing of Scotland at Maine Road in October, which caused Stan Cullis, the Wolves international, later to remark 'This was the finest football I have ever seen', was still fresh in the minds of all concerned.

Scotland had once more called on West Ham's Archie Macaulay. Before the Wembley game, Scottish officials had argued about introducing numbered shirts. The idea was 'scotched' by the Scottish FA chairman's casting vote after he remarked, 'Numbers are all right for horses and greyhounds, but not for humans.'

Many of the players would spend the night before the game watching a rapid air raid which made sure many Londoners had a sleepless night. Following their aggregate 12–0 destruction over 2 games in 1943, the Scots were again on the receiving end. Sadly, Hammer Macaulay deflected a Smith shot beyond Jimmy Crozier. This was the prelude to Tommy Lawton, Jimmy Hagan (2), Joe Mercer and Raich Carter adding to the Scottish pain. There was only a flicker of consolation when Jock Dodds scored his second goal in the last minutes of the match.

Macaulay retained his place for the Hampden Park return match, which attracted the largest crowd recorded during the Second World War (133,000). The Glasgow police made no attempt to restrict numbers, seemingly seeing such an exercise as futile following the 'invasion' of the previous year.

This match was a 'sturdy' encounter, although many saw it as a battle of a game, showing an aggression rarely expressed in professional sport. Tommy Lawton was to remark that the encounter was 'the toughest match I have played in – ever'. Later, even the ardent Scottish supporters were to agree that their side had gone over the top in their efforts to stop the English advance.

Jim Caskie's curling drive opened the scoring, beating Frank Swift with 20 minutes played. The hopeful Scots were quickly brought back to reality when Tommy Lawton replied with a couple of characteristically opportunist strikes. Raich Carter put the visitors 3–1 up by half-time.

Dodds, the Scottish skipper, seemed to be fighting for possession constantly. In the second half he and Cullis rose together, contesting a high Caskie cross. Frank Swift, having rushed off his line, could only watch the ball wing its way into the unprotected goal, by way of the head of Cullis. The game ended in a 3–2 victory and Scotland being left to think again.

A history-making figure in the England team was inside forward Hong Ying 'Frank' Soo. In his time he played for Luton Town and Stoke City, and he was the first player of Chinese origin to play in the Football League, and the first non-white player to represent England (albeit in the unofficial wartime matches).

The Anti-Aircraft Command met N. Command at Chesterfield on 18 March, but with more than half the former being made up of West Ham players – Macaulay, Cater, Woodgate, Wood and Dunn – N. Command came away 2–0 victors. The first day of April saw Macaulay in the Army team that bested the RAF 4–0 in Edinburgh (a 50,000 crowd was happy to cheer on players for the most part based in England). Nearly 31,000 came to watch Archie the Hammer in action again at the end of the month in the cause of a Combined Services side, raiding alongside Ted Drake. However, the England side that gathered at Stamford Bridge took the game 3–1.

West Ham beat Watford 4–1 in a friendly at Upton Park on 8 April, but lost by the same score at Selhurst Park later in the month.

With the much-awaited second front invasion of Europe seemingly imminent, come the end of the season hope and optimism were infecting most facets of British life, including football. However, as plans for the invasion heightened, the AGM of the Football League was postponed indefinitely. It seems no one wanted to premeditate too much.

In the League South, which this time went through to May, Tottenham finished 5 points ahead of West Ham, who seemed at this point to be specialists in coming second.

On 10 May, Charlie Bicknell, George Foreman and Len Goulden ran out for the Police and Civil Defence team that lost 5–2 to the Combined Services at Wembley.

Also in May the Football League Cup pool stood at £30,377 – seventy-four clubs received £420, up by £31 from the previous year. The popularity of this tournament is clear from these figures.

League South, 1943/44 – ending 6 May 1944							
	Played	Won	Drawn	Lost	For	Against	Points
Tottenham Hotspur	30	19	8	3	71	36	46
West Ham United	30	17	7	6	74	39	41
Queens Park Rangers	30	14	12	4	69	54	40
Arsenal	30	14	10	6	72	42	38
Crystal Palace	30	16	5	9	75	53	37
Portsmouth	30	16	5	9	68	59	37
Brentford	30	14	7	9	71	51	35
Chelsea	30	16	2	12	79	55	34
Fulham	30	11	9	10	80	73	31
Millwall	30	13	4	13	70	66	30
Aldershot	30	12	6	12	64	73	30
Reading	30	12	3	15	73	62	27
Southampton	30	10	7	13	67	88	27
Charlton Athletic	30	9	7	14	57	73	25
Watford	30	6	8	16	58	80	20
Brighton and Hove Albion	30	9	2	19	55	82	20
Clapton Orient	30	4	3	23	32	87	11
Luton Town	30	3	5	22	42	104	11

Paynter called on thirty-eight men to fight the league. Almost predictably, George Foreman made the most appearances in Cup and League combined (35), although it was a close-run thing with Small and Len Goulden (34). Foreman scored more goals than any other player by a long way – 26. For the third season running he played in every league game. The *London Evening News* reported Charlie Paynter as referring to Foreman, along with Billy Lewis and Small, as 'war workers' and this would go some way to clarifying why these players, compared to those in the Services, were so often in the Hammers side; Lewis played 32 games in defence while Small chalked up 34 appearances playing a number of positions.

EIGHTEEN

BIRMINGHAM BEATEN

(1940 WAR CUP – FOURTH ROUND)

I played a couple of first-team games for West Ham in 1944, but I was around the place quite a bit at that time. The pitch was a mud-patch in the rain and of course the balls held the water, so there were games when the ball didn't bounce at all!

I suppose it was all new for me, but it wasn't hard work. Mostly it was fun. Everyone made everyone else feel at home. It was a lively atmosphere. Playing games was mostly instinctive. I think we learned to express ourselves, although while the older players were always ready with advice, they would also let you know when you slipped up. As would the crowd.

Eric Parsons

On 25 May 1940 destiny wafted the Hammers to Upton Park for round four of the Football League War Cup and their meeting with the 1931 FA Cup finalists, Birmingham FC (they would not adopt the 'City' appendage until 1943).

On the morning of the match, the commander of 10th Panzer Division, General Ferdinand Friedrich Schaal, demanded the surrender Calais, letting the defending forces know that if they did not yield, he was determined to lay waste to Calais. It was the task of Brigadier Claude Nicholson, who had taken command of all British units in the port, to respond – his rejoinder was polite but to the point: 'No, I shall not surrender. Tell the Germans that if they want Calais they will have to fight for it.' Schaal made good his threat, and a fierce bombardment ensued, deploying artillery and Stuka dive bombers. Following this Schaal repeated his demand that the British surrender. Nicholson remained defiant: 'The answer is no, as it is the British Army's duty to fight as well as the Germans'.'

Schaal was to be involved in Operation Valkyrie, the attempt to assassinate Hitler in 1944. Unlike the majority of his fellow conspirators, he avoided execution and survived the war.

West Ham's opponents had finished twenty-first (out of twenty-two) in the final peacetime season of the First Division (then the top flight of the English game), but when football began to return to normality, Birmingham won the Football League South, finishing with a better goal average than bitter rivals Aston Villa.

Birmingham left Upton Park disappointed after an entertaining match in front of Upton Park's biggest crowd of the competition so far. The game was reported thus:

Hammers Win Again
And Reach Cup Semi-Final
West Ham United 4, Birmingham 2

The game in the Football League Cup, fourth round, at Upton Park, was one in which there were many missed scoring chances. It was deservedly won by West Ham, who thus qualified for the semi-final, in which they play Fulham on Saturday. To achieve their success they had to overcome a reverse in the first quarter of an hour, when Trigg netted for Birmingham. They quickly got on terms, for in two minutes Foreman equalled and a goal by Macaulay 10 minutes before the interval gave them a narrow lead at the change over. A third goal by Foreman 10 minutes after the resumption seemed to have well cleared the way for victory, but a slip by Conway seven minutes later, when he allowed a shot from Trigg to pass through his hands, narrowed the issue. A brilliant goal by Goulden three minutes later, however, clinched the argument, and the Hammers might have had some more but for poor finishing.

The team: Conway: Forde, C. Walker, Fenton, R. Walker, Cockroft, Small, Macaulay, Foreman, Goulden, Foxall.

Att: 18,500

Slightly contrary to the above, the official record of the game has it that Foreman, Goulden, Macaulay and Small scored the goals.

On the same day the first transport of prisoners arrived at the Mauthausen-Gusen Concentration Camp in occupied Austria. The Belgian forces had been driven out of Menin by attacks of units from Army Group B, a 300,000-strong combination of three German Army Groups that had come together for the first time during the Western Campaign of 1940 in Belgium and the Netherlands. At this point Army Group B was commanded by Field Marshal Moritz Albrecht Franz Friedrich Fedor von Bock (which sounds like a firm of Teutonic solicitors or the back row of the Eintracht Braunschweig team of the time). A monarchist, he was known to revile the Nazi order, but was tolerated because of his skill as a commander. He was known by his men as 'Der Sterber' ('The Dire') and/or the 'Holy Fire of Küstrin', alluding to his habit of preaching to them about the honour of laying down their lives for 'Das Vaterland', which Bock more or less did on 4 May 1945 when, on the way to Hamburg, his car was strafed by a British fighter-bomber.

Army Group B went on to fight on the Eastern Front and under Ewin Rommel ('The Desert Fox') in Italy and northern France.

Before May was out, the last pockets of resistance in Boulogne had been eliminated.

On 31 May 1940, the *Daily Express* reported that football might be closed down until peace was restored 'due to team raising and transport problems'.

NINETEEN

GOLDEN LEN GOULDEN

Moral courage is the most valuable and usually the most absent characteristic in men.

General George S. Patton

Leonard 'Len' Arthur Goulden might arguably be thought of as one of West Ham's most skilful outfield players ever. Certainly, this majestic inside forward was one of three great strikers of the pre-war history of the Irons, alongside Syd Puddefoot and Vic Watson. Goulden was able to move effortlessly between midfield and attack, having a remarkable capacity to completely alter the trajectory of a Hammers assault via an extraordinarily precise, long-distance, left-foot pass. He possessed a remarkable capacity for the unexpected and was able to render opposing teams dramatically susceptible in a single move.

Born in Hackney, London, on 9 July 1912, his family had relocated the short bus ride away to Plaistow by the time Len reached 3 years old. Moving from his school team to West Ham Boys, he was selected to play for England Schoolboys in 1926 to face both Wales and Scotland. Five years later he signed as an amateur with West Ham. This was an era before youth football at Upton Park so, as was the convention with young players at the time, the teenage Goulden was sent to learn his trade at first with non-league Chelmsford, and then Leyton. His first paid job, like many young people in the West Ham area, was as an employee of Tate & Lyle, in their gigantic sugar refinery in Silver Town (on the north bank of the River Thames).

Outside of the playing season, Len (before signing professional) had many jobs, but spent one summer employed by the Cearns family on the redevelopment of Highbury, helping to convert the Arsenal home ground into the finest football stadium in the nation during that period. Len's role was (according to his son Paul) 'throwing a bit of concrete on the North Bank' – something many of us have yearned to do over the years. While doing this work, the young Len was able to watch Cliff Bastin train. Len had played with Bastin as a schoolboy international (*v.* Wales) and looked forward to the day when he might equal Cliff's achievements. The next time they played together was in Berlin under the gaze of Adolf Hitler.

The eldest of Len's two sons, Roy (born in Ilford, Essex, in 1937), would play for Arsenal between 1959 and 1961 before moving on to Southend United and then Ipswich Town. His second son, Paul, was born in 1944 and became a head teacher.

Len Goulden came from a sporting lineage, his father Dick, a sheet metal worker, was amateur featherweight champion of England. Len's older brother, an amateur footballer who, in 1934, played for Marseille Olympic, was an engineer with the famous Marconi organisation, which was based in Chelmsford, Essex. It was from the company's factory, on 15 June 1920, that the first official publicised sound broadcast in the United Kingdom was made, featuring Dame Nellie Melba. A couple of years later the world's first regular wireless broadcasts for entertainment started from the Marconi laboratories at Writtle (close to Chelmsford), although the 'studio' was not much more than a modest wooden hut.

Marconi was prominent in the development of a number of technological innovations that helped Britain survive and ultimately prevail in the Second World War, most notably – and critically in terms of the Battle of Britain – radar.

Unlike many players of his era, Len's ability was so marked that he spent little time in reserve football. Len broke into the West Ham League side in the last part of the 1932/33 season, shortly after signing professional forms, making his debut at The Valley *v.* Charlton Athletic on 8 April. This marked the start of what was to be an historic partnership with Jimmy Ruffell. Len swiftly became a regular in the first team. A fortnight on, he scored his first goal for the Irons in a 4–3 defeat of Nottingham Forest. In June 1936, three years after first signing as a Hammer, Len married Irene Hamilton (registered in West Ham, Essex).

Ernie Gregory had watched Len from the terraces as part of the Upton Park crowd. Many years later the Hammers' goalkeeping great was to say:

> We've had some great forwards over the years at West Ham but Len was the greatest – the daddy of them all. He was the one I paid my money to see … I can still see Len now – controlling the ball, he killed it instantly … But don't just take my word for it, ask any of the old-timers – they'll tell you the same, Len was the tops. He wasn't a big bloke but he could out-jump anyone.

Such were his obvious qualities that, although for most of his career his skills were confined to the second flight of the English game, Len gained England honours *v.* Ireland in 1937. The following year he was a member of the squad that made the longest-ever England tour up to that point in time, which included the notorious 'Nazi salute' game in Berlin, during which he scored the blistering, literally net-tearing final goal in the defeat of 'the master race'. For Stanley Matthews this was 'the greatest goal I ever saw in football'. The great England outside right still remembered the strike many years later:

> Len met the ball on the run; without surrendering any pace, his left leg cocked back like the trigger of a gun, snapped forward and he met the ball full face on the volley. To use modern parlance, his shot was like an Exocet missile. The German goalkeeper may well have seen it coming, but he could do absolutely nothing about it. From 25 yards the ball screamed into the roof of the net with such power that the netting was ripped from two of the pegs by which it was tied to the crossbar.

During wartime Len served as a police officer, which allowed him to play 192 games in the Hammers' colours, scoring 77 goals. He was selected for 6 'unofficial' international games for England during the conflict, scoring 3 goals:

11 November 1939	Cardiff, Ninian Park	*v.* Wales
13 April 1940	London, Wembley Stadium	*v.* Wales
8 February 1941	Newcastle, St James' Park	*v.* Scotland
3 May 1941	Glasgow, Hampden Park	*v.* Scotland
7 June 1941	Cardiff, Ninian Park	*v.* Wales
14 October 1944	London, Wembley Stadium	*v.* Scotland

Goulden also ran out for Chelsea as a wartime guest and in 1945, helping the west London Blues win the Football League South Cup. The move to Stamford Bridge and Division One became permanent as peace broke out. The £5,000 fee retrospectively looks like something of a 'give-away' price.

In 1945 Len was in the Pensioners side that met the renowned Moscow Dynamo at the Bridge and over his five-year stint in SW6 he appeared 111 times, hitting 19 goals for Billy Birrell's boys. However, his assists for his centre forward, the remarkable Tommy Lawton, did much to preserve Chelsea's status. He moved to wing half after a while, but the nearest he came to glory was an FA Cup semi-final *v.* Arsenal in 1950 that ended in defeat. The Gunners went on to Wembley to better Liverpool with 2 goals from Reg Lewis. Lewis scored 143 goals in 130 wartime appearances, including 4 during the War Cup Southern Final of 1943, a 7–1 annihilation of Charlton Athletic. In the final stages of the conflict he was in the British Army of the Rhine. In 1946 he came back to London and continued to turn out for Arsenal.

Len was offered a chance to manage Chile around this time, but after a spell on the coaching staff at Stamford Bridge, in the summer of 1952 he moved on to coach Watford in Division Three South, under manager Ron Burgess, the renowned former Spurs player. Together they guided the Hertfordshire side to fourth place in 1954. After four years with the Hornets, Len left to work with his son Roy in the latter's post office (he never, as some authors claim, became a 'postmaster'). Following a three-season return to his coaching role at Watford, alongside Burgess guiding the club to his first promotion (from Fourth to Third Division), in 1965 Len took a two-year coaching role in Libya, North Africa.

Returning to the UK, for a while Len managed Banbury United (not 'Town' as is often reported – this team was formally 'Banbury Spencer') before taking up a coaching position with Oxford United reserves (January 1969 to February 1970). From 1969 he found employment at a USAF base in Northamptonshire (at this point Len made his home not too far away in Fritwell, Oxfordshire).

Len remained a Hammer at heart all his life; he was often in the crowd when West Ham were playing in the midlands before he retired. A number of writers have erroneously claimed that Len relocated to and passed away in Cornwall. In fact, after retiring he moved to Chelmsford, to be closer to his son Roy, but he and Irene found it hard to settle there. Paul had ambitions to develop his gifts as an artist, and in connection with this, had bought a place in the Cape Cornwall area. He suggested that his mum and dad move there with him (the family had holidayed in Newquay from when Roy and Paul were babies until well into their teenage years). But again this did not work for the couple. The cottage was set in quite an exposed position, close to cliffs, and during their first winter the roof was blown away. So after approximately a year they moved once more, this time to Humberstone Road, Plaistow, E13; a five-minute stroll from Upton Park.

But, like Ron Burgess, Len developed dementia and Alzheimer's, and although Paul was on hand as much as possible (Roy had immigrated to Australia at this point), Irene, like many relatives of folk who suffer with this awful condition, couldn't cope. Len was moved to a care home in Muswell Hill. Less than a year on, West Ham's greatest striker contracted pneumonia. He died in Chase Farm Hospital on 14 February 1995.

A supremely creative player, Len was capped for England at a time when there were many forwards of tremendous quality to choose from, and of course he played with the best of them, the likes of Stoke's Freddie Steele, who for Len was hugely underrated. Indeed, for Len, Steele was amongst the best centre forwards he had played alongside. The legendary Tommy Lawton once said of Len Goulden that: 'He would have played for England in any era.' Certainly in another era he would undoubtedly have played many more games for his country.

Len had been selected for fourteen peacetime England sides between 1937 and 1939. He would score the first of his 4 goals on his debut in 1937 during the 6–0 destruction of Norway in Oslo. As a player from a middling Second Division club, this is a testament to his outstanding prowess.

For all this, Len's first love had been cricket. Soon after he was approached by West Ham, Essex County Cricket Club invited him to try out for the team. Len always said he preferred the summer game to football (he played at a good amateur level during his football years), and had Essex been the first to ask he would probably have never played for the Hammers. Cricket's loss was certainly football's gain. However, when Len moved to Chelsea he was able to pit himself against some of the best cricketers in England in the annual Chelsea *v.* Arsenal match held near Box Hill, Surrey – the likes of Arthur Milton, Don Roper, and Les and Denis Compton. It's a shame (in terms of squaring the circle) that West Ham's Jim Standen was with Arsenal a little too late to have played against Len.

Len was great pals with Archie Macaulay and Stan Foxall, and like the latter he enjoyed a joke. It was ironic when Macaulay joined Arsenal because the Gunners had approached West Ham for Goulden's signature when Alex James stood down in 1937. Goulden, like many footballers of his era, had always looked up to Arsenal; those who played for the giants of North London, and/or knew the club as an institution, understood it to be what any good player would aspire to be part of at that time. Highbury was where the best graduated to. However, the Hammers board had rejected the approach immediately. Alex James and Len Goulden became close friends, and Len was with Alex when the great Scottish international breathed his last.

In 1996 Paul Goulden invited Sir Geoff Hurst to the school where he was working in Plumstead to give out prizes. Talking to the former Hammer, Paul told him that his father was Len Goulden. Hurst's immediate response was to say that if he had commanded the same affection that the fans had for Len, he would be a proud man. At the same school Paul had met a parent by the name of Puddefoot. It seems he was the great-great-nephew of the celebrated Syd. In the words of Harry Hill, 'what are the chances?'

Paul Goulden, an interesting, generous and intelligent man, confirmed to me that his dad's first football loyalty was always to West Ham. He passed me a letter sent to Len on West Ham headed paper, dated 9 October 1945, written in the fine hand of Charlie Paynter. The first part of the letter read:

> Dear Len,
> Just a personal note to endorse the sentiments expressed by my Directors.
>
> In my long career I have had to say 'Goodbye' to a good many players, some by transfer, others by the way that comes to all players in time, but frankly I have never felt the parting from others hit me so hard as it does in your case.

This shows both the quality and humanity of Len and something of the bond Paynter had with his players. One wonders if there is anything more worthwhile that can be achieved in football. Maybe Charlie had it right after all?

TWENTY

MUTINY AT UPTON PARK

> Football has nothing to do with fair play. It is bound up with hatred, jealousy, boastfulness, disregard of all rules and sadistic pleasure in witnessing violence: in other words it is war minus the shooting.
>
> *George Orwell*

Over the Whit weekend (20–30 May 1944) one of the largest contingents of troops ever to arrive in London from the north of England and Scotland was taken to the Boleyn Ground. As in established camps, barbed wire and fences were erected and sentries posted, so effectively isolating the troops from the outside world. To many this must have felt like prison.

On 1 June the servicemen confined in the ground were divided into groups and each group in turn was addressed by their commanding officer, who told them that they were bound for France 'any day now'. The troops were also given an approximate picture of what they would be tasked with when they got to occupied Europe, which included a look at relevant maps of where the tank-landing craft would be transporting them to – the Ouistreham beaches, Normandy.

Following this the troops were instructed to form queues to be given their first payment in francs (the currency in France before the Euro) from their supply sergeants for use in France. When this was completed the groups came back together on the West Ham pitch for an address by the army chaplain. His tenor was grim and depressing, talking of the 'perils that lie ahead of us all' before leaving the men to contemplate their fate in the canteen.

All the available beer had been consumed by 7 p.m. and there were no cigarettes to be begged, stolen or bought within the confines of the Upton Park stadium. Irate troopers, on approaching supply sergeants about their plight, were sharply reminded that it was Whit weekend and as such the NAAFI depots were closed.

Faced with the lack of the traditional basic resources for the amelioration of understandable dread (booze and fags), dozens of these D-Day bound men resorted to sneaking by the sentries, edging and undercutting their way through the barbed wire, clambering on one another's shoulders or even tunnelling their way out. A few of the men remembered 'bunking' into the ground as kids and merely reversed the process to liberate themselves from it. In this way, it wasn't long before every local pub was stacked with servicemen clamouring for drink and cigarettes, a few managing to pay in francs that some landlords continued to display in their bars well into the 1960s.

The chief inspector of police for the district, Reg Smith, was later to recall:

> By this time everybody from Montgomery down was telling us to get the soldiers back inside the stadium. My office had already been on the job and the bulk of the AWOLs had gone back quietly. Only about thirty remained, but they were carousing in pubs as widely apart as Limehouse and Canning Town and were in no mood to respond to the orders of the military and civilian police who had been sent to round them up.

Reg was faced with something of an imponderable situation, basically being told to get lost by an appreciable number of men who would be relied upon to help liberate Europe – putting them in jail would be self-defeating, to say the least. However, hanging out in Canning Town nick, a retired police sergeant, who had returned to the force in a voluntary capacity when war broke out, asked Smith for a truck and a driver, assuring him that he felt able to collect the erring servicemen without too much fuss. The old cop, a veteran of the Great War, picked up a few of his old comrades living locally, including my material grandfather, George, and was as good as, maybe better than, his word. He and his little crew of 'Old Contemptibles' by 5 a.m. had all the men back in the stadium, plus half-a-dozen who hadn't been there in the first place. Some of the men and a couple of landlords were held in custody for a while, but that was the extent of official consequences.

BUZZ-BOMBED BOLEYN BOYS

In the summer of 1944, at a point when Londoners started to feel more secure about the RAF's control of the skies, the first V1 'doodlebug' or 'buzz-bomb' – a pilotless monoplane powered by a jet motor, armed with a 1-ton warhead – was unleashed on the capital. By September the first V2 rocket had hit London. As this weapon flew at supersonic speed, it was impossible for even the latest fighters to intercept. By March 1945 close to 9,000 civilians had been killed by these flying bombs. The attacks provoked a feeling of panic, with people leaving London in their tens of thousands.

It had been decided at War Cabinet level that no information would be released about the V1 attacks. However, the *Evening Standard* broke ranks, telling how 'a raider was brought down in the East End'. A couple of days later the Nazis launched 200 bombs, seventy-three of which got through to London, obliging Herbert Morrison, the then home secretary, to make public knowledge of the V1 – which the press at first called the 'P-plane'. The Boleyn

Ground was hit in a V1 attack on 2 August, destroying part of the West Stand and damaging most of it; the impact crater was about 3ft deep and some 20ft wide in the south-west corner of the pitch. However, there was much to be thankful for; had a game was been in progress at the time, losses would probably have been calamitous.

Looking ahead to the new season, the *Stratford Express* carried the headline, 'West Ham FC's Ground Trouble. Away Matches Only at the Start':

> West Ham United will commence the season under ground difficulties, and Mr Charles Paynter, secretary and manager, says that it is probable that all matches for the first two months will be played away. He told a reporter that this does not mean that the club will lose any of its home matches, but that they will be played later in the season. 'Clubs have co-operated and met us in our trouble, and the difficulty is being met by reversing fixtures' said Charlie Paynter.

No mention was made of the rocket as the press was kept tight-lipped in terms of giving away the slightest information to the Axis foe.

In the face of all this, the 1944/45 football season got under way at the end of August. The 'spotter' system was now being used widely, although even if one managed to get sight of a V2 before it hit, the potential for doing anything about it was negligible.

On 6 June, under the command of Generals Eisenhower and Montgomery, years of methodical preparation culminated in American, Canadian and British troops landing on the coast of Normandy. The Allies had managed to keep the Nazis speculating about where and when the invasion to liberate Western Europe would start. Consequently, the German defensive positions were strung out along the whole of the northern coast of France. Even when it was clear that Normandy was the centre of the Allied effort, Hitler refused to see the landings as anything more than a diversion, so convinced was he that Calais would be the focus of any invasion. 'Confirmation bias' (the more you tell yourself something, the more it feels like a fact), the curse of strategy from the personal to the global, proved to be a blessing to the Allies.

The Axis command understood that if the Allies gained a foothold, the chances of repelling them were doubtful, so they concentrated their resources on the beaches, mining them extensively and setting up tank traps. The Nazis correctly anticipated that the inevitable attack would take place at high tide, so also set in place structures designed to tear out the bottoms of landing craft.

But as history shows, the Allies prevailed and within three weeks Cherbourg was liberated. An Army XI started a Scottish tour on 6 August with Archie Macaulay, Harry Medhurst and Ted Fenton in their number. They kicked off with a 2–0 win at Aberdeen *v.* Combined Services. By that time the British Army had captured Caen. Under three weeks later, West Ham held Tottenham to a 2–2 draw in North London (George Foreman and Jackie Wood were on target for the Hammers) in the opening game of the season. By the end of that month the Army tourists north of the border had defeated Moray Services in Elgin (8–3), N. Scotland Services in Fort George (6–3) and Combined Services in Inverness (7–1), and Charles De Gaulle, the leader of the 'Free French' forces, had followed the Allies into Paris.

With seventy-five pre-war clubs in action (the highest figure since 1939/40), a total of 310,000 people had watched the Western, South and North Leagues on the opening day of the league schedules. In the League South, 72 goals were scored in the 16 games. Only Exeter and Ipswich had failed to play in wartime leagues.

The 9 September saw Archie Macaulay, alongside the likes of Tommy Lawton, Frank Swift, Matt Busby, Stanley Matthews and Stan Mortensen, turn out for the Combined Services' 8–4 win *v.* Ireland in Belfast.

The Irons made their way to Shepherd's Bush on 16 September with Ephraim 'Jock' Dodds joining the squad. The 28-year-old Blackpool centre forward had been scoring prolifically throughout the war for club and country (Scotland). Although he didn't register at Loftus Road, over the following 8 games that he took part in he struck 11 times, including a hat-trick during a 7–4 Irons victory at Craven Cottage.

With Dodds in such scintillating form, George Foreman moved temporarily to Spurs.

BOMBING ALONG

The footballing structure, which seemed to have worked well enough throughout much of the war, was again put into operation for the 1944/45 term as the advance into Europe from D-Day continued.

However, on 9 September 1944 the FA embarked on a 'wartime tour' in Belfast, at Windsor Park. A crowd of 49,875 watched an Irish side take on a Combined Services XI, which included Hammer Archie Macaulay. A compelling game produced a dozen goals, with Ireland's Peter Doherty hitting 4. Raich Carter matched Doherty's contribution for the Combined Services; Jimmy Mullen added a brace, while Tommy Lawton and Stan Mortensen rounded off the tourists' 8. This was not considered a wartime international, although the Combined Services side was made up of internationals from England, Scotland and Wales.

The tour went on to Paris (30 September) where a French XI was defeated 5–0 and (1 October) in Brussels, Belgium were beaten 3–0.

On 14 October Terry Woodgate was knocked out cold after 10 minutes at Kenilworth Road. However, he made a remarkable recovery, appearing for the Hammers the following week for the 3–0 win *v.* Arsenal.

On the same day Wembley staged its first international of the season, attracting 90,000 for England *v.* Scotland, with Hammer

Len Goulden taking over at inside left from Hagan. Len scored from an assist by Lawton in the 6–1 destruction of the Scots.

Scotland had recalled Matt Busby when Bill Shankly was deemed to be unfit, although Shankly felt he was more than able. Busby, however, was in Aldershot. In the end the raw Bob Thyne came into the team, a youthful centre half who was available because he was getting over shell shock and shrapnel wounds, picked up while in action on D-Day!

Towards the end of 1944 the peppering of London with V1s lessened as Allied forces, advancing through Normandy, reached the former launching sites. Anti-aircraft batteries alongside RAF fighters had also been downing a good number of the V1s. But aerial attack continued with the use of the V2 rockets, which continued to terrorise Londoners and those living in south-east England.

Transport problems prior to the build-up of men and materials before D-Day had led to the AGMs of both the FA and League being postponed until October when there were some unexpected setbacks on the European Western Front, with the German breakthrough in the Ardennes. It was agreed that if and when a transitional season could be started, the number of guest players would be restricted to six per club and then gradually reduced. However, the post-war committee of the FA reported the establishment of eight subcommittees to deal with a variety of topics for the time when hostilities would be at an end.

West Ham went on a 9-game winning streak, starting on 16 September with a 1–0 away win over Queens Park Rangers (Len Goulden was the scorer). The side's ninth win on the bounce was a 7–4 thriller at Craven Cottage; a hat-trick from Jock Dodds was added to by a deuce from George Ludford and singles from Goulden and Benny Fenton (brother of Ted). Two nets from Harry Potts, and one each from Johnny Arnold and Arnold Lowes were the Fulham reply. This win was doubly impressive as the Hammers had no fewer than six players turning out at Burton Park for the Anti-Aircraft Command *v.* W. Command. Up to 18 November the Irons had only been beaten once (a 3–2 reversal at The Valley on 2 September) in a dozen games.

Following a fifteen-month discussion, on 21 October, the Post-War Planning Committee proposed, when football normality was restored, a rise in player wages to between £8 and £9 during the winter and £6 and £7 in the summer. A £100 increase in benefits was also recommended from the £650 ceiling. On the same date, at Selhurst Park, Charlie Bicknell was back playing for the Police and Civil Defence, defeating the National Fire Service 3–1.

A week later Archie Macaulay was in the forward line of the Army Scotland *v.* Army in England at Hampden. The English won the day 2–1 to the disappointment of the crowd of 41,558. Archie was again on call, this time for Anti-Aircraft Command *v.* W. Command, alongside fellow Hammers Terry Woodgate, Ron Cater, Dick Dunn and Jackie Wood; the latter struck twice in the 3–3 draw at Burton Park. On 25 November Macaulay was selected to play in the Scottish side *v.* the RAF at Hillsborough. The Scots did well to beat a strong side, which included Raich Carter, Stanley Mathews, Bernard Joy, Stan Mortensen and Ted Drake, 7–1.

The return to Upton Park on 2 December was marked by the game *v.* Tottenham Hotspur. This was to be Jock Dodds' first and last appearance at the Boleyn Ground, battling for the West Ham cause. Kids, sitting like sparrows in the lintel and metal beams of the open (roofless) stand, were among the expectant 25,000 crushed into the available areas of the home of the Hammers. However, 3 minutes off the half-hour, Harry Gilberg met Bill 'Sonny' Walters' centre to beat Harry Medhurst.

There was a rumour that Dodds was happy enough at Upton Park but joined Fulham after there were whispers that George

Foreman was to make a return to the Boleyn Ground following his stint with Spurs.

Macaulay was in the Army line-up *v.* an FA XI at Bradford on 9 December, scoring his side's goal in the 1–1 draw.

With Millwall due to visit Upton Park on 30 December, QPR manager Dave Mangnall, a Hammer between 1934 and 1936 (29 goals in 37 matches), looked to Charlie Paynter a few days before the League South game to help him field a side . On the day of the match Reg Attwell and Ernie Gregory wore Rangers colours. It was a good game that the home side won 4–2 (a hat-trick from George Foreman was added to by a Terry Woodgate net).

The New Year saw 300,000 attending matches; however, it was still astonishing for many when Fred Howarth, the League secretary, revealed that there had been a 40 per cent rise in turnout on the previous year. For all this, bad weather at the end of January meant postponements and what had become the usual pleas for an extension to the season, which were ultimately granted; the term would continue for three extra weeks to 26 May.

Brighton and Hove Albion came to the Boleyn Ground on 13 January 1945. This was to be a 9-goal game, not least because of some uncharacteristic rickets on the part of Harry Medhurst and his defence. The visitors were 4–1 up with half an hour left on the clock. It was looking like a distinctly bad day at the office for the Irons. But out of the blue, with the Seagulls missing a penalty to add to the drama, the home team produced 4 goals as Brighton snatched defeat from the jaws of victory.

The sad footnote to this encounter was that it brought the curtain down on Jim Barrett's noble career of two decades. The England schoolboy international, at the time a sergeant in the Services, had a proud reputation for breaking the netting by way of penalty kicks. Ernie Gregory recalled how Jim could 'knock a man out from 20 yards' with his powerful drive.

Archie Macaulay started 1945 in much the same way as his previous wartime career, playing representative football. On 6 January he was in Brussels in the Scottish Services team that beat Belgium 3–2. The day after he was in the side that lost 6–4 to Flanders in Bruges. Five days later, along with Ron Cater, Dick Dunn, Jackie Wood and Terry Woodgate, he was playing for the Anti-Aircraft Command *v.* SE Command at Selhurst Park; Dunn scored in the 6–3 defeat of his side. On the same day Ted Fenton lined up for E. Command *v.* London District at Griffin Park in what was to prove a close and entertaining match (London District won 7–6).

Harry Medhurst was in goal for an Army XI at Ipswich *v.* the Royal Navy on 17 February. He kept a clean sheet in the 2–0 victory.

Following 3 straight losses from 9 December to 14 April, West Ham won 10 successive League South contests. When these are added to the 4 victories in the Football League (South) Cup, Group 3, the Hammers were looking irresistible. Indeed, the only blots on the copy book were made in the latter competition, a 1–1 draw away to Queens Park Rangers, a 4–0 reverse against Spurs at White Hart Lane (one of only 3 matches in which West Ham would fail to score all season), and the 2–1 defeat by Chelsea in the semi-final of the latter competition at White Hart Lane.

The League South Cup, 1945 – Group 3							
	Played	Won	Drawn	Lost	For	Against	Points
West Ham United	6	4	1	1	14	6	9
Queens Park Rangers	6	3	2	1	7	8	8
Tottenham Hotspur	6	3	1	2	13	4	7
Aldershot	6	0	0	6	3	19	0

A crowd of around 35,000 turned up in North London on 25 March for the meeting with Chelsea in the last four of this competition. Laurie Townsend (guesting from Brentford) scored for the Hammers, but the Irons were foiled by goals from

George Wardle and Alf Whittingham. Maybe if Len Goulden had been playing for the Irons, things would have been different, but as it was the Blues went on to win the competition, beating Millwall 2–0 at Wembley in front of a crowd of 90,000. The £29,000 of receipts were cut into to the tune £13,300 by entertainments tax. Showing the persistence of the 'guest system' (which by now the football authorities were looking to outlaw), of the twenty-two players who ran out for the final, just ten were representing the club they were registered with.

Ironically, paradoxically, sardonically and slightly sickeningly, West Ham were thereafter to defeat the Stamford Bridge crew twice in League South matches.

England were again victors over Scotland (3–2) at Villa Park on 3 February. Archie Macaulay of West Ham was once more on duty for the Caledonians. Macaulay was also with the Scotland side that lost 6–1 to England on 14 April 1945. This was the heaviest defeat Scotland had ever suffered at home.

Players, like so many other people, were now thinking of demob. Footballers also needed to think about which clubs they would join and what sort of contract they could demand or hope for. Despite some derision about the 'Aldershot Commandos', they had done a great job for Britain's morale.

Hitler committed suicide at the end of April; a man who had never cared for football, but then football had not cared much for him.

Despite the Hammers losing just 5 matches all season and from the start of December to the final game of the season, in mid-May, winning 13 out of 15 games and tasting defeat just once (5–3 at Upton Park *v.* Southampton), Tottenham were once more confirmed as League South champions, 5 points ahead of West Ham.

By May an end to conflict in Europe was in sight. The FA announced the approval of friendlies to mark the celebrations on VE Day.

League South, 1944/45 – ending 26 May 1945							
	Played	Won	Drawn	Lost	For	Against	Points
Tottenham Hotspur	30	23	6	1	81	30	52
West Ham United	30	22	3	5	96	47	47
Brentford	30	17	4	9	87	57	38
Chelsea	30	16	5	9	100	55	37
Southampton	30	17	3	10	96	69	37
Crystal Palace	30	15	5	10	74	70	35
Reading	30	14	6	10	78	68	34
Arsenal	30	14	3	13	77	67	31
Queens Park Rangers	30	10	10	10	70	61	30
Watford	30	11	6	13	66	84	28
Fulham	30	11	4	15	79	83	26
Portsmouth	30	11	4	15	56	61	26
Charlton Athletic	30	12	2	16	72	81	26
Brighton and Hove Albion	30	10	2	18	66	95	22
Luton Town	30	6	7	17	56	104	19
Aldershot	30	7	4	19	44	85	18
Millwall	30	5	7	18	50	84	17
Clapton Orient	30	5	7	18	39	96	17

The sixth term of wartime football concluded three weeks after VE Day (8 May). It had been decided that the following season the forty-four clubs would be split into North and South leagues and that the 1946/47 season would be a return to the normal, pre-war organisational pattern of football.

Despite not being able to play a home game until 2 December (contesting 14 straight away fixtures) because of the bomb to the Boleyn Ground, the season had been one of the best of the war years for West Ham. But it could have been even better had Stan Foxall not been prohibited from playing that season by a knee injury picked up at Lotus Road in the first few weeks of the Hammers' schedule. A broken leg had also deprived the Irons of their wartime goal-machine George Foreman. He sustained the fracture in the League South Cup game *v.* Aldershot on

24 February. That had been his last game until the opening match of the following season.

Len Goulden, with 31 outings, made the most appearances for the club. Thanks to his 7 goals in the Football League (South) Cup (Group 3), Len was also West Ham's leading marksman with 17 hits, although George Foreman with 15 strikes in the League South was 5 ahead of Len in that contest.

Paynter called on twenty 'guest' players during the 1944/45 term, probably an effect of the commotion at the start of the liberation of Europe. He was obliged to chop and change his side perhaps more than in any other wartime season, calling on forty-six players (over 50 per cent of whom scored for the club). There had nevertheless been some notable performances, including an 8–1 victory over Aldershot at Upton Park in the last part of January and a 9–1 annihilation of Luton in East London in the penultimate match of the season.

At Villa Park, Birmingham, on 3 February 1945, Hammer Archie Macaulay was again on call for Scotland. Only some extraordinary saves by Royal Navy petty officer Bob Brown, a Queen's Park amateur at the time, kept the margin down, particularly in the later stages of the game when a distinguished home attack was looking fearsome. Bob Brown and Stan Mortensen (2) were answered by Jim Delaney and Jock Dodds in a close game.

Archie Macaulay was once more summoned to the cause of Scotland at Hampden Park, Glasgow, on 14 April. While Les Johnston made it 1–1 at half-time, following Raich Carter's opener, in the second half Tom Lawton (2), Bob Brown, Stan Matthews and Les Smith made it far and away Scotland's heaviest defeat at Hampden. It was an English achievement which has yet to be surpassed; a 6–1 humiliation in front of 133,000 tartan supporters.

However, this was the end of England's outstanding run of 7 consecutive wins, a period that had seen the Scots ship 36 goals. Frank Butler of the *Daily Express* asked, 'Will there ever be another wing partnership to rival Matthews and Carter?' The answer is 'no', not so far anyway.

THE ATOMIC BOMB

> The atomic bomb made the prospect of future war unendurable. It has led us up those last few steps to the mountain pass; and beyond there is a different country.

So said J. Robert Oppenheimer (the so-called 'father of the atomic bomb') when reflecting on the results of the 'Manhattan Project', which had culminated in the detonation of the first atomic bomb in the desert of New Mexico on 16 July 1945. With this new weapon President Truman could shelve Operation Olympic, the proposed invasion of Japan in November that year, which would have been tremendously costly in terms of Allied lives. Taking Iwo Jima, an island with an area of 8 square miles, had cost 25,000 Allied casualties in February 1945, while Okinawa took nearly three months to subdue.

'Olympic' would have required a simultaneous Soviet invasion. Many US officials did not want Stalin involved in the post-war settlement in Japan, while Churchill and Truman had agreed not to share the results of the Manhattan Project with the Soviet Union. Thus at the Potsdam Conference in July 1945, Truman decided to use the bomb as soon as one was ready, to try to shock Japan into submission.

At Potsdam the Allies, excluding the Soviet Union, had demanded the unconditional surrender of Japan, darkly threatening 'prompt and utter destruction'. Capitulation was not forthcoming and Hiroshima was more or less destroyed by the A-bomb on 6 August. The Soviet Union declared war on Japan two days later and started to seize Japanese territory. On 9 August, with the original target Kokura obscured by cloud, Nagasaki was laid waste by the bomb 'Fat Boy'.

Elements of the Japanese Army resisted moves to surrender and it required an intercession from Emperor Hirohito for the war to be ended; Japan surrendered on 14 August. The next day was declared 'VJ Day'.

BEYOND INTO A DISTANT COUNTRY

West Ham had drawn 1–1 with Arsenal at White Hart Lane on 5 May (the week before the mashing of Luton); Sam Small and Ted Drake had done the respective honours. Three days later the world, and in particularly Britain, celebrated VE Day. However, hostilities continued in South-East Asia, where Iron Charlie Walker was serving.

A friendly at Griffin Park produced 7 goals, and unfortunately West Ham only got 3 of them. Seventeen days later, on 26 May at Upton Park, the Bees left East London on the end of a 5–0 victory. Ted Fenton was in Zurich on 24 July with the FA XI that beat Switzerland 3–0.

As the war with Japan drew to its history-changing atomic conclusion, plans for the transitional season of 1945/46 were cemented. The Management Committee had pushed for the return to a near pre-war situation, but this was prevented by the clubs, anxious about the shortage of players and constant difficulties with and costs for travel and accommodation. However, guest players were limited in League matches to six per team. Starting on 3 November 1945, this level was reduced to three. The reintroduction of the FA Cup was to prove remarkably popular. Following its seven-year absence it was perhaps an indication that things were returning to normal and clubs didn't complain given that ties over two legs helped stack up the profit (this was a 'one-off' arrangement for the transitional season only).

The League War Cup, in its various incarnations, which had been such a helpful wartime distraction for many millions, as well as a source of desperately needed income for the clubs, was consigned to history. But with the restoration of the FA Cup and, at the behest of the professional clubs, it was agreed that the War Cup principle of home-and-away legs from the first round proper would be continued in order to maximise revenue from the competition (apart from this, the organisation of the Cup reflected pre-war practice).

Players continued to draw £4 a game, although it was widely recognised that this did not constitute a living wage.

The 'real' war was now over. The only job left for the world and for football was the transition to and winning of peace.

TWENTY-ONE

BRIDGE OF SIGHS

(1940 WAR CUP SEMI-FINAL)

Set the elevation!
Traverse on for line!
Stratton's just a'loaded,
There's still a little time.

Me, I'm on the left side!
Bob, he's on the right!
Dingus yells 'You Ready Subs?'
The method's 'Battery Right'.

From 'Echo Gun' by Mike Subritzky (161 Battery)

On 1 June 1940 the Hammers' semi-final of the War League Cup with Fulham was scheduled to kick off at Stamford Bridge. They had already disposed of the home side Blues at this venue, but it was also the ground where they had defeated favourites Derby County 5–2 in the 1923 FA Cup semi-final and the place where they had, as a Southern League side, beaten West Bromwich Albion 3–0 in a replay of the second round of the FA Cup in 1913. The Baggies had been a First Division outfit at the time. George Hilsdon, known as 'Gatling Gun', had scored twice for the Southern League Irons.

In the early years of the 1940s the stadium was a huge edifice, certainly compared to Upton Park. The bridge had provided and would provide a venue for greyhound racing, rugby, speedway, athletics, baseball, Grid-Iron football, cricket and, of course, football (see Belton 2013c). Just five years previous to the War Cup semi-final it had drawn a crowd of nearly 83,000 for a Chelsea *v.* Arsenal game. It was a sprawling and potentially intimidating place.

The day before the Fulham *v.* West Ham War Cup encounter, the *Daily Express* was calling the game 'the greatest wait-and-see match of any consequence ever played'. This might feel like a bit of an exaggeration, but the writer had a point as the two teams that came together in West London boasted players they might have only dreamed of fielding in peacetime. The *Daily Express* elaborated:

> What with some of the players in the army and others of them in the national workshop effort, there's no way of knowing just what bunch of lads is likely to trot on to that field.

The article, if it did nothing else, summarised the difficulties confronting football in the early years of the Second World War. For all this, Fulham, who only had to take a stroll from Putney Bridge to play the game, sent a good side out to represent the club. The Cottagers had made the quarter-finals by leaving Brentford, Norwich and Nottingham Forest in their wake. In the last 8 they had met Everton (a side that had finished third in the small but demanding Western League, just 3 points shy of claiming the championship) and caned the proud Liverpool Blues 5–2, with the wartime Welsh cap Viv Woodward (not to be confused with the great England player, Vivian John Woodward) banging in a couple (the Fulham hard man would score 19 goals in 43 outings that term and strike for his country *v.* England in June 1941) whilst wartime England international Ronnie Rooke racked up his fourth goal of the tournament in front of a Craven Cottage crowd of 14,705. The bandy-legged goal-machine would lead his side's scorers with 27 in 35 appearances in the 1939/40 season.

Just a few days prior to the semi-final, Fulham had beaten West Ham in the 'C' Division league competition. It had been a close game at the Cottage, with Jim Barrett hitting home for the Hammers, but it wasn't the best psychological preparation for the Irons with Rooke and McCormack on target. That said, at Upton Park in early March the Hammers had knocked Jack Peart's Craven crew all over the place with a 5–0 obliteration.

The semi-final kicked off at 6.40 p.m. on a Saturday evening to accommodate war workers, although as many were committed to shift-work it would have been a moot point to what extent this advantaged the working public.

The game was reported with understandable gusto as '"Blitzkriegs" At Chelsea':

> West Ham United go to Wembley with Blackburn Rovers for the final of the Football League War Cup. They defeated Fulham in the semi-final at Stamford Bridge on Saturday [1 June] evening, after an amazing match. It was a match of 'blitzkriegs'. West Ham leading two goals to nothing at half-time were the first to indulge in the lightening wars and within five minutes of the resumption had increased their total to four clear goals. It seemed all over, but it was then that Fulham staged their 'blitzkrieg', and between the 12th and 29th minutes scored three times, and came within an ace of forcing an extra period of play. It was great stuff all through, with Fulham's grand effort as a fitting climax in a match that was all action from start to finish.
>
> Brown put through his own goal after eight minutes play and Goulden scored a second for the Hammers in just under half an hour, to give them an interval lead that they thoroughly deserved as the result of their greater power in attack. Then a grand goal by Foxall, and another by Small five minutes after the restart seemed likely to be the forerunner

of a big score, but the Hammers' defence suddenly went all to pieces. Woodward led the revival of Fulham with a neat header. Rooke scored a second and later netted a third from a penalty kick and spectators saw West Ham changed from a team who appeared easy winners to one up against it for the first time in the match.

The excitement was terrific and a crashing shot by Rooke, which might have meant the equalizer, cannoned off a defender's legs, and at the other end, when Foreman showed a clean pair of heels to the Fulham defenders and might have relieved West Ham's anxiety, he tried to dribble round the goalkeeper, who anticipating the move, fell on the ball and cleared. While they were scoring their four goals, and until the time Fulham secured their first, West Ham played grand football in attack, with Macaulay and Goulden the inspiration of most of the moves that frequently had the Fulham defenders out of position. Behind, the Hammers had great wing halves in Fenton and Cockroft, and powerful defenders in C. Walker, R. Walker and Forde, and with everything running well for them they were the complete side.

The team: Conway: Forde, C. Walker, Fenton, R. Walker, Cockroft, Small, Macaulay, Foreman, Goulden, Foxall.

Att: 32,799

West Ham were 2 up at half-time thanks to Len Goulden and an own goal, and led 4–0 in the second period by way of strikes from Foxall and Small. But in a typical Hammers way they allowed Fulham to put 3 past them in 17 mad minutes. Ronnie Rooke, with a penalty, got 2 and Vivian Woodward completed the damage.

The situation had the Hammers followers praying for the final whistle. You, like me, are probably familiar with this type of torture – when football is agony and the supporter is obliged to ask themselves why they put themselves through such trials. There is always the effort to rationalise it. The final result doesn't really matter very much in terms of the entire stream of life. After all, a football match, a whole football season, the game in general, doesn't amount to a great deal in comparison to history, world events, one's own existence.

But this kind of logic doesn't work. Every minute is a lifetime and the guts of the hopeful, the doubtful and/or the faithful twist and turn. Even though this is your team, you want to leave, but you must stay. You hate every one of the players for throwing the security of something like a 4-goal cushion away; your contempt for the referee giving the 'so-called' goals knows no bounds; you detest the opposing fans, envisioning their gloating when they ultimately, predictably (in the case of West Ham's history) score the equaliser/winner in the second minute of injury time. But you are blindly, stupidly, angrily loyal, as you rain curses down on everyone from the owners of the club to the mascot (especially the mascot, who is accused of the most disgusting crimes and social deviations).

The last minutes of the game crawl by. However, as soon as the final whistle is sounded, the mighty if fickle Irons have scraped through, and recriminations dissipate with victory. Every one of 'our' lads out there on the park is a great bloke, a hero who has given his all for you, the club and, in terms of West Ham, the East End of London. We all become 'Artful Dodgers', 'cheeky chappies' or unconvincing impressionists of Danny Dyer, Bob Hoskins, Ray Winstone, Russell Brand, Kenny Lynch or Eliza Dolittle (who are all the same person really, have you ever seen them together?), well up for a quick chorus of 'Knees Up Muvva Brown' while indulging in a bit of Cockney patois – 'Know wot I mean, my son?'; kinda surreal really.

West Ham won the semi-final. They were going to Wembley. It is such moments and the anticipation of the same that keeps the supporter going until the next time, and it is why you pay to see a game. Nearly 33,000 fans had done just that for the pleasure (or purgatory) of seeing West Ham escape the last four – the largest crowd for a wartime club match to that point. Those who made their way home to the east felt they had got value for money.

It's always good to beat another London side. The FA Cup winners might be defeated or the Champions of the Premiership routed, but it still does not compare to coming away from another Cockney ground having just plundered 3 points or bundled them out of the Cup, especially in the early rounds … even more so if it's Spurs … at White Hart Lane. No offence, it's nothing personal …

TWENTY-TWO

BLACKBURN

(1940 WAR CUP FINALISTS)

> The first season was very strange. It was quite enjoyable but a lot of the matches were played in a half-hearted manner. No one knows what was going to happen in the war. It wasn't easy to concentrate on football.
>
> *Frank Broome (Aston Villa and England)*

Throughout the Second World War, getting serving players and war workers together for a match took some foresight. Where possible they would be informed by telegram on the Wednesday before the Saturday match that they had a game. This was unlikely to have been the case for the first Football League War Cup Final, however. Many of the Blackburn players had a long and relatively successful association with Rovers and there was an affinity between them, gelled by the ethos of the club. All had played together in the War Cup and/or the North West League throughout the season. All of them had been involved with the 1939/39 Second Division Championship side. They were a tight unit who knew each other well.

The Riversiders had started their campaign of 1940 with the defeat of Bolton Wanderers 8–2 over the two legs. The Trotters had finished well above Rovers in the North West League. Blackburn then faced Manchester United (from the Northern

Regional League), beating them 3–1 at Old Trafford. In the third round Sunderland had been vanquished and in their quarter-final, runners-up in the Midland League, West Bromwich Albion had been eliminated (2–1). In the last four Rovers had faced the runners-up from the North-East League, Newcastle United; Blackburn made the final with the only goal of the game.

So it was a good, talented and well-established side that awaited West Ham at Wembley on 8 June 1940.

James 'Jim' Barron (goalkeeper) was born in Burnhope, County Durham on 19 July 1913. He made his debut for Rovers *v.* Sheffield Wednesday at Hillsborough on 11 April 1936.

Starting his career with Durham City and Blyth Spartans, Jim moved to Ewood Park in March 1935 and was with the side that won the Second Division Championship in the 1938/39 term.

Jim guested for a number of sides during the Second World War, including Bradford City (1941/42), Gateshead (1941/42 and 1943/44), Darlington (1943/44), York City (1944/45) and Newcastle United (1944/45). In June 1946 he moved to Darlington.

In Football League and FA Cup, Jim made a total of 83 appearances for Rovers. During the war years he was employed in a steelworks in his native north-east, so restricting his opportunities to turn out for Blackburn.

Post-war, Jim made 23 League appearances for the Quakers. His son, also called Jim, kept goal for Nottingham Forest and Wolverhampton Wanderers during the 1960s. Jim senior died in Newcastle on 15 September 1969.

William 'Billy' Arthur Hough (right-back) made his first appearance for Rovers at Edgeley Park on 23 October 1937. Born in Greenfield, Wales, in the summer of 1908, after playing for Connah's Quay and Shotton, Holywell Arcadians and making 4 appearances at inside forward for New Brighton (scoring 1 goal), he left the ranks of amateur football in September 1930. Three months later he was with Preston North End, and it was at

Deepdale that he converted to the full-back role, showing himself to be a solid rather than extravagant performer. He made the move to Ewood Park in 1936 to start a six-year stint with Rovers, winning the Second Division Championship with the club in the 1938/39 season. In all he played 56 peacetime games for Blackburn, 31 of these in the latter championship term.

Rovers brought in Billy just before selling Jimmy Gorman to Sunderland, but Hough was obliged to wait the best part of eighteen months to break into the first team. He started the 1938/39 season as first-choice left-back, but injury kept him out of the team. When he was back to match fitness he couldn't displace Ernie Lanceley. Billy appeared in 40 wartime matches before leaving Ewood Park and the professional game.

Walter Crook (left-back) played his first game for Rovers at Ewood Park *v.* Liverpool on 19 March 1932. Walter represented England *v.* Wales in the wartime international (18/11/1939) at the Racecourse Ground, Wrexham. He led Rovers as club captain to the 1938/39 Second Division Championship (in which he was ever-present, making 42 appearances and scoring twice), 'doing the double' over West Ham (who finished eleventh that year) having experienced relegation in 1935/36.

Making a total 237 turnouts for Blackburn (although he was never to score before or after the 1938/39 term), Walter had made his way through the junior ranks at Ewood Park prior to getting a secure foothold in the Rovers first team. This included a couple of seasons in the tough Central League. But he was rewarded with a protracted run in the First Division in the 1934/35 campaign, and from December 1934 he was ever-present in the senior side up to the outbreak of war and the suspension of the League programme in September 1939.

Walter played in the initial 17 games of the 1946/47 season, establishing a personal niche in the record books with 208 successive Football League appearances for Rovers.

A natural left-footer, despite playing a few games on the right, Walter made the left-back position his own. A rugged personality with, at times, an aggressive approach, he was something of an inspirational character for both his teammates and Blackburn's supporters.

Military service meant that for most of the war years Walter was unable to turn out for Rovers. When he returned to Ewood Park, his former manager Bob Crompton had passed away and he was unable to see eye to eye with Eddie Hapgood. At his own request he was placed on the transfer list in May 1947.

From Rovers he joined the Wanderers of Bolton (May 1947), roving not too far of a wander to Burnden Park. However, injury caused him to call it a day in football and take premature retirement. In 1948 he moved into coaching with the then struggling Ajax club of Amsterdam, staying with de Godenzonen (the Sons of the Gods) up to 1950. Walter returned to east Lancashire in June 1951 to take command of Accrington Stanley. However, his spell at Peel Park was less than idyllic; he resigned in February 1953.

Walter went back to Ajax for the 1953/54 season, but he had been out of football for a time when, in October 1954, he was offered the post of manager of Wigan Athletic. However, he had left the Latics before the start of their 1955/56 campaign. He later spent eighteen years on the coaching staff of Preston North End before becoming disenchanted with the game. Born in Whittle-le-Woods, Lancashire, on 28 April 1912, Walter died in the same county, in Mellor, on 27 December 1988.

Arnold Whiteside (right half) was born in Garstang, Calder Vale, Lancashire, on 6 November 1911, and made his debut for Rovers at Ewood Park *v.* Liverpool on 12 November 1932 in a 2–2 draw.

Arnold was with Woodplumpton Juniors when the Blackburn chairman was on his way to Brunton Park for a game, which had been cancelled before he got there. Not wanting to completely waste his time, he found a village game to watch and the 16-year-old Arnold Whiteside was playing in that match. Rating the sinewy but skilled lad, the next day he asked Arnold's dad if he could sign his boy as an amateur. In March 1931 Arnold turned professional.

Another member of the Second Division Championship side of 1938/39, Arnold made 33 appearances that season, scoring once. In all he would fight the Rovers' cause 239 times, netting 3 times in peacetime.

A weaver by trade, Arnold had to be bought out of the Calder Vale mill where he worked before he moved to Rovers. This is indicative of the time, reflecting how skilled workers, which included footballers, were not easily given up by employers.

As a lad Arnold had been judged to be too slight to make the professional game, but his work-ethic playing in the Central League impressed enough to win him a first-team debut, although it took him well over a year to make himself a regular.

By March 1934 Arnold was playing at right half and he remained the automatic choice in that role until the conclusion of the 1936/37 season.

During the 1937/38 term Arnold only managed 11 outings and was placed on the transfer list. But manager Bob Crompton was minded to give him another shot in September 1938. Arnold took his chance, being central in Rovers' successful Second Division title campaign.

An engine in midfield, Arnold made 150 wartime appearances for Blackburn. He also turned out for Liverpool as a guest on a couple of occasions. When the peace was won, he was one of those players who provided experience and steadiness in a struggling side. Blackburn let Arnold go at the end of the 1948/49 schedule. He spent the following season with Wigan (playing 24 matches). He passed away in 1994.

Arnold was good enough to be pursued by the likes of Tottenham, Liverpool and Arsenal. But such was his skill, tackling and ability to create and stop opportunities in terms of attack and defence that he wasn't going to be allowed to leave Ewood Park.

While his playing credentials were part of the rationale for Rovers hanging on to Arnold, he was also a great favourite of the supporters. Known as the 'little gentleman', it was recognised his stature was against him, and he was greatly admired for the way he overcame this disadvantage. Arnold would travel to games on the same train as the Rovers crowd, and such was his diminutive build that he would sometimes get half-price admission.

After two decades in football Arnold became a chimney sweep and he did well; the business has continued for three generations. Andy currently runs the firm his grandfather founded and continues to service some of the houses Arnold worked on at the start of his second career.

Robert 'Bob' Ireland Pryde (centre half) was born in Methil, Fife, Scotland, on 25 April 1913 and signed for Rovers in May 1933. While at Ewood Park he was twice selected to play for the Football League.

On leaving school Bob started working life in motor-mechanics, playing part-time football with St Johnstone. A loan spell with Brechin City preceded Bob's Rovers debut *v.* Chelsea at Ewood Park on 21 October 1933 – a 4–2 victory over the London Blues.

Standing at over 6ft and weighing in at 13st 7lbs, he stepped into Norman Christie's boots, turning out 41 times in Blackburn's Second Division Championship season of 1938/39. Missing just 1 game, he scored a single goal in that campaign but his part in this achievement was pivotal. In all, he would make 345 peacetime appearances for Rovers, finding the net 11 times.

Initially Bob joined Rovers as trialist, plying his trade in the Central League. Although he got into the Football League side relatively quickly at the left half spot, he had to wait until the 1936/37 season to make his place secure, taking the role of centre half.

Bob was a comparatively tall player and not always consistent in terms of his performance in his early years in England. He was slim but tough, able to read the game well, and this made up for his not being the fastest defender in the world. A born leader, the war years saw him at the peak of his powers. His skill and inspirational qualities worked to hold a frequently changing team together.

Bob hit the rigging 11 times in 180 wartime appearances for the club between 1939 and 1946. But he also turned out for West Ham once in the 1941/42 London League (21 February 1942 – a 2–1 Upton Park win *v.* Brentford). On 19 April 1941, Bob was called up to represent the Football League *v.* a British XI. He played alongside Ken Willingham, Huddersfield Town's wing half, Tommy Lawton and Chelsea's Alf Hanson at outside left.

The British XI also included Billy Cook and Alec Stevenson (Everton), Sam Jones (Blackpool), Don Dearson (Birmingham), Stan Cullis (Wolves), George Mutch (Preston), as well as Liverpool's Matt Busby, South African Berry Nieuwenhuys (who would also turn out for West Ham in the war years) and Willie Fagan. The Anfield Reds supplied both goalkeepers, Alf Hobson, coming in to cover for Frank Swift, who couldn't get leave, and George Poland at the other end.

Bob was selected to play again for the Football League *v.* the League of Ireland at Dalymount Park in April 1947, rubbing shoulders with the two 'Stans', Matthews and Mortensen, Joe Mercer, Jimmy Hagan and Albert Stubbins in a side that won 3–1. At that time it was an uncommon honour for a non-Englishman to represent the League, as the matches were effectively practice games for the England national side.

Bob was 33 when peacetime football returned, but he was still a dominant figure in the Blackburn side. After sixteen years in the service of Rovers, at the end of the 1948/49 season, Bob moved to take up the challenge of player-manager at Wigan Athletic. In the 1949/50 term, he played 22 matches, scoring a couple of goals in the Lancashire Combination as the Latics claimed the runners-up spot. Ending his playing career, he led the club to the League title as manager. He left Springfield Park in January 1952. Bob passed away in June 1998.

Francis 'Frank' Cornelius Chivers (left half) hailed from Drybrook, Gloucester. Frank was 29 when he got his initial run-out for the Blackburn first team on 19 March 1939 *v.* Luton Town at Ewood Park almost a year after joining the club.

Another veteran of the successful Division Two campaign of 1938/39 (Frank made 38 appearances for Rovers that term), Chivers was the dynamo of that side. Working with Arnold Whiteside and Bob Pryde, Frank was part of a half-back line acknowledged to be among the best in England.

Frank arrived at Ewood Park from Huddersfield Town as a centre forward. Coincidently, his second goal for the Terriers was scored at Leeds Road *v.* Blackburn in February 1936. He found the back of the net a total of 16 times in his 50 League games for Huddersfield.

Frank played in the last 10 matches of the 1937/38 season at Blackburn as either a centre forward or an inside left, but missing the opening 5 matches of the 1938/39 campaign, he came back into the team as a left half. It was in this role that he experienced his greatest success with Rovers. A persistent and gritty defender, Frank was not only resolute in his exploits to win the ball; he was indefatigable in his support of the team's forward line.

With the outbreak of war Frank returned to the work he had done before breaking into the professional game: coal-mining – he had started his football with Goldthorpe United, in the colliery town of the same name. As an amateur he played for Barnsley before turning professional in October 1930. His tough wartime job did not stop him turning out for Blackburn 88 times during hostilities, claiming 3 goals. He also guested for Huddersfield Town during the 1940/41 season.

Tragically, Frank was one of thirteen men killed in a mining accident, an explosion at Barnburgh Main Colliery, on the outskirts of the village of Barnburgh, about 2 miles north of Mexborough in the Dearne Valley, South Yorkshire, on 16 February 1942. In most biographies he is recorded to have lost his life in the Dom Valley in April 1942, so he may have died of his injuries after the initial explosion. He was just 33. He had played 55 peacetime games for Rovers, scoring 3 times.

William 'Billy' Rogers (outside right) played his first Football League game for Blackburn *v.* West Ham United at Upton Park on 29 August 1938 (an Archie Macaulay goal had ultimately not counted for very much as Rovers won 2–1). He was born in Ulverston in Lancashire on 3 July 1919. Bill was to appear 83 times for Blackburn, netting 27 times in the process.

Billy was brought to Ewood Park by new manager Bob Crompton in the summer of 1938 and instantly tasked with the outside right role following the opening game of the 1938/39 season. Crompton had accepted that Jack Bruton was no longer up to the job and the athletic Billy proved a competent replacement. He scored 18 goals in 41 League appearances as Blackburn lifted the Second Division title.

During the war Billy struck 26 goals in his 72 outings for Rovers. He also guested for Leeds a couple of times during 1943/44. Following the conflict he returned to the first team, but was unable to achieve the consistency that had been a cornerstone of the team throughout 1938/39. In October 1947 Billy moved to Barrow and went on to score 14 goals in 197 League appearances for the (then) Ziggers.

Billy started out in football with Preston North End, but before he got the chance to make a first-team appearance he was grabbed by Crompton. He hung up his boots in June 1953. A crowd favourite during his time at Ewood Park, he died in 1974.

Leonard 'Len' Butt (inside forward) died in Macclesfield, Cheshire in June 1994, in the month of August. Sixty-six years earlier he took the leap to become a professional footballer. His baptism into the game was at Wilmslow Albion. He went on to turn out for Ashton National Gas and from 1929 to 1930 Stockport County. Len made just 8 appearances, scoring 1 goal for County before moving to Macclesfield in 1931. He joined the ranks of Huddersfield Town in 1935, making 67 appearances, scoring 11 goals in two seasons.

Born in Wilmslow, Cheshire, on 26 August 1910, it was at Carrow Road that Len made his debut for Rovers on 23 January 1937. In total he would make 117 appearances for the club in peacetime, putting his name against 48 nets. A player who could both create and score goals with equal assurance, Len was the ideal inside forward. Recognised as one of the most intelligent practitioners of his time, he was a regular member of the team that brought the Second Division title to Ewood Park in 1938/39; contribution: 16 goals in his 41 League games that term.

Len was a wartime guest for Manchester United (1939/40 and 1940/41), Huddersfield Town (1940/41 and 1941/42), Wrexham (1940/41), Manchester City (1941/42), York City (1941/42), Chelsea (1942/43), Stockport County (1943/44), Aldershot (1943/44) and, in 1943, Hibernian in Edinburgh.

The success Len enjoyed at Blackburn was in marked contrast to his early days in football when, after his time Stockport County, he drifted back into the non-league game. Providentially, he recaptured the form that would take him to Ewood Park along with Jock Wightman.

Len's pace and astuteness swiftly endeared him to the Blackburn crowd. The war years and a knee operation took a toll on him to the extent that after League football returned he left Ewood Park for York City in January 1947. He played for Mansfield Town from October 1947 before becoming player/coach with Mossley in June 1948. In the 1948/49 term Len made 50 appearances, scoring 23 goals for the Lilywhites. He led Mossley to victory in the Manchester Junior Cup and the Ashton Challenge Cup. The following season Len inspired Mossley through the qualifying rounds of the FA Cup to the second round proper, defeating Ashton United, Altrincham, Northwich Victoria, Buxton, Droylsden United, Runcorn and Witton Albion in what for Mossley was historically a phenomenal run, which was only stopped after a replay with Southern League big boys Nuneaton Borough. Len made 37 appearances, scoring 10 goals. However, he resigned at the end of the season. He died in 1994.

John Robson Weddle (centre forward) scored 18 goals while wearing the red rose over his heart 49 times, the first of which was against another group of Rovers, those of Tranmere, on 27 August 1938 at Ewood Park.

Born on 5 November 1905 in Whitburn, South Tyneside, Weddle started his working life in the pits. He had joined Rovers after a decade with Portsmouth, although he started his football with Fatfield Albion.

At a time when Portsmouth seemed to be fated to relegation in their first season in the top flight of English football, J.W. Tinn, the club manager at the time, discovered Weddle in his native north-east. Tinn introduced the youngster as leader of the Pompey attack. After his debut on 3 March 1927 Portsmouth didn't taste defeat for half-a-dozen games. Weddle scored 9 times in 14 outings, making him pivotal in his side's First Division survival that term. In 368 appearances Weddle would find the back of the net 171 times for the Fratton Park fraternity.

Jack (as Weddle was known) gave eleven seasons to the Pompey as the busy, enthusiastic leader of the Hampshire team's attack. 'Steamboat' Weddle, as he was dubbed by the Pompey supporters, was in the Portsmouth sides that contested the 1929 and 1934 FA Cup finals, but Jack was probably best remembered for his performance in the semi-final of the latter competition *v.* Leicester City. The tie was staged at St Andrew's, Birmingham, and in front of a ground record crowd of 66,000 Weddle completed a hat-trick in his side's 4–1 victory.

The best of his playing days were probably behind him when he headed back north to fight the cause of the Riversiders in May 1938, but Weddle was to repay the faith Bob Crompton had in him, fitting well between Len Butt and Albert Clarke.

Regarded as something of the 'father figure' of the side that secured the Second Division title in 1938/39 (in which he donned the blue and white an ever-present 42 times and hit 16 goals), after the Second World War, Jack joined the club's training staff, graduating through the third and second teams to become, in July 1949, head trainer at Ewood Park.

Twice taking charge of Football League XIs while coaching Blackburn, Jack played a crucial backroom role with the side that got to the FA Cup Final in 1960. Weddle left the club in May 1961. He passed away in Blackburn on 21 November, eighteen years later.

Albert W. 'Nobby' Clarke (inside left) was something of a utility striker (he was also able to play inside right or centre forward). He was born in Sheffield on Christmas Day 1916 and was well travelled as a player before rocking up to Ewood Park in July 1938 (in an exchange deal that took Wally Halsall to St Andrew's), appearing for Mosborough Trinity, Frickley Colliery, Mexborough Town, Torquay United and Birmingham. His wartime wanderings were equally impressive, guesting for Torquay United (1939/40), Newport County and Cardiff City (1941/42).

Albert shared his first Blackburn outing (of his 42 for the blue and whites in peacetime) with Jack Weddle. He claimed a brace in this match and went on to finish as the leading goalscorer during the club's Second Division Championship season – 21 strikes in 38 appearances. However, over his Rovers career his goal tally was to grow by only a couple, although his assists were much more numerous.

Albert figured in one season of peacetime football for Rovers, but his stamina and eagerness were long remembered at the club.

A tricky and at times dazzling dribbler, capable of making searing runs, Albert was hard to mark. At Rovers he quickly struck up a useful connection with Jack Weddle. This was particularly telling when (as was his wont) Weddle drifted out to the wings; Albert was always ready to dart into the centre forward role. This not only covered for Jack but confused opposition defences.

Albert was ever-present in Blackburn's 8 Football League War Cup ties of 1939/40 and made 2 more appearances in that competition in 1940/41. However, while he continued to be registered with the Rovers, he made no further appearances for the Riversiders in wartime football.

Albert was killed in action whilst serving with the Devonshire Regiment in June 1944 during the D-Day operations.

The plan for the Devonshires on D-Day was for them to land at Le Hamel, on Gold Beach, to the rear of the 1st Hampshires. On the day, in poor sea conditions and with an unexpected high surge tide, things went wrong. Three of the four companies were carried more than a mile to the east before they could reach the beaches. When they finally did make landfall they were obliged to fight their way to their designated assembly point on foot. Two of the four company commanders were wounded and another was killed. Those who did get to Gold Beach as intended were among the first to land in the first few minutes of the invasion from some of the more than 4,000 ships involved in the invasion. Many jumped off the landing-craft into neck-high water. Holding their rifles above their heads, to wade ashore, more than a few vanished beneath the waves before they made the beach; others were killed as they got out of the water, while some drowned in bomb craters. But the 'Bloody Eleventh' went on to help win the Battle of Normandy and forward the liberation of north-western Europe from the Nazis.

Albert's War Cup medal was stolen in a burglary of his daughter Ann's home in August 2012, causing understandable distress to Ann and her 96-year-old mum.

William 'Billy' Francis Guest was a hard-working player with a powerful shot. He joined Rovers in part-exchange when Jack Beattie moved to Birmingham in January 1937. The energetic Guest seemed to resolve Blackburn's on-going difficulty with the outside left role. Billy was a consistent member of the side the following season, until after 4 games of the 1938/39 season when he was dropped in favour of Bobby Langton. Billy ended up playing just 8 matches in the Second Division glory season, adding just 1 goal to Blackburn's total.

Born in Brierley Hill, near Dudley, West Midlands, on 8 February 1914, Guest shared his first game with another debutant, Len Butt. He came to the Riversiders in January 1937 via Brierley Hill Juniors, Bromley Juniors (Kingswinford) and Birmingham FC (he had joined the Blues in 1932, scoring 15 goals in 76 League outings).

Following 1946/47, after being deployed as an inside forward for a number of games, with Bob Langton making the left wing his own, Bill departed Ewood Park with 94 peacetime appearances and 32 goals to his credit. He joined Walsall but signed for Peterborough United around eighteen months later. He also played for Kidderminster Harriers, Lovell's Athletic, Hinckley United and Bilston United, and ultimately took on the job of trainer with Brandwood Rovers.

Guest scored 9 goals in 35 appearances during wartime football with Rovers. He died in November 1973.

As can be seen from the above biographies, the clash at Wembley in the summer of 1940 was a true north *v.* south confrontation with which the likes of the modern game has nothing to compare.

TWENTY-THREE

THE LEGEND THAT IS DICK WALKER

I am not going to defend myself. I have nothing to defend myself against. The War Moguls ordained that I stayed in England to do my war job. I appeared in hundreds of charity matches and helped raise vast sums for the Red Cross and Service Charities. Let me make it quite clear – I didn't ask to stay in England and my conscience will answer my case.

Tommy Lawton in Football is My Business, *referring to the Army tourists being booed and heckled while playing in Italy, the Middle East and Greece. They were dubbed, amongst other names, 'the 5th Army D-Day Dodgers' and 'the PT Commandos'.*

Dick Walker was once more in the West Ham side that overcame Fulham; he played every game in the Hammers' War Cup campaign of 1940. His name has been etched into the history of the Irons by a love affair between the player and the Upton Park crowd, which spanned three decades and almost 600 matches in all competitions, 311 in the first team. Walker scored only 2 goals for the club in first-class games, 1 a season over the 1947/49 period: West Ham's first goal of the 1947/48 term in the 4–1 Valley Parade defeat, and at Oakwell in the 3–2 win during 1948/49. Despite first seeing the light of day in view of the sacred football marshes of Hackney, Dick took up the game at a relatively mature age for a future Upton Park icon. It was when he and his family relocated to Dagenham that Dick began to develop his play, on Sunday mornings, as an inside forward with the local Becontree Athletic side.

He was invited to turn out for a few games for West Ham in the London Midweek League and for the 1932/33 schedule he joined the West London club, Park Royal, on a sort of informal loan arrangement. After he turned out for the Royals against West Ham at Upton Park, the Hammers brought him home to begin a relationship which was to encompass more than twenty years.

Walker made his first-team debut at right half, *v.* Burnley at the Boleyn Ground in August 1934 at the age of 21 (the first game of the season, which the Lancashire Clarets, despite a Vic Watson goal, won 2–1). Dick performed a range of defensive roles before finally taking over from the formidable Jim Barrett at centre half in 1936, at a point when the nature of this position was changing dramatically. Had the war not interrupted Dick's progress, it is highly likely that he would have played for his country and maybe threatened Jimmy Ruffell's appearances record for the Irons. If West Ham had been allowed to fulfil their promise and won promotion in the early 1940s, Walker would have been a strong candidate for an England spot. Ultimately this would have made him an attractive option for the management role at Upton Park, but of course, that is a massive line of 'ifs'.

Like Stan Foxall, Dick Walker was known for his humour and love of a practical joke. During his wartime leave he would play for West Ham. His listing in programmes was premised by speculation about his current rank, which seemed to be on a sliding scale between private and sergeant and back to private again. His time in the services was not without its 'drama', but he hadn't taken the usual footballer route of awaiting call-up and becoming a PTI; he volunteered for active service. While some writers tell how Walker saw action as an infantryman in North Africa and Italy, where his bravery was recognised in dispatches, the Hammers programmes of the time record Dick being a paratrooper. As a footballer he represented the Army in the Middle East and played for West Ham 24 times in the war years up to 1945. In 1945/46, in the League South, Walker turned out on 44 occasions. After the war, Dick was elected by his fellow players as captain of the West Ham side following the retirement of Charlie Bicknall.

It must have been a melancholy end to his first-team career when Walker made his final appearance in the Second Division (*v.* Plymouth Argyle, 18 February 1953). The lowest crowd of the season at Upton Park watched Dick and the rest of the Irons lose 1–0, but the centre half turned in his normal impeccable performance, earning the respect of each of the 8,000 Upton Park stalwarts who had turned up to cheer Dick Walker into the sunset of his career.

Walker's testimonial on 11 October 1957 was against Sparta Rotterdam. West Ham won 5–0; Dick completed his first and final hat-trick in claret and blue as Vic Keeble made his scoring debut.

Dick Walker once said:

> ... the idea of West Ham being more interested in playing attractive football than winning is rubbish. Winning is what managers, players and supporters all want. The only difference is that West Ham wouldn't stand for winning by kicking people ... it wasn't 'win at all costs' but no one went out to lose; no one liked getting beat and if you could avoid that you would!

The end of Dick Walker's career was sad and perhaps unjust. When Ted Fenton returned to Upton Park he had to face the problem of all new managers – how to assert his authority over players who had grown accustomed to the previous regime. Dick Walker, the captain and probably the most popular player at the club, was the first to have problems with Fenton. Walker's description of the situation is simple: 'I didn't like him and he didn't like me.' It was a clash between, in some ways, very similar men. Walker saw Fenton's actions as 'A matter of taking over from somebody popular and wanting to show you're in charge.' However, Walker's physical power was reflected in his mental strength. In his time at Upton Park he had become an icon and someone whom players and supporters looked up to. Walker was above all an honest man. Eric Parsons, who played for West Ham in 1943 and much of the 1950s, told me: 'If you were good, or had a good game, Dick would tell you so … if you were crap, he'd tell you that too.'

Walker once remarked:

> The club put pressure on players after the war to save money and buy houses, but it had little effect … other players didn't think or talk about the future. It was the times. Most people got a job and did it … we didn't think a lot about money; we were doing a lot better than most people we knew.

Walker and Fenton were never going to find a way to co-exist, and for Dick by 1957 Ted 'had made it unpleasant for me long enough. It was finally time to go.' West Ham didn't renew Dick's contract at the end of the season. The club offered him a job 'to attend to the players' boots' at £4 a week – something less than 25 per cent of his playing wages. As the new season started, the former club skipper was doing the job he had done as a groundstaff boy a quarter-of-a-century previously. Again, Tommy Dixon, a post-war stalwart of the West Ham side, recollected:

> Dick used to stud my boots for half-a-crown [about 13p]. He'd ask if I wanted them ordinary or deluxe, so I went for deluxe. That meant he'd paint the tips white!

Following his testimonial match against Sparta of Rotterdam, Walker became a scout with Spurs, a role he played for many years. He was a popular professional, respected by players and fans alike, a bit like Julian Dicks in another era. As Tommy Dixon remembered, 'You would walk round Plaistow and Poplar with Dicky and go in a pub. All the people would say "Hiya, Dick!"' The Boleyn crowd adored Walker; he would make jokes with people in the infamous 'Chicken Run', discuss the game with them and even, usually at Christmas time, take it on himself to conduct them.

Maybe it was the general esteem and regard that Walker inspired that made Fenton anxious about him. The former captain and centre half would have been a popular choice as manager, but that would be a bit like Malcolm Allison or Julian Dicks taking over from Ron Greenwood or Alan Pardew.

It may be a bit harsh to judge actions from today's standpoint. What seems like injustice now, may well have appeared to be generous over eighty years ago. Walker saw himself as being well treated: 'After all, they even gave me three benefits.' Former players who fell on hard times were occasionally helped, although rather than being given money they were allowed to sell programmes or chocolates at the ground.

For example, Jim Barrett had been ill and unemployed for many months when his situation became known to friends and supporters. One of them wrote to West Ham in January 1956, asking the club to hold a collection before a match to raise funds for Barrett. For years, West Ham had allowed charitable organisations to raise money at certain matches, but that ended in 1951 when the club limited charitable activity to pre-season practice matches. The board's reply to the request reminded the writer of the club's policy about collections and added, 'We have helped Barrett on many occasions and we're still trying to help him.' The admission that the club had been helping Barrett was unusual, as West Ham preferred to keep its charitable acts confidential, looking to avoid embarrassment to the recipient. At the same time, the club would not have wished to encourage other ex-employees to look to their former employer for assistance.

Walker represented, perhaps more than any other player, the traditional nature of West Ham as a football club. He came to Upton Park soon after the Hammers fell out of the top flight of the game. His popularity was not instant: filling the boots of Jim Barrett, a massively revered player amongst both pros and supporters, meant that for years he was obliged to play through both media and the crowd's demands for a return of 'Big Jim'. Malcolm Allison had to deal with a similar situation when he moved into Walker's role.

Dick did not exude skill; he admitted, 'I couldn't play, but I could stop those that would. West Ham was a hard club.' This casts doubt on claims that West Ham have always looked to play a dexterous and stylish game; certainly before the war, the Hammers were known more as a tough and uncompromising outfit. That said, Walker exemplified the unique character of West Ham, and how Upton Park was an inimitable arena in football. Walker gave his all in every game, and it is this that finally won the supporters over, together with his often self-deprecating sense of fun. But never was his light-heartedness seen to compromise his commitment. This was clear to any opposition that faced him or the teams he led.

Walker embodied the requirement of East London life to put in hard graft for what was needed or wanted. In many ways his penchant for comedy was a cushion against the difficulty of existence that he had known at first hand and understood to be the lot of others. He personified the Cockney confidence and concomitant 'cheek' so resented by those from other British cities. He brought this into his game and infected the team with a similar spirit, and this made the Hammers a singular entity in the grey days of football, reflecting their locality and their people.

Walker came to Upton Park because he saw it as an opportunity to draw a wage for playing. At that juncture he probably would have played for anyone who paid him. Dick hadn't seen a West Ham game home or away; in fact, he hadn't attended any professional games. As he was to relate, 'The first [professional] football match I ever saw, I was in.' His older brother supported Spurs, so Dick had only a very vague knowledge about West Ham and no particular affection for the club.

The backdrop to Walker's childhood years was a massive, newly built Dagenham council estate; a sprawling but isolated location. It was not a hotbed of football support, although the game was played widely. When, at 13 years of age, Dick was selected to represent the district, his most profound obstacle was purchasing a pair of boots. He paid 3*s* (15p) for his first pair, which by removing the studs doubled up as his everyday footwear. Dick's sisters were in work but his father was unemployed and unable to apply for any benefits because as far as the authorities were concerned the family, via his sisters, was bringing in money. For Walker, avoiding the pangs of hunger required 'scrounging a bit', while cold evenings and mornings caused him to 'nick a bit of wood from a construction site to use in the fire'. This wasn't poverty in the context of the times; this was 'getting by', which involved struggle.

The young Walker was picked by West Ham playing Sunday football. The telegram inviting him to attend an 'A' team match *v.* Arsenal was delivered to him at the labour exchange.

Following his initial appearance with West Ham, Walker was inducted into the sharper practices of professionalism. He was instructed to go to a shop in Shepherd's Bush, the owner of which ran an amateur football team (this was the Park Royal connection). To hold on to amateur status but draw an income, Walker was found work as an electrician's mate, although he was to confess, 'I didn't know how to change a light bulb.' He hardly had time to learn either, as from that point Walker and other team members 'trained like professionals', as he put it.

Park Royal were a successful side, winning most of what was available to them, giving Walker a showcase for his abilities. Subsequently, he was selected for a side to play in Paris. He recollected he got 'terrific money – £4 or £5 a week in 1933 made me the richest man on our street'.

The following year Walker was of an age to turn professional with West Ham. This was quite a leap from playing for Park Royal. Unable as he was to hold on to a first-team place, a drop in wages followed (£4 instead of £5). But that was far better than the dole or returning to his previous work as a barman. This said, by this point money was not his only motivation:

> I loved playing football ... and there were other things. I moved back with my mother. I might not have been very well known yet for my football, but we were famous because we were paying the rent.

A couple of years later, back in the Hammers first team, he thrived on the notoriety that came with the job. He told that he:

> ... knew what fame was when bus conductors wouldn't take a fare and people would start to talk to me in pubs. It was like having people put out flags on the street when I walked down. I always wanted to stop and talk to them.

Walker married and moved to the more select Chadwell Heath district of Essex. In his words, it was 'a little posher – it had curtains on the windows'.

Walker came to Upton Park during the years of the Great Depression. People were coming to East London in their droves looking for work at a time when there was little work to be had. Make no mistake, as captain of West Ham, Walker had 'made it'.

A transitional character in the history of West Ham United, Walker was around Upton Park to see a new approach to football and the effective reinvention of the club. This was largely ushered in by Malcolm Allison, brought to the Boleyn Ground from Charlton for a £7,000 fee. His passion for success, grasp of the game and ability to drive and motivate others was really the exact opposite of the conventional West Ham player. Allison had no time for the club's principles or what he saw as an outdated culture, or players who were not prepared to commit to his way of doing things. Errors were not 'one of those things' in Allison's eyes; they were the result of carelessness. The perspective of the crowd and the management were of no import to him. Allison would analyse the game with a select group of fellow players and move from that point. This attitude certainly lifted the collective performance of the team. The paying public often found him enigmatic; Allison was both admired and reviled because while, his commitment and leadership qualities were evident, his arrogance was a stranger in terms of what supporters recognised as proper deportment for a footballer. The latter was made flesh by Dick Walker.

When Walker's career neared its end and he was no longer an automatic choice, he switched his attention to helping the younger players with the same enthusiasm he had shown for the game. After his final first-team appearance in 1953, it was another four years before he hung up his boots, completing over 200 appearances for the reserves and 'A' team. His final appearance in a West Ham shirt was in 1957.

Walker's later life was not happy. He was beset with poor health that required him to spend long spells in hospital. Tom Dixon recalled, 'They didn't treat Dick Walker too well. He died a tramp, so they tell me. Sad, sad.' Walker's death, in February 1988 at the age of 75, did indeed represent a sad demise for a man who had helped so many young players make their way in the game.

The end of Dick Walker's career with West Ham marked a transition at the club. As the old West Ham captain left the field for the final time, he closed an era. The man who came in to take his position and leadership role, Malcolm Allison, ushered in a new dawn.

TWENTY-FOUR

CROMPTON

No one won the last war,
and no one will win the next war.

Eleanor Roosevelt, The Wisdom of Eleanor Roosevelt

Perhaps the biggest individual asset Blackburn Rovers had, and so the most potent threat to West Ham's ambitions, going into the Football League War Cup Final at Wembley in 1940 was their manager, Bob Crompton. He was a giant of the first half of football history, probably one of the best players on earth in his day, remaining arguably the finest performer the blue and whites have ever fielded, taking context into consideration. In all honesty, for all my personal bias, West Ham had nothing to match him. Ernie Gregory told me:

> Crompton was the best defender anyone had seen. But he was also a thinker. I think, in his time, there was no one who could read the game in the way he could. He was one of the best at that ever!

Bob was born in Blackburn on 26 September 1879, the third of four sons to Robert and Alice (née Utley). At this time the Crompton family lived at No. 1 Harwood Street, Blackburn. The young Bob attended Moss Street Boarding School and Moss Street Higher School. His father was a pub landlord. By 1891 the family had moved to No. 148 Harwood Street: the Rose and Thistle Inn.

In September 1896 Bob moved from Blackburn Trinity to First Division Rovers as an amateur. He made his debut for Rovers on 10 April 1897 at Stoke City. He was 17, playing at centre half, and for many years remained the youngest player to take that role in the Blackburn first team. Three games on, Bob was playing at left-back, but he was ultimately to settle at right-back. In 1898, after gaining his plumbing indentures, he signed professional.

Bob started his working life as an apprentice plumber. He was also a keen swimmer and water polo player. But in 1891 his occupation was listed as 'assistant farmer'. A decade on, he was still living with his parents at the Rose and Throstle Inn, along with his older brother, his wife Ada (née Ingham) and their son. Bob and Ada had married in September 1901.

Looking to extend his income independently of football, Bob became a partner in a firm of plumbers, patenting a number of significant innovations in the trade. Throughout his life rumour had it that these inventions had made him rich. While he consistently claimed that the stories were exaggerated, he owned a car in an era when few people did; he was said to be the first footballer to own one. Bob also had a business partnership with his Rovers teammate, Billy Davies, the Welsh international centre forward, in a motor engineering concern.

Renowned for the force and skill of his shoulder charge, and a natural leader, Bob never made less than sure that his players adhered to his own high principles in terms of fair play, and he won most of the honours which the game had to offer during the era in which he played. He skippered the club for two championship wins (1912 and 1914). Alongside Arthur Cowell, George Chapman and goalkeeper Jimmy Ashcroft, Bob was the fulcrum and leader of this remarkable team.

By 1911 Bob was also a publican, living at No. 185 Audley Range in Blackburn. He and Ada had four children: Harry, Robert, Alice and Wilfred (another child had died young).

A private man, Bob remained detached from playing colleagues, but he had authority and commanded the respect of those who played under his captaincy. A gifted footballer, he was possessed of aerial power, rarely beaten in a jump, while being an accurate passer of the ball. Bob was also capable of a legendary, cannon-like kick.

Although he made a couple of appearances in the 1919/20 season, the First World War was the terminus of Bob's playing career, but in 1921 he was invited to take up a position as a director at Ewood Park. Five years later he was appointed 'honorary' manager and started to create a side around leading players like Henry Healless, Jack Roscamp and the former West Ham star Syd Puddefoot.

Bob was well liked by the Blackburn crowd, who recognised the man as the finest player that the Riversiders had ever produced. The win against Huddersfield Town in the FA Cup Final of 1928 added to Bob's storied status. Huddersfield and been hot favourites for the Cup and this, together with Bob achieving the one honour he never managed as a player (having been on the losing side in the final of 1912), boosted the club's morale and status.

This said, Bob Crompton's despotic approach to management started to provoke turbulence among the players. Like Malcolm Allison in a later era, Bob had a definite vision of how he thought football should be played and how players needed to conduct themselves, on and off the field. While he was ready to give ear to others, he was no compromiser. The situation boiled over during February 1931 when the chairman received a letter from the players relating to grievances against Bob. While still a director, Bob instantly withdrew from his duties as manager. In March 1931 the annual meeting of the club was convened. Astonishingly, there was no mention of the dispute involving Crompton, but after a vote, he failed to be re-elected to the board. At a stroke, a thirty-four-year relationship was ended and Bob took a punt at being Bournemouth's manager.

Subsequently, Rovers were relegated to the Second Division for the first time in their history. Local newspapers that had been critical of Bob Crompton's departure campaigned for his reinstatement and in March 1938, with the club floundering close to the basement of Division Two, Bob was approached by the board. He retook charge on 2 April 1938, and Blackburn avoided a second relegation, this time to the Third Division North.

Lauded as the club's redeemer, in May 1938 Crompton was officially appointed the Blackburn manager, and started to assemble a side to resuscitate the club. During the spring of 1939 Rovers had ensured their return to the First Division as champions of the Second.

In the first years of the Second World War, Blackburn played in the North-West Regional League. On 15 March 1941 Bob collapsed with a heart attack during a match at Ewood Park (a 3–2 victory *v.* Burnley). He died that evening at No. 24 Eldon Road, Blackburn. Blackburn had lost their most outstanding figure ever, and the last link with Rovers' glorious history. His funeral, at St John's, Blackburn, was attended by the mayor, civic leaders and more than a hundred representatives of the press, the football authorities, other clubs and businessmen.

Crompton was an England international player for more than a decade. He was first selected to represent his country on 3 March 1902, playing at right-back; a goalless draw *v.* Wales at The Racecourse Ground, Wrexham. He gained 41 caps up to 1912, 22 as skipper, a role he took as a 24-year-old. There was no younger England captain until Billy Wright in 1952. This distinction was achieved on 13 March 1911, and before the record-breaking match against Wales, Bob was awarded an enlarged framed photographic self-portrait (a big 'selfie'). He scored just 1 goal for his country; sadly an own goal. England had won 27 of the games Bob was involved in and drawn 8, scoring 115 goals and conceding just 39 – a 76 per cent success rate.

It was also Wright who surpassed Bob's record number of caps; however, it has to be remembered that when Bob was playing, England international matches were mostly confined to Home International Championship games. Playing consistently in the England side today, over the same period of time that Bob was called to his country's cause, would mean a collection of around 120 caps.

Crompton played alongside one of West Ham's greatest. In 1913 Lawrence Cotton, Rovers' chairman, broke the British transfer record by buying Danny Shea from West Ham United for £2,000. Shea hit 12 goals but Rovers managed only fifth place that season.

In the four League campaigns running up to the First World War, Blackburn came first, fifth, first and third in the top flight of English football. At this point in time there was no greater force in football and it was led by Bob Crompton.

Apart some wartime games for Blackpool, while serving as PTI in the First World War, Bob was a one-club man, playing 529 Football League games for Rovers between 1896/97 and 1919/1920, over 600 in all, a feat bettered only in the Ewood chronicles by Ronnie Clayton and Derek Fazackerley.

During the Great War, looking forward to Bob's Blackpool coming to Anfield, the *Liverpool Echo* expressed the general excitement about the appearance of the now 38-year-old legend. It told of how Bob invariably drew the crowds, and savoured the prospect of his impending battle with Fred Pagman, the Liverpool striker:

> ... to-morrow a piece of football worth going a long way to see will be witnessed at Anfield. Pagnam will need to dribble cleverly to get past a man of Crompton's solidity, and there may be a charging bout which will be rousing. The crowd loves to see healthy charging between men of Crompton and Pagnam's build, and to-morrow's game will doubtless produce some big cheers.

Nicknamed 'Mr Blackburn Rovers', Bob was the first professional England captain at a time when it was believed that only amateurs should be bestowed this honour and responsibility. But as an outstanding tactician, no one was better placed to lead the side.

In February 2013 one of Bob's purple velvet England caps (embroidered with the England badge and 1907 date) was auctioned at Bonhams for £1,750 – probably more than Bob ever earned from football.

Charlie Buchan, who played with Crompton for England in 1913, claimed in his autobiography that 'Crompton was undoubtedly the outstanding fullback of his time. A commanding personality, he was the best kicker of a ball I ever ran across.' Bob had formidable physique but he was never to allow his strength to dominate his play; he was amazingly quick on the turn. But as a sporting figure, he was well respected as a gentleman of the game.

For West Ham, his mere presence at Wembley must have been intimidating. According to Eddie Chapman, 'Bob Crompton was one of those men who had charisma; even in a stadium full of people he stood out. He was a force in his own right.'

TWENTY-FIVE

THE 1940 FOOTBALL LEAGUE WAR CUP FINAL

The war? What you going to do about the war?
You just got on with it!

Ernie Gregory

By the time the 1940 Football League War Cup Final took place, the Phoney War had come to an end. On 10 May 1940, Adolf Hitler launched his Western Offensive and invaded France. The game was played out just a few days after the historic and remarkable events on the beaches of Dunkirk.

When West Ham United appeared at Wembley they looked like a force to be reckoned with: Herman Conway, in goal, had Charlie Bicknell, Charlie Walker, Ted Fenton and Dick Walker in front of him. However, with Sam Small, George Foreman, Archie Macaulay, Len Goulden, Stan Foxall and Joe Cockroft (an amazingly consistent wing half) the East Londoners appeared to have come prepared to attack.

The War Cup Final brought West Ham face-to-face with a strong Blackburn side. Rovers were a long-established northern club, founded in 1875. They had won the Cup five times in the 1880s and 1890s. Alfred Wainwright, later famous for his guide-books to the Lakeland fells, was a co-founder and chairman of the

Blackburn Rovers Supporters Club. He came down by coach for the final.

Herman Conway, having been released by West Ham at the end of 1938/39, was unattached at the time of the final, so officially he was a guest, but in practice both sides named teams that were genuinely attached to the respective clubs. The team that took the field to oppose Blackburn on that 8 June 1940 could easily be accepted as an authentic West Ham XI. Every player, including Conway, had long stints of recent first-team duty. The match programme listed five of the Hammers team as working in an aircraft factory.

It was originally intended to play an extra half an hour in the event of a draw at 90 minutes, but this was altered to 20 minutes. If there was still a stalemate at that stage, then the match would continue until one team scored and thereby ended the match. It would have been the first ever 'golden goal' in a major tournament final.

Wembley was allowed a capacity of only 50,000, which made the atmosphere a bit different from the Hammers' first visit in 1923 when around a quarter of a million people had effectively wrecked the new Wembley Stadium (see Belton 2006). The crowd of 42,399 paid either 1*s* (5p) or 2*s* (10p) to stand on the terraces. Better seats ranged in price from 3*s* (15p) to 10*s* 6*d* (52.5p). The audience for the wartime final were mostly East Enders. But most attending that day were deeply affected by the sight of the survivors from the British Expeditionary Force, who had their own seating area. They received a great ovation. Scores of them still carried their wounds. Seeing them dressed in their hospital uniforms, blue jackets, white shirts and blood-red ties, there were those in the crowd who may have felt ashamed that they were safe at Wembley when the enemy were just a few dozen miles away across the sea.

Although it was not an 'official' cup final, being at Wembley was a satisfying experience for those who attended, players and fans, but it also carried the flavour of a wartime match. This was something that is hard for us to imagine today; the exuberance of a cup final, tempered by a background of war, and a consciousness that the next event under the twin towers could well happen in the shadow of occupation. 'Abide With Me' was very special on this occasion. Britain, an island surrounded and under siege, needed all the help it could get. Never had the opening verse of the hymn been so relevant:

Abide with me; fast falls the eventide;
The darkness deepens; Lord, with me abide;
When other helpers fail and comforts flee,
Help of the helpless, oh, abide with me.

After the First Lord of the Admiralty, Mr Albert Victor Alexander (1st Earl of Hillsborough and Baron of Western-Super-Mare to be) met both teams, the Band of the Irish Guards played the national anthem followed by the 'Marseillaise', in honour of the fight the French had put up against the onslaught of Nazi Germany.

Mr Dutton, the referee, from Warwick, awarded Rovers a corner in the first minute that signalled the start of a pressurised opening period for West Ham. But having weathered the early storm, the Hammers came close to taking the lead by way of Foxall. This was followed by a good effort from Foreman that brought the very best out of munitions worker Barron, the Blackburn keeper, who was playing as if he was old Blighty's last line of defence against the Hun.

For all this, the Hammers' 'down-the-middle' tactic was being thwarted by the Riversiders' precise use of the offside trap. However, West Ham's flexible attack was able to respond. The Irons switched to wing offensives. It was this that delivered Stan Foxall's 34th-minute strike; it was he who ignited the move. Goulden and Foreman, with notable finesse and a deal of cunning, moved the play into Rovers' box, the speed and guile of the move leaving Rovers bereft of a response. Barron, seemingly mesmerised by the complexity of the West Ham attack plan, could only watch as Foxall hung over the ball. The claret-and-blue executioner focused on the goal for a fraction of a second, which to Barron must have felt like an age of scrutiny. The shot came in like a meteorite. The Rovers keeper pulled a parry from the depths of the protective instincts that inhabit the souls of those who defend the net, but it was only deflected to the feet of ambulance builder Small. Sammy, from close range, made no mistake, taking the goal like a Russian harpooner might once have taken a whale. As is the way with all momentous goals, there was a small droplet of silence before Wembley roared and engulfed the moment in sound.

The second half saw skipper and key defender Charlie Bicknell, together with the pivotal Len Goulden, play on with injuries. This, coupled with the verdant Wembley surface and the break-neck speed of the game, obliged the Hammers to temper their more adventurous instincts and at points, according to Dick Walker, the Irons 'struggled a bit'.

The game went backwards and forwards with Blackburn outside left Billy Guest never giving up the effort to pressurise the Hammers' defence. However, following the goal Goulden and Macaulay dominated the midfield, ably supported by the Fenton/Cockroft partnership at the heart of the Irons' defence. Thus, for the most part, West Ham seemed to be in control.

The First Lord of the Admiralty was back in action (the man was indomitable) to present the players with their medals (the award of a trophy and medals for the finalists was due to the relaxation of earlier decisions in this respect), and handed the Cup to Charlie Bicknell. For the first time the Irons paraded victorious around the Wembley turf. Ted Fenton was to recall in his book that, although the competition was considered worth winning:

> ... victory was not followed by the customary high jinx ... Austerity was the watchword everywhere ... The Wembley crowd was restricted in numbers by the police and after the game we players quietly split up and went straight back

> to our service units ... it was hilarious as a wet Sunday in Cardiff. But then the rest of the world wasn't exactly having a fancy-dress ball.

However, in Denis Signy's *The West Ham United Football Book* of 1968, Dick Walker recollected:

> Most of the lads had an informal cup winning reception in the Boleyn Pub near the ground. We got back there in time to get in a few pints before closing time. I remember my medal going round and round the public bar.

After the match, the Blackburn players got together at the Great Northern Hotel, Kings Cross, for a celebratory banquet. That would be the final gathering of the 1938/39 championship-winning side as those proud, strong and talented men went their separate way into the war years.

The War Cup victory against top-flight Blackburn Rovers was accomplished by the side that Charlie Paynter regarded as the best of his career at West Ham. It was the club's first major trophy. Goulden and Macaulay were the leaders. For many players it was their last chance for a victory of national note and the culmination of long careers at West Ham United. However, Ted Fenton and Dick Walker both made significant post-war contributions to the club. Other team members, who were not on the pitch at Wembley due to wartime duties and commitments, included Eddie Chapman and Ernie Gregory. The latter explained:

> We'd all joined the TA before the war, they thought that it would encourage other lads to do the same if we did. So we were called up straight away when it started. Archie Macaulay got away to play in the final and the rest of us didn't even know what the score was until he got back to the unit again.

The war in general and the Dunkirk evacuation in particular meant that West Ham's triumph did not have the impact it deserved outside the team's dockland home. The *West Ham Mail* gave a sober match report:

> A solitary goal scored after 34 minutes gave West Ham United a victory which they just deserved in the Football League War Cup at Wembley Stadium on Saturday evening. Summed up briefly: The Hammers had the better of Blackburn in the first period and scored once while Rovers dominated the second period without success. It was neither a poor game or a great match. It was purely and simply a battle between two grand defences – probably the best in the country.

The *Stratford Express* reported the match with sporting grace and a certain amount of solemnity that reflect the context and time:

> B.E.F. See Hammers Win
> Cup Comes to Boleyn
> Blackburn's Great Effort
> West Ham United 1, Blackburn Rovers 0

> Members of the evacuated BEF, many of them in hospital blue and white, were among the 43,000 spectators who saw West Ham United win the Football League War Cup Final at Wembley on Saturday by the only goal of the match. The last time the Hammers were at the Stadium was in 1923, when they took part in that first sensational final there for the FA Cup and were beaten by Bolton Wanderers by 2 goals to none. There was nothing sensational about the substitute final on Saturday, and perhaps the most remarkable thing about it was that, despite the bitter times, the intimate little

ceremonies that always provide interest for the spectators were carried through as usual. There was the presentation of the members of the teams to the guest of honour – on this occasion Mr A.V. Alexander, the First Lord of the Admiralty – the playing and singing of the National Anthem with the addition this time of that of our French Allies, and finally the parade of the players to the Royal box for the presentation of the trophy and medals by Mr Alexander. The only difference from the usual atmosphere was the prolonged cheers that greeted the B.E.F. party when they entered the arena and took seats provided for them.

Battling Defence

In the match itself there was a keen and hard struggle, with the Hammers defending grimly in the closing stages to hold on to the slender advantage they had gained in the first half. For nearly half an hour their defence battled against determined opponents, who threw everything into attack on the principle that they had everything to gain and nothing to lose, but an equally determined set of defenders ultimately emerged victorious. In this struggle two Hammers, named Walker, one Richard and the other Charles, played a great part for their side, and the former, at centre half, was the outstanding defender of the match. It was seldom that Weddle, the Rovers centre forward, could escape his attentions.

Taking the match as a whole there was little to choose between the teams. West Ham held the balance of attack in the first half, and deserved their lead at the interval, but later in the play it certainly appeared that the Rovers would gain the equalizer as the result of their efforts. That they failed was a tribute to the steadiness and strength of the Hammers' defence, despite the fact that Bicknell, the captain, felt the weakness of an injured knee practically throughout. That goal scored by Small after 35 minutes proved to be the all-important one.

Centre Forwards

West Ham's attack, Macaulay and Goulden, was supported by two grand attacking wing halves in Fenton and Cockroft, but after a while they started to tire and the long swinging movements of the Rovers' front line began to tell. Weddle tried hard to force a passage through the middle, but he had not the support from his inside wingers that Foreman had from Macaulay and Goulden, and the most danger to the West Ham goal came from the two wingers, Rogers and guest. The Rovers, like the Hammers, had their scoring chances, but there were not many for either side, a tribute to the fine covering work by both sets of defenders. Pryde, the Blackburn centre half, ran R. Walker very close for chief honours in defensive play.

The early stages of the game were marked by some fine passing movements between West Ham's three inside forwards, but although they were several times within shooting distance, something generally went wrong at the last moment. The first real chance fell to the Rovers when Weddle, running out on the right wing, got across a good centre, but the ball travelled too fast for Guest, who could only make a wild lunge, and it slid from his foot many yards wide of the goal. Then a series of attacks by West Ham resulted in Barron saving from Foxall, but in other efforts Foreman, Goulden and Macaulay were all wide of the mark with shots. The clever footwork of Macaulay and Goulden frequently opened the way for attacks, and from one of these a centre by Foxall was headed a few inches on the wrong side of the goal by Foreman.

The Winning Goal

When West Ham scored 10 minutes before the interval, the Rovers' defence was badly at fault. An excellent bit of dribbling by Goulden, and a pass to Foxall on the wing, looked like being wasted as the winger stood still with the ball. The defence, however, held off, and allowed him to 'fiddle' with it until he was able to return it to the unmarked Goulden. The latter quickly pushed the ball through to Foreman, who sent in an admirable shot. Barron made an equally smart save, but the ball ran out to Small, who closed in and crashed it into the net before the goalkeeper could recover. Immediately after, the Hammers' goal had a remarkable escape, when Conway came out of goal to meet a long free kick by Hough, and missed the ball, which passed a few inches wide of the empty net. Shots by Foreman and Macaulay were saved by Barron just before the interval.

Blackburn's swift attacks in the early part of the second half looked like carrying all before them, and a great rising shot by Clarke was cleverly saved by Conway. Butt was just too high with a header, and Rogers sent over from a centre by Guest. The Hammers' defenders stood up well to the constant attacks of the Rovers, in which the wing halves joined as extra forwards. Once Weddle was stopped only by a prompt tackle by R. Walker, and later on Conway brought off a fine save from Rogers. An injury to Goulden had rather put the Hammers' attack out of gear, although Macaulay made two spirited efforts, Blackburn crowded all their strength into attack in the last few minutes in an effort to force extra time, and in the last minute Conway fisted away a shot from Guest.

West Ham: Conway; Bicknell, Walker, C; Fenton, Walker, R., Cockroft; Small, Macaulay, Foreman, Goulden, Foxall.

Blackburn: Barron; Hough, Crook; Whiteside, Pryde, Chivers; Rogers, Butt, Weddle, Clarke, Guest.

To their credit Rovers had managed to field a team composed entirely of Blackburn-registered players.

Wembley and West Ham's War Cup victory was the culmination of what had been an interesting season, which had taken place in an odd and frightening time. It had, as much as anything else, provided a relief from national tension, but in more ways than one it was to be a false dawn. Just two days later, on 10 June 1940, Italy declared war on France and Britain.

Thus, the winning of their first (and last) major wartime trophy coincided with Britain's darkest hour. It was as if night had closed in with no certainty of a dawn to follow it. Before the War Cup Final there had been talk of football closing down for the duration of the conflict, but the miracle of evacuation from Europe's beaches helped to revive in a stunned populace the realisation of how close they had been to a catastrophe. The subsequent 'Dunkirk Spirit' flourished as a reflection of this 'victory in defeat', even after everyone's senses were restored. Poetically, this is very much like following West Ham.

CLARET AND BLUE ARMY

A poignant example of what I mean by this was manifested in the FA Cup semi-final defeat at Villa Park in April 1991. This exposed the soul of the Irons, transforming a time and a situation that would have been accepted as hopeless by many, into a beautiful and glorious celebration of the progeny of the Blitz, evoking an ancestral spirit wrought in the fire of Nazi bombs and the unremitting, unforgiving shipyard furnaces that roared day and night on the banks of the Victorian Thames.

West Ham were thrashed 4–0 by Nottingham Forest in a match that was over as a contest in the opening minutes after referee Keith Hackett sent off Tony Gale, a pivotal player in the Irons' defence. What seemed a harsh decision in effect put the encounter beyond the reach of the East London side from the Second

Division. Forest were then in the top flight of the English game, under the leadership of Brian Clough, and were the League Cup winners of 1990. For all that, the West Ham supporters who had made the trip to the midlands (I was one of their number) not only took it all in their stride, but made a carnival out of the disaster with an unparalleled expression of loyalty hardly seen even in the most passionately supported of games.

Throughout the half-time break and the whole of the second half, 20,000 claret-and-blue-clad Cockneys chanted 'Billy Bonds' claret and blue army' (Bonds was at that point manager of the Irons) with a stirring intensity and volume, many doing a sort of rain dance to the rhythm as the hapless Hammers were being overrun and battered; we never wavered, the chant did not falter or alter as Forest's fourth went in – it made no difference at all, we just went on and on; 'Billy Bonds' claret and blue army'.

As the intonation of the chant seeped into the entire atmosphere of the stadium, the Hammers players begun to take long gazes into the heart of the crowd, incredulous at the will and the endurance of the hymn. Echoes melded with the chaotic descant that had been generated. As the word 'army' ended, it was shadowed by a repeat of the word coming out of the ether until there seemed to be no separation between the phases; 'Billy Bonds' claret and blue army, army. Billy Bonds' claret and blue army, army …'

We were the last of the Mohicans; we were 'Men of Harlech' facing the massed Zulu troops. It was a mantra of inner power, the external was irrelevant. 'We-ness' prevailed; that which was 'us' overcame the rest of reality. The game itself had transformed into something symbolic; a means to show the defiance of the East London soul and our total self-sufficiency as a community. 'Billy Bonds' claret and blue army, army.'

It reminded me of a story I once read about a Confederate military band that were surrounded by a crack Union regiment in the American Civil War. The Union commander sent a messenger offering to take the surrender of the band; the answer was a passionate rendition of 'The Yellow Rose of Texas'. 'Billy Bonds' claret and blue army, army'.

After the game hundreds of fans took to the pitch to make merry. Most were West Ham supporters. Ian Bishop, the Irons captain that day, looked bewildered as the travelling Hammers carried him shoulder high off the field in front of the massed ranks of Billy Bonds' still-chanting claret and blue army. 'Billy Bonds' claret and blue army, army, army, army!'

There are more than a few Hammers fans who were around at that time who see that bright Birmingham afternoon when Villa Park became the site of the commodious, sacred East London ritual of joyous insubordination, the 'knees-up', as the moment when we demonstrated that we were seemingly ready to put up with anything. But do not mistake defiance for compliance and solidarity for stupidity.

We didn't celebrate defeat that day; we were demonstrating that we could not be defeated. No one has ever really beaten West Ham; not *the* West Ham; those who *are* the club and the area. These people were not beaten by the starvation brought by Victorian capitalism and being whipped into the docks as industrial slaves; they were not defeated by the Kaiser and the hell of the Western Front (the nickname given by the Germans to the British soldier had that telling Cockney ring; 'Tommy Atkins' was the warrior whom the enemy revered and respected). These people were not destroyed by the poverty of the Depression, but stood firmly, disallowing Mosley's Brown-shirted racists to walk through 'our manor', with another repeated chorus: 'They shall not pass!' Hitler, Goering (another little fat bloke!) and their Luftwaffe were met with a similar force of attitude. Despite the murder of tens of thousands of East Enders, the destruction by fire of homes and workplaces, the evil of fascism was resisted on the very streets. Thatcher's rape of the union protection which had long been looked to by those who have inhabited the Docklands as their one defence against the past did not overcome us. So, the idea that we can be defeated has always been ridiculous – the real tragedy might be that a generation of supporters will at some point fail to recognise this. This is one reason I write about West Ham; to keep the 'fuck you' flame flickering. BILLY BONDS' CLARET AND BLUE ARMY!

LIGHT AT THE START OF THE TUNNEL

Yet in 1940, for football as a whole the outlook seemed bleak. The nation was enveloped by her enemies. Invasion seemed imminent. It never happened, but the Battle of Britain did – a contest few might have bet on the RAF winning, but win it, alongside the people of London and Britain, they did.

The entire War Cup competition of 137 games, including replays and final, had been condensed into just over two months of 1940.

Eddie Chapman, who had been in the squad for the final against Blackburn Rovers, but was unable to play, said of the game:

> West Ham rose to the occasion. I think they looked fresher than Blackburn, but in the end it was a win of the new over the old. West Ham played in a more modern way and I think the West Ham players were slightly more experienced.

West Ham's oldest player in the final was the 35-year-old Charlie Bicknell. Archie Macaulay was the youngest; he would be 25 a month after the game. The average age of the team was 28. As a 35-year-old, Weddle was the oldest Rover. The 21-year-old Rogers was the baby of the Blackburn boys. Like the Hammers, the average age of the Riversiders was 28. In fact the combined age of the Irons was 311, while the sum of the Blackburn players' years was 310. So Eddie was right – there was *slightly* more experience in the West Ham side.

According to Ernie Gregory, the difference in the sides was Ted Fenton:

> Ted was interested in anything new. He'd try things out. He'd learnt a lot from other players as a PTI in the army. He asked a lot of questions and had a good memory. West Ham moved the ball about more in 1940 and that was Ted.

That said, it seemed Ernie thought the Hammers were probably overall the better side:

> But West Ham also had Len Goulden who could do that too. Play it on the ground. He wasn't a big feller but he could out-jump anyone. I think on the field him, Archie Macaulay, Stan Foxall and Ted Fenton made the difference. And it was hard to get past Dick Richards.

Relatively few guest players were deployed in the initial wartime season before West Ham's Football League War Cup campaign instigated something of a fixture pile-up that exposed the lack of depth in terms of playing staff. Two matches were planned for the week prior to the final at Wembley, which obliged Paynter to bring in guest players to cover the gaps and the only 'true' West Ham player to line up for the match *v.* Charlton on 5 June was Jim Barrett.

West Ham reached the War Cup Final by beating the combined opposition 22–11: Chelsea (3–2 and 2–0), Leicester City (1–1 and 3–0), Huddersfield Town (3–3 and 3–1), Birmingham City (4–2) and Fulham (3–2).

The final had gone ahead despite the fears that London would be bombed by the Luftwaffe; those who came to Wembley in their tens of thousands had decided to take something of a risk. For many the day marked their first – for some their only – winning glory in the game, although Archie Macaulay won his third major medal in his football career.

TWENTY-SIX

TRANSITION

At first there was just a rock. The rock was not a hammer, but it was a tool. The rock was eventually tied to a stick; then the hammer was born. But today, we don't hammer with rocks on sticks. Human beings do not just make tools. We improve and develop tools. This is one of the things that separate you from a crow, taking a stone in its beak and dropping it on an egg; something crows have done and not improved on for perhaps millions of years.

The main purpose of tools is to make them better and finding the tools to do this. Today, you don't have the skill, the knowhow, the tools to curve that ball; it seems impossible. The tools you have are not good enough. But then someone does what you thought was impossible. They found the means to make their tools up to the job. Humanity can do this.

This is the most valuable lesson for kids coming into our game; they can do what they thought or was told was impossible for them. They will hold on to that even when they are like me, too weak and old to even want to curl a ball. But do you know, I still take joy in seeing a young kid finding, making the tools to do it and eventually doing what they thought was impossible for them. Do you think we convince ourselves of our own limits sometimes?

Jimmy Andrews (West Ham United)

The season 1945/46 would be a term of transition but the Football League decided to stick with the regional format for the last time. Normal football, the kind interrupted by Hitler in 1939, would pick up the pieces on 31 August 1946. It already seemed an awfully long time since spectators had first been told what to do 'in the event of an air raid'.

As suggested by the idea of transition, the football authorities did not go directly back to the way of things prior to the war. The season of 1945/46 would be organised to give clubs a chance to adapt and normalise their affairs. Many players remained in the Services, and this would be the case long after hostilities ended, particularly for those who were stationed in the Far East.

Although there were a few modifications, the organisation of the season reflected what had gone before in the war years. The Division One and Two clubs that had commenced the 1939/40 season were grouped together and divided into North and South divisions at a point approximately between Stoke and Derby.

Newport County were the only club in the League South that West Ham had never met in a Football or Southern League competition. The Hammers' longest journey would be Plymouth and Swansea in the west and Nottingham and Derby in the north.

As was usual, teams designated 'Colours' and 'Blues' played public trials at Upton Park. The Blues were the club's likely reserve side for the season and Jack Wood was in the ranks of that XI. He had just got over a serious motor-bike accident. Charlie Walker was in the Colours team, the probable first team. Charlie had been serving in the Far East for the best part of the previous three years. He was playing alongside Dick Walker, who had been with the Parachute Regiment since September 1942.

Many supporters couldn't believe that just before the start of the 1945/46 campaign Len Goulden was sold to Chelsea. The fee of £4,500 was a huge amount of money for most people. The average wage of a bricklayer in London was 2*s* (10p) per hour, and a loaf of bread would cost you 8*d* (about 4p), but for the aficionados, doyens and denizens of Upton Park, Len's dozen years with the club had been sold cheaply. That said, he was probably past his peak and, a bit like Joe Cole when he moved to Stamford Bridge in 2003, he was never to play as well as he did with the Hammers. Len Goulden was at Stamford Bridge in time for the historic game *v.* Moscow Dynamo (played on 13 November) and Len scored the opening goal in the 3–3 draw. Tommy Lawton and Reg Williams were also on target.

West Ham's first game of the League South campaign took the team to St Andrew's, where a crowd of 30,000 saw a penalty from the boot of Charlie Bicknell beat Birmingham, who had no retort. This was followed by 4 consecutive Boleyn Ground matches resulting in just the one win. The Hammers were more roofless than ruthless as Upton Park continued to bear the scars of the V1 attack; West Ham's first home game *v.* Arsenal was referred to in the programme as 'the Roofless *v.* the Homeless'. The will and the money were in place to put the stadium back together, but this wasn't possible because of a shortage of skilled labour and the necessary materials.

Len Goulden was back at the Boleyn Ground on the first Saturday in October and it was odd to see him run out in the blue of Chelsea. Scoring twice, he helped his side to a 4–2 victory.

Seven days later, 45,000 went to Stamford Bridge to see their new striker denied and, with goals from Bicknell and Almeric Hall, the home side were defeated 2–1. Goulden was effectively taken out of the match in a second-half 'collision' with Norrie Corbett. Goulden had as good as run into a brick wall … an animated one.

In November 1945 a meeting of players from fifty-three clubs voted in favour of a strike; it took a lot of hard bargaining before the League agreed to compromise on the pre-war maximum of £8 a week – change was on its way. As with many workers, the conflict had given footballers a clearer picture of the worth of their services by way of war conditions.

The rebirth of the formal organisation of international football was heralded by the FA agreement with Stanley Rous that England should have a team manager. Walter Winterbottom was later to be given the job. It was not, however, agreed that he should be allowed to actually manage. The FA reformed its pre-war Selection Committee, and its new members insisted on touring the country and voting for the professionals who most accorded to their amateur standards; it was from among these individuals that the England team would be selected. The old guard seemed to have some fight left in it.

Derby County (on 17 November) put an end to a run of 5 unbeaten games when the Irons were systematically and totally destroyed at the Baseball Ground (5–1) and then beaten by the Rams at Upton Park (3–2), undone by the magic of Peter Doherty and sheer ability of Dally Duncan. Doherty had turned out for the Irons for a friendly *v.* Portsmouth in 1943.

Twenty-six goals over half-a-dozen games in December and January equated to entertainment galore from the Hammers. However, for everyone associated with West Ham, the 6–0 defeat of Arsenal at Upton Park on 5 January, as the FA Cup returned to the footballing schedule, was the game of the season, with Hall and Wood getting 2 apiece, and Foreman and Ken Bainbridge making up the half-dozen.

The Football Association, as a one-off, had organised the competition as two-legged ties. The Irons lost the away leg at White Hart Lane (Arsenal would not return to Highbury until the following season), but only by the 1 goal early on (from Horace Cumner), so went through to meet Chelsea.

Under the headline 'Blitzkrieg at Upton Park', the East London press was effusive:

> This 'first leg' in the third round tie of the FA Cup between these old rivals at Upton Park was without doubt the sensation

> of the day. The Arsenal were pulverised by a side that worked like a machine, with speed and accuracy allied with any amount of 'devil'. The Arsenal knew they were beaten at the end of half an hour. During that period the West Ham attack was devastating. Time after time it split the Arsenal defence wide open and scored 4 goals.
>
> The defenders had no answer to the Hammers Blitzkrieg and although the home forwards lost some of their effectiveness in the second half, they were still the masters and added 2 further totals. The score might have reached double figures so overwhelmed was the Arsenal defence, had it not been for the gallant display of Joy at centre half and Swindin in goal. These two and, in a lesser degree Scot, stood firmer than others in opposition to West Ham's sweeping raids, but their efforts were in vain.
>
> The teams on this momentous occasion were: West Ham United: Medhurst, Bicknell, Cater, Small, Walker, Fenton, Woodgate, Hall, Foreman, Wood, Bainbridge.
>
> Arsenal: Swindin, Scott, Wade, Nelson, Joy, Collett, O'Flanagan, Henley, Lewis, Drury, Bastin.

With 35,000 inside the Boleyn Ground, the gates had been closed. However, hundreds of people found free access through the bomb-damaged parameters of the ground. Bill (W.J.) Cearns, the chairman of the club, was to ask those who 'bunked in' to pay for their entrance retrospectively, saying that he would pass anything coughed up to East Ham Memorial Hospital (there had been a collection at the ground for the hospital before the tie with Arsenal). It is unclear if the dosh came flooding in.

On 26 January, West Ham dropped Ken Bainbridge in favour of the returning Archie Macaulay. There were 65,726 at Stamford Bridge, the biggest crowd of the fourth round of the Cup that term (the only Cup game to better this attendance that season was

Aston Villa *v.* Derby County on 2 March with a crowd of 76,500) and the largest attendance to watch a Hammers side since the first Wembley FA Cup Final of 1923. Indeed, so far that season way more than half-a-million people had watched West Ham play. This type of support was repeated all over the country. Sport, and it seemed football in particular, along with speedway, was experiencing a boom.

Len Goulden was not in the Chelsea side due to a bout of the flu. But it was only the Irons' defence that averted a goal avalanche. Machin got Chelsea's opener and late in the game Dick Spence made it 2–0, picking up on a cocky back-heel from the £110,000 man Tommy Lawton. Lawton was in blistering form but Dick Walker, for the most part, matched him on the ground and mastered him in the air.

In the return game at Upton Park, despite incessant attacks that had the Chelsea defence at sixes and sevens throughout the match, only 1 goal from Almeric Hall, laid on by Ken Bainbridge just before half-time, was produced. West Ham were eliminated.

For that match, on 30 January 1946, the 31,000 crowd were, through the lack of anything resembling shelter in the ground, pitted and doused by a torrential hailstorm. The pitch was also turned into a mud patch.

Goulden, although now flu-free, had his collarbone broken following a 'mishap' with the West Ham defence after 8 minutes. The local press reported:

> West Ham started like giant eaters and their 'game' seemed assured when Goulden left the field. They attacked desperately but the Chelsea backs weathered the storm and the perfidious minutes ticked steadily by as Hammers began the second half with tremendous determination. For a long period there was only one team in it. How the Chelsea goal escaped was a little short of miraculous but it was also a tribute to a very gallant defence.

> In a few minutes that remained Chelsea packed their goal and when the ball was occasionally transferred there was frequently the spectacle of Lawton being entirely on his own. The West Ham defence had an easy time and the attack failed to save the game.

It was on 9 February 1946, at Home Park, that George Foreman made his last appearance for the West Ham first team; he had made 207 wartime appearances for the Irons. He was bettered by other Hammers, but they had played for a couple of clubs – Len Goulden 178 for West Ham, 35 for Chelsea; Joe Cockroft 199 for Sheffield Wednesday, 19 for West Ham. Foreman had scored 212 goals during the hostilities, which placed him sixth in the list of wartime marksmen nationally. Len Goulden with 102 was the only other Iron to break the century mark. The hosts became the guests at the Boleyn Ground the following week, where Plymouth faced George's heir-apparent at centre forward: the 21-year-old Don Travis, who had signed as a professional with West Ham after being registered as an amateur with Blackpool. He had impressed in a trial *v.* Chelsea Reserves, hitting 4 goals in that Combination game. He repeated that feat against Argyle, so emulating the accomplishment of Billy Grassam, scoring 4 on his first-team debut. Bill had achieved this in the opening game of the 1900/01 campaign *v.* Gravesend in the Southern League (1 September 1900). The 7–0 whacking of the Pilgrims in 1945 was to be their heaviest defeat of the campaign.

Another record had also been equalled; Terry Woodgate, West Ham's outside right, hit a hat-trick in just 7 minutes. Syd Puddefoot had been the last Hammer to complete such an exploit *v.* Chesterfield, in the first round of the FA Cup, on New Year's Day 1913.

Travis and Woodgate scored again the following week when Pompey came to East London. West Ham were 1 goal down with

30 minutes to play, but ultimately turned things round to win 3–1 (Ken Bainbridge scored too).

Both goals in West Ham's 2–1 Upton Park victory *v.* Wolverhampton Wanderers on 13 April were scored by Travis; in all he had hit 7 nets in 6 games by the end of the season. But with no more goals in 5 more outings over the next couple of seasons he left Upton Park for Southend in 1948. However, he was on the losing team only once in 11 first-team games for West Ham.

League South, 1945/46							
	Played	Won	Drawn	Lost	For	Against	Points
Birmingham City	42	28	5	9	96	45	61
Aston Villa	42	25	11	6	106	58	61
Charlton Athletic	42	25	10	7	92	45	60
Derby County	42	24	7	11	101	62	55
West Bromwich Albion	42	22	8	12	104	69	52
Wolverhampton Wanderers	42	20	11	11	75	48	51
West Ham United	42	20	11	11	94	76	51
Fulham	42	20	10	12	93	73	50
Tottenham Hotspurs	42	22	3	17	78	81	47
Chelsea	42	19	6	17	92	80	44
Arsenal	42	16	11	15	76	73	43
Millwall	42	17	8	17	79	105	42
Coventry City	42	15	10	17	70	69	40
Brentford	42	14	10	18	82	72	38
Nottingham Forest	42	12	13	17	72	73	37
Southampton	42	14	9	19	97	105	37
Swansea Town	42	15	7	20	90	112	37
Luton Town	42	13	7	22	60	92	33
Portsmouth	42	11	6	25	66	87	28
Leicester City	42	8	7	27	57	101	23
Newport County	42	9	2	31	52	125	20
Plymouth Argyle	42	3	8	31	39	120	14

In the spring of 1946 Charlie Walker and Ted Fenton left Upton Park and West Ham United completed the club's final wartime season. The side had twice defeated Birmingham City (the Champions) and drew maximum points from 10 fixtures away from Upton Park. But, ever bitter-sweet, wartime football at the Boleyn Ground ended in defeat. The last goal of the war at the 'Home of the Hammers' was scored by centre forward Ronnie Rooke for Fulham; it completed his hat-trick. Hall (2) and Wood had kept the Irons in the fight but on 29 April 1946 the Cottagers faced the peace with a 5–3 victory behind them.

Harry Medhurst played in all West Ham's matches in the final wartime season (the only 'ever-present' player) and Almeric Hall, with 19 goals, was the leading scorer. 'Temporary Hammer' Jock Dodds, with 289 strikes, had finished behind Tommy Lawton, 336, as top goalscorer of the war. Dodds had been the best seasonal scorer with his 65 for Blackpool in 1941/42. His 8 wartime goals for his country made him Scotland's best marksman of the years of conflict.

West Ham held the English wartime record for the longest unbeaten run on the road: 9 games between 16 September and 11 November 1944. In Great Britain only the mighty Glasgow Rangers (with 10) had done better.

The biggest wartime crowd had been the 139,468 that had been at Hampden to watch the Scotland *v.* England match of 13 April 1946.

At the Football League's annual meeting on 1 June it was decided that the normal League programme would start in 1946/47 under a new wage structure: players would receive £10 a week in the winter and £7 10*s* in the summer (before the war this had been £8/£6). Player benefits were upped from £650 to £750.

All in all, the war years had been a relatively successful time for West Ham. Perhaps in the leagues they contested, Arsenal and Tottenham fans might argue that those sides came out better in terms of results, but they did not innovate and modernise to the extent that the Hammers did. Hence, within two decades Upton Park had caught up with White Hart Lane and was on Highbury's tail. That the club lost ground after that is another story, part of which I have told elsewhere (see Belton 2013a, 2013b).

The years from 1939 to 1945 set the scene for the greatest period in the history of the Hammers, the 'golden' age of Upton Park. With the move to the Olympic Stadium, it's pretty safe to say – the wonders of Sam Allardyce and the arrival of Slaven Bilic notwithstanding – that the era which had started with the coming (and going) of Ted Fenton, the push of Malcolm Allison and the executive maturing of Reg Pratt, and finished with the best days of John Lyall, would be the greatest the Boleyn Ground had ever known.

ABOUT THE AUTHOR

Brian Belton was born just a five-minute walk from West Ham United's Upton Park home. Every other Saturday, as a baby in his cradle, he was able to hear the Irons fans giving vent to the 'Bubbles' anthem; as such it was his childhood lullaby. Brian's father, during and just after the war years, played for West Ham boys and his grandparents and great-grandparents supported the Irons. Brought up and going to school in the docklands district that is the stomping ground of the 'claret and blue' fan army of East London's football team, Brian is genetically, body and soul, an authentic Hammer.

Brian has been employed in youth work around the world, including the Falkland Islands, Sri Lanka, Malaysia, Hong Kong, Zambia, South Africa and China, and today he is an internationally recognised authority on the subjects of identity, ethnicity and youth work. He currently works as a senior lecturer at the YMCA George Williams College in Canning Town teaching students preparing to go into youth work, and he has produced close to twenty books associated with West Ham United, encompassing almost the entire history of the romantic, capricious, and sometimes unfathomable Irons. Many a lecture on the expression of identity has included a chorus of 'Bubbles', finishing with a holler, arms wide in the air, of 'COME ON YOU I-ONNNS!'

REFERENCES

Belton, Brian, *Birth of the Blues – Chelsea, the First Decade* (Endeavour Press, 2013c).
Belton, Brian, *'Brown Out': The Biography of West Ham Chairman, Terence Brown* (Pennant Books, 2007).
Belton, Brian, *Bubbles, Hammers and Dreams* (JMD Media, 2013).
Belton, Brian, *Days of Iron: The Story of West Ham United in the Fifties* (JMD Media, 2013a).
Belton, Brian, *Founded on Iron Thames Ironworks and the Origins of West Ham United* (The History Press, 2003).
Belton, Brian, *The First and Last Englishmen: West Ham United in the 1960s* (JMD Media, 2013b).
Belton, Brian, *The Lads of '23: Bolton Wanderers, West Ham United and the 1923 FA Cup Final* (Tony Brown, 2006).
Belton, Brian, *The Men of '64* (The History Press, 2005).
Belton, Brian, *War Hammers I: The Story of West Ham United during the First World War* (The History Press, 2014).
Hitchens, Christopher, *Letters to a Young Contrarian* (Basic Books, 2002).
Joy, Bernard, *Forward Arsenal* (London: Phoenix House, 1952).